Instant-Effect Decorating

Instant-Effect Decorating

Hundreds of easy, inexpensive
ways to make your home
exciting and livable

by MARJORIE P. KATZ

Drawings by the Author

Photographs by David Sagarin

Published by M. Evans and Company, Inc., *New York*
AND DISTRIBUTED IN ASSOCIATION WITH
J. B. Lippincott Company, *Philadelphia and New York*

Contents

I. All About Instant-Effect Decorating and Me   7

Sore Thumbs and You · If You're Starting from
Scratch · On Buying Antiques, or "Antiques" · Dis-
cover-a-Color Scheme · Found Furniture and What to
Do with It · Turn a Room into a Live-in Environment

II. Cover-ups   31

Cover-up a Window · Cover-up a Window Shade ·
Cover-up a Bed · Cover-up a Wall · More Cover-
ups · Cover-up a Floor · Cover-up a Seat · Cover-up
a Lampshade

**III. Everything You Always Wanted to Know
About Throw Pillows . . .**   65

Where Should Throw Pillows Be Thrown? Why Are
Really Nice Throw Pillows So Expensive? Why Can't I
Make one Myself? What Should a Throw Pillow Be
Stuffed With? What Can I Use to Cover a Throw Pillow?
How Do You Get It All Together? Eight Basic But
Fabulous Throw Pillows · The Greatest Throw Pillow
Dress-ups Ever

IV. Hang-ups   95

What to Hang Up: the End of the Empty Wall · A
Gallery Is Where You Make It Happen · Arranging a
Wall Arrangement · How to Hang Up · The Frame-
up: Frames and Mats to Make Yourself · Mounting
Sculpture—Too Much Fun to Be Left to Professionals ·
How to Attach Sculpture to a Base · Investing in the
Real Thing

V. Art Hang-ups   125

"Found Art" · Collages and Assemblages · "Found
Sculpture"

VI. **And More Hang-ups** 151

Hang a Wall-Hanging · How to Hang a Wall-Hanging · Make a Wall-Hanging · Hang a Room-Divider · The Art of Nature · Shadow Box Display Case · Shell and/or Pebble Mosaic

VII. **Stow-aways and Stash-its** 179

Storage Space and How to Find It · Put it on Wheels · Up the Bathroom Walls · A Kitchen Should Look Like a Kitchen · Create a "Kitchen Sculpture" · Pegboard Can Be Beautiful · Closets and How to Stretch them · "Dead" Storage

VIII. **Put-ons** 207

Put-on Patchwork · Put-on a Pillowcase · And Still More Put-ons

IX. **Getting It All Together** 233

A Glossary of How-to Techniques and Materials · Acrylic Paints and Mediums · Adhesive-backed Materials · Crewel · Crochet · Embroidery · Felt-tipped Markers · Fixatives · Fringe · Glue · Needlepoint · Painting · Polyurethane · Pompons · Rugs · Shelves · Tassels · Tie-Dyeing · Wood

X. **Design Portfolio** 261

Dozens of designs to use for appliqué, embroidery, needlepoint or painting

XI. **Something Else** 289

Or, What Something You Would Otherwise Throw Away Can Be Turned Into · A Second Use for Newspaper · Use broken Crayons and Candle Stubs · Turn a Wooden Trimming Rack Into · · · New Uses for Old Boxes · What You Can Do with Pill Containers · Use Empty Egg Cartons · Use Old Wrapping Paper · And Use Frozen-Juice Cans

Index 315

∾ I ∾

All About Instant-Effect Decorating and Me

"Instant-Effect Decorating" is my own way of describing the ideas in this book. Each of them is capable of giving a new look to a room. Each can be made with ordinary, easy-to-find materials. Best of all, each can be achieved in very little time and for very little money. In every chapter you will find dozens of ideas that you can adapt in your own home right now. You will discover ways to create both the broad strokes and the significant details that can make a home livable, a room lovable and life visually more agreeable.

Many of these decorating ideas and projects I have incorporated into my home; others I have created expressly for this book. I hope it will be a starting point for you—a place from which you can go on to add your ideas to my ideas and create something that will reflect only you.

A great many of the things described in this book have grown out of my own experience struggling to keep a more-than-fifty-year-old apartment from showing its age, and trying to overcome the inflexibility of its walls to make it work for me and my family the way we want to live in it. This has meant not only putting in plumbing and electrical wiring but building walls, removing doors and making closets. More interestingly, it has meant camouflaging structural problems, converting liabilities to assets and creating a visually exciting home for four individualists.

Fifteen years ago, my husband and I started furnishing our first apartment. Three apartments, two children and a dog later, we still have, and love, most of our earliest acquisitions. We have been through only one major redecorating episode, which didn't really change the basics. But we are constantly making minor changes—the kind of changes that can bring a room up to date.

It is never necessary to live with out-of-style rooms. You aren't wearing the same clothing, hairdo or makeup that you wore fifteen, ten or even five years ago. If your home has that unfashionable feeling, it should be brought up to date too. But this does not mean that a major overhaul is necessary. It's the details that make the difference.

You probably never discarded an entire wardrobe and replaced it at one fell swoop. Instead, you tried for a new fashion feeling by changing a hemline and switching accessories, while gradually replacing major items in your wardrobe as they became worn or outdated.

Fashions in interior design change, too, and anybody would tire of looking at the same old surroundings year after year, day in and day out. Just as you can perk up your wardrobe with a new scarf or pair of shoes, you can perk up a tired room with the right Instant Effect.

Use this book to find the Instant Effects that will perk up your home *now*. And when, in a few years, the "now" look of today becomes the "then" look of a bygone day, turn again to Instant Effects to create a fresh, new environment.

There was a time when I never thought of applying my do-it-yourself skills to the furnishing of my own home, even though I had learned needlework before I learned to read, and had been an arts and crafts instructor while I was going to college. However, when the time came to decorate a room for our first baby, I had to start using my ingenuity to get the effect I wanted. I had decided upon a basically gray room—gray walls and gray tweed carpet—as a background for splashes of intense color. For curtains I had chosen an orange, gray, black and white geometric print and an orange daybed cover. For the wall over the daybed, I envisioned three large, white-framed pictures. My husband and I found the pictures we wanted in one of those oversized coloring books whose illustrations are taken from classic children's stories. But a visit to a framemaker brought me up short. Frames the size I needed, in white enamel, would cost more than the baby's crib! So, hesitantly, I decided to do it myself.

In the five-and-ten I found wooden frames in the exact size I needed; I also bought a small can of paint and a brush. For a few hours and a few dollars, I had my white frames. Then, to set off the black-and-white pictures and to disguise the mats that had come with the frames, I found an old set of poster paints, mixed orange to match the daybed cover and brushed away.

Danny is now eleven, and the coloring-book pictures have been replaced by color photographs of jungle animals, but the white frames and orange mats are still in service over his bed.

Danny's room, also the scene of my second do-it-yourself decorating venture, held twice as much as the usual toy chest. So I bought a stock piece of unfinished furniture: a phonograph-and-record cabinet. That, too, got enameled white. Several years later, it turned up, now enameled hot pink, in my daughter's room. And in between, I discovered that creating my own special decorating effects was both practical and rewarding.

My own taste seems to reach backward with one hand and forward with the other. In our furnishings, we have struck what my husband and I feel is a workable balance between "modern" and "antique." Our lamps are a good example, because they fall into both categories. Among our cherished old ones are a pair of nineteenth-century brass oil lamps and some Austrian porcelain vases of the same vintage. Wired for electricity and adorned with creamy antique-silk shades, they share rooms with the polished chrome light fixtures of Now.

This combination of old and new is everywhere I look. On the wall in front of my desk at this moment is an old print of an eighteenth-century London scene. It is displayed against the stark simplicity of a black plastic rectangular frame—which enhances the delicate lines and tints of the print to perfection. In my kitchen, the warm wood tones and sturdy curved backs and seats of the Victorian oak chairs both blend and contrast with the angularity and brightness of a Parsons table in orange Formica.

I adore the furnishings of the past and the attention to fine detail, the love of good woods, the care with which pieces were constructed. And I'm entranced by the furnishings of the present and the experiments with new materials, the use of color, the clean lines and functional shapes.

What I don't like are dishonest furnishings—those pieces called "French Provincial," "Early American" or "Oriental Modern" that all too often have excessive detail, fancy hardware and out-of-proportion curves just added onto them. These are only half-baked imitations of the sturdiness and mellow woods of real French Provincial or genuine Early American pieces, of the clean lines, handsome lacquered finishes and balanced proportions of good Japanese pieces.

Once, because I needed storage space, I bought a low black chest with a very deep double drawer. While he was writing the receipt, the salesman remarked, "This is our Oriental model. We have the same thing over there in French Provincial." And indeed they did—the identical chest, in fruitwood finish. That salesman's remark almost cost him the sale—but the thought of all the stuff I could cram into that deep drawer saved his commission. However, that chest was forever spoiled for me and was the first thing to go during a minor redecorating episode. It was my first "sore thumb."

Sore Thumbs and You

I define a "sore thumb" as any detail in a room that screams at you "I'm not right! Do something!" No home is ever completely free of sore thumbs, I'm sure. There's always *something* that was a mistake or that still needs working on. But you *can* minimize them. Sore thumbs fall into three categories:

1. Those you've "inherited"—as gifts or giveaways.
2. Those you've bought and have outgrown.

3. Those you've acquired with the house; that is, they're built-in, or structural.

The first thing to do is get rid of as many sore thumbs as possible, by passing them along to somebody else. (One man's sore thumb is another man's treasure; this is the principle on which thrift shops and white-elephant sales thrive.) And this is the way to get rid of them: Sell them if you can, and try to recoup some of the loss; or give them away, preferably to Goodwill Industries or the Salvation Army. Both organizations will call for almost anything and will put your sore thumbs to good use by having them reconditioned and then offered for sale at bargain prices.

After you've disposed of as many sore thumbs as possible, take a tour of your domain and list, room by room, the sore thumbs that remain. These will be things like ugly windows and misplaced doors, empty walls and other structural problems. Or unattractive furniture that is necessary for its storage capacity or is too expensive to replace. Or a room that just doesn't work because the overall effect is drab and colorless. Now you know what you have to work on.

For instance, if your "sore-thumb list" includes a dull bed or sofa, you'll probably find at least one idea that will work for you in Chapter II, "Cover-ups," or Chapter III, "Everything You Always Wanted to Know about Throw Pillows." If your sore-thumb list includes a dull wall, rethink your color scheme using the ideas in this chapter (below), or look in Chapters IV, V and VI for all sorts of things to hang on a wall to give it and its room a lift.

We'll start in this chapter with two problems that everybody has to cope with at one time or another—color and furniture. With the Discover-a-Color Scheme you'll learn an easy way to plan the colors for any room in your home, depending on your taste alone, instead of on rules and charts. And you will learn how to update old and ordinary pieces of furniture and turn them to new uses, when you read about Found Furniture. You'll also find out how to create a Live-in Environment, the newest way to furnish an empty room.

Think of a room—every room in your home—as a setting that must make an immediate effect on the viewer. Only after a while do the details become apparent. In planning a room, therefore, think first of the overall effect you want, because you will be spending much more time living with and looking at your furnishings than anyone else.

If You're Starting from Scratch

If you have the luxury of beginning with an empty room, or even an empty house or apartment, don't be overwhelmed by the task that lies ahead. Planning your own interior design is fun. Just take one step at a time, and don't panic.

Window-shop relentlessly. Visit every home-furnishings department within traveling distance. Read the decorating magazines to find out what's new, and how it's being used by the "name" decorators. Study advertisements. And keep notes about what you like.

If what you like is priced outside your budget, use your eyes and ingenuity to find or adapt lower-cost versions. The ideas in every chapter in this book should help.

Plan your color scheme first. It is the biggest effect of all.

Then plan the major furnishings—those necessities that fulfill the room's function, like a bed for a bedroom, seating for a living room, a desk for a study or den. You can always add the less important, satellite pieces around them.

Don't feel you have to buy a whole "suite" of matching pieces for a room—that everything-of-a-kind look is too limiting. The varied, eclectic approach—adding the secondary pieces as you come across them, and seeing your room progress by stages— is where your creativity really begins to show up.

"Blow your wad" on one magnificent piece, something you'll always love. Buy a splendid sofa, a wonderful table, a well-designed shelf system. Whatever your extravagance is, you'll never regret it. It will bring your whole room into focus. It will make tolerable the inexpensive touches, the alternative solutions that must be added, you hope temporarily, to the room. And if you pass up the one magnificent piece, you will see it regretfully in your dreams for years afterward. Friends of mine had a $2000 budget for their first apartment, and spent half of it on a sofa that they loved. Otherwise, their apartment was furnished inexpensively. But that one luxurious piece made them feel like millionaires.

My own first extravagance was gold wool-velvet carpeting. Fortunately, I had the foresight to have it installed throughout our small first apartment. When, a few years later, we moved to larger quarters, the carpeting went with us. With a few seams hidden close to the walls where only I could find them, there was enough of it to cover a large L-shaped living room. For the next six years I was thankful that I hadn't covered only the floors of the very narrow living room of that first apartment.

Buy the best *quality* you can afford. Don't be afraid to ask questions about the construction of furniture, whether of cabinet or upholstered pieces. The way a piece is constructed will give it a long, trouble-free life in your home. This is true of the minor accessories, too.

On Buying Antiques, or "Antiques"

I was with a friend when she bought a lovely crystal, hundred-or-so-year-old chandelier, all gilt-bronze and black, to hang in her dining area. And she actually spent less for it than one of my neighbors had spent only a month earlier for a lucite and chrome contraption that turned out to be the chandelier Ford-of-the-year. That comfortingly proved a theory of mine: you can buy a one-of-a-kind old piece for no more money, and frequently even less, than you'd pay for a mass-produced new one that serves the same function. This is true for chairs and tables, headboards and dressers, armoires and rugs, as well as for the smaller accessories.

I made this discovery shortly after we were married, when we started looking for lamps. Our first apartment had only three built-in lighting fixtures—in the bathroom, the kitchen and, of all places, inside a closet. So a lamp was an immediate necessity, a floor lamp, of course, since we didn't yet have any furniture to stand a table lamp on. We bought practically the first one we came upon, and carried it with us from living room to dining area to bedroom, plugging it in and unplugging it a dozen times every evening. It was a handsome lamp, a reproduction of an old piece. And it was expensive.

Later, after our furniture arrived, we went looking for table lamps, and found several century-old brass oil lamps in an antique shop. Each one with its custom-made shade cost less than our floor lamp had without its shade. A sudden pang at the realization that I had unwittingly squandered a portion of our decorating budget sent me, too late, to do some comparison shopping. I discovered that new "oil lamps," made to look exactly like the ones we had just purchased, but shiny and lacquered instead of mellow with age, cost twice what we had paid. Antiques, I was discovering, could be a good buy after all. It was the new copies of old pieces that were overpriced.

Right, and wrong, too. One day I found a large French porcelain lamp, a truly majestic piece, beautifully decorated and authentically eighteenth century. I fell in love with it; the living room needed it; I must buy it. But the price was—well, not quite astronomical but almost. The salesman was apologetic. He explained patiently that antiques are rather like puppies: they cost more when they are pedigreed and popular.

We bought the lamp because we loved it. And we decided that we would never pay more for something just because it was an "antique" than we would have to pay for a contemporary item of similar quality and function. Unless, of course, we fell in love with it.

The U.S. Customs Office defines an antique as an object at least a hundred years old. But for practical purposes, an antique is anything made in an earlier period. And if the piece of your choice was made in a period that has not yet become popular, you can get a very good buy indeed.

Among the "antiques" that can still be found at reasonable prices are things made in the relatively recent past, thirty, forty or fifty years ago. And surprisingly, although a room furnished completely in the style of forty years ago would look uncomfortably overdone and overstuffed today, individual pieces—if they are in good condition and if they were handsomely designed to begin with—can be used in the most modern homes. (If, however, your "find" of this vintage is functional but has nothing else—like shape or finish—going for it, treat it as Found Furniture to which you must add your own finishing, or refinishing, touches; and see below.)

Discover-a-Color Scheme

Whether you are starting from scratch, or whether your sore-thumb list includes a dull color scheme, color is the thing to begin with. There's no excuse for blandness in today's rooms. They are likely to be sparsely furnished and to depend on strong color accents for their character. This is a far cry from the overfurnished rooms of only a few years ago, which featured elaborate draperies and large upholstered pieces in a setting of brown and tan with beige walls.

Color schemes today are likely to be combinations of different shades of red—wine, crimson and fuchsia, perhaps; or they may combine several different black-and-white prints against which flashes of brilliant color—yellow, orange, green— stand out clearly.

You have only to think about your own reaction to the bright colors on display in housewares and linen departments to know that color, lots of it, should be a part of everyone's life. You wouldn't think, probably, of dressing yourself in browns and beiges and tans without the glitter of some jewelry or the splash of a bright scarf. The same thing goes for the rooms you live in. Color adds interest, perks up the atmosphere, lifts the spirit.

It is sad that so many articles and books on home furnishing start by explaining color wheels and harmonizing colors and warm and cool shades and so on. This makes people feel that since the subject is so complicated, with so many rules, they're better off away from it. But this is absolute nonsense, and if you are unsure of how to use color in a room, there is a simple way for you to find out. Use your own eyes!

What use of color have you seen that you liked? That you kept looking and looking at? A print dress? A picture of a room in a magazine? One of the new decorator-designed bedsheets or bath towels? An English bone-china dinner plate in a department store, a Chinese vase in the Metropolitan Museum of Art, a ceramic bowl from Mexico?

Whatever it is, buy it—a scarf or a tea cup, a pillowcase or a swatch of fabric, a museum picture-postcard or a book jacket. If it's a page in a magazine, tear it out. If it's a store display, take or ask for a color photograph.

This is your color-scheme sample. Keep it with you constantly—on your night table, in your handbag, draped across the sofa, heaped up on the kitchen table. Look at it last thing at night and first thing in the morning. If your sample is small, take it to a fabric department and buy some inexpensive cotton material in your chosen colors—a quarter or a half yard of each color should be enough.

When you get home, bunch them up, twist them around, place them on top of, next to, across each other. Add swatches of other colors. Place favorite objects—a figurine, an ash tray, a painting—on top of or next to your color choices. Spend a lot of time looking at your colors, and make sure you like them. Pin them to your window shades. Tape them on your walls. And if you still like them, that's it. You've found the color scheme for your room. Start figuring which of the colors you like in large doses and which work better as streaks or accents. Add other colors. Perhaps subtract. But work with fabric, which you can stretch out stiffly or crumple up.

Cut 2-inch swatches of your fabric choices; or pick up a standard color chart in a paint store and cut out your colors. Put these small color samples in an envelope and carry it around with you at all times. If you're decorating more than one room, keep a separate envelope for each. When you discover a carpet or a wallpaper, get a small swatch and tuck it into the envelope too. You never know when you'll come across something that seems right for your room, and have to match the color.

(You could also tuck a floor plan of your room into the same envelope, marking off the arrangement of furniture as you buy. Use pencil so that you can erase if you decide to move things around. Then you'll always be able to figure out whether something you've just seen is the right size for your room.)

Perhaps you already own something that suggests a color scheme to you. Or perhaps you have seen something that you like—a painting, perhaps—but are afraid to buy it because it might not "go" with your room. Buy it and decorate the room around it. It's much easier to find a blue carpet than a blue oil painting.

I faced this problem a few years ago. Our bedroom had been furnished in a pleasing, serene combination of blue, gold and white. But, after several years, it came to seem only dull. Out of sheer necessity we had just bought a large, unfinished closet (old apartments frequently have large rooms and minuscule closets). We could not decide what to do with the room and with the new closet, which didn't quite fit well enough under our high ceiling to pass as a "built-in." So, hoping for an inspiration, we used the interior and let the large but nondescript wooden giant stand unfinished in a corner. Then one day we discovered a Chinese-red bedspread. Instantly we had our new color scheme. The closet was enameled a glistening red. A few sore thumbs disappeared, such as the old draperies and bedspread, and one not-very-good painting. A friend just back from a trip brought us a fragment of red cloth from North Africa, embroidered in darker winy shades of red and blue. We hung it against a white linen mat in a white frame directly over the bed. A large black leather lounge chair was added, along with a red wall-hung lighting fixture. And at the window, a white Roman shade with red-and-black braid trim completed the transformation.

Found Furniture and What to Do with It

Found Furniture is any piece that is worth all the fixing-up you care to give it because it cost you next-to-nothing, or perhaps absolutely nothing. It is the stuff other people give to thrift shops but you are clever enough to disguise and adapt and give new life to.

I first realized the potential of this approach when I came across several sets of drawers, from an old oak sewing-machine console, for sale at $3.50 each. My husband said, "What do you want that junk for? You'll never be able to do anything with it." But I insisted and finally selected a matched pair.

Within a few days, I figured out what to do with them, and started to do it. I took them apart, replaced the old hardware with new screws and new drawer-pulls of brushed chrome, re-

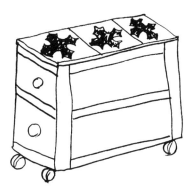

stained the wood, lined the drawers with adhesive-backed white vinyl and put enormous chrome casters on the bottom. The top of each set of drawers was covered with three Mexican tiles whose terra-cotta-on-white design picked up the new dark walnut finish. For a total cost of under $20, I had a pair of unique chairside tables, which we had long been needing.

Shortly afterward, we decided we needed some sort of stand which could hold plants and small sculptures in the living room. One evening my husband telephoned me. On his way home from the office, he passed one of the neighborhood used-furniture shops that displayed some of its wares out on the sidewalk, and he noticed something that he thought we could fix up and use. "It's about forty years old and just awful—one of those things they used to call a what-not table—but we could paint it white and it costs only . . ."

That was all I needed to hear. So he brought it home and it was indeed awful. It was covered with so shiny a varnish that it was impossible to tell what color the wood was supposed to have been. But it did have two large shelves that would be fine for displaying a few of our African wood-carvings. I decided to operate.

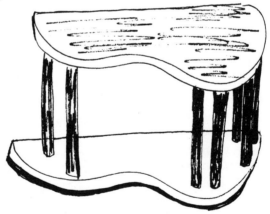

Since no enamel could possibly stick to all that varnish, my first step would have to be to get rid of it. But I wasn't sure that the standard paint and varnish remover I'd previously used would work on this. I tested it, brushing a patch along the rear of the bottom shelf. Holding my breath, I waited out the fifteen minutes recommended and watched the stuff bubble up into a sickly-looking orange blister. Then, using a damp rag, I wiped the orange gook away. Where it had been, the wood grain showed through clearly, the beautiful dark red-brown of fine mahogany. What a relief! This was one sow's ear that I knew I could turn into a silk purse. White enamel indeed! We were going to have a lovely mahogany plant-and-sculpture stand as soon as I could get to work.

I prepared carefully for the day when I would operate on my "patient." It was so large that I decided to work in the bathtub. I bought a large can of varnish remover to supplement my old supply. I saved up rags and newspaper. I bought new, strong rubber gloves, and a large brush. And the next available opportunity, which was a Sunday, I waved goodbye to my husband and children as they left for Central Park, and got down to work.

First I lined the tub with several layers of newspaper. Then I started brushing remover over every inch of varnish. It took all day and two applications of remover to get all the 1920's varnish off. But when I was through, the piece was a beauty. I finished by rubbing it with two applications of lemon oil, letting the old wood literally drink it up before I wiped it with a dry cloth.

Although we have no more room for Found Furniture in our apartment at the moment, I find myself peering into every junk and thrift shop I pass, looking for pieces that could be rescued and planning how they could be redesigned. Here are my suggestions:

1. If possible, choose a piece whose basic lines are good, because that is what you have to work with. It is difficult to ignore the finish, but you must; it will be refinished anyway. Look for good construction, drawers that slide easily in and out, legs that don't wobble (although you can always simply remove and replace them with others), wood that is not too chipped or cracked. Good sources of supply include used-office-furniture dealers, movers, house wreckers, Goodwill Industries and Salvation Army stores and other thrift shops. Even better are hand-me-downs.

2. Decide how you want the piece to look when you're done with it—brightly enameled, or stained in dark or light shades. In general, it's best not to think in terms of restoring the piece

to its original condition, unless you're sure it was a first-rate piece of furniture to begin with. If the wood has an open grain, such as oak, the best effects are usually obtained by simply cleaning the piece and perhaps staining it. Enamel is best applied to a close-grained wood such as mahogany. In any case, don't feel so committed to your design plan that you can't shift gears if the cleaning process uncovers a beautiful finish that you never suspected was there.

3. Remove any of the old hardware that is in less than great shape. Any old screws and nails that show on the outside are likely to be rusted and worn. Replace drawer-pulls and cabinet handles with new metal or ceramic ones. However, if the old drawer-pulls are really lovely, remove them anyway so you can clean them up separately and so they won't get in the way when you work on the wood itself. Remove old casters from legs.

4. To clean old hardware, buff with fine steel wool, or use a suitable cleanser. Remove rust from iron with naval jelly (available at a hardware or paint store).

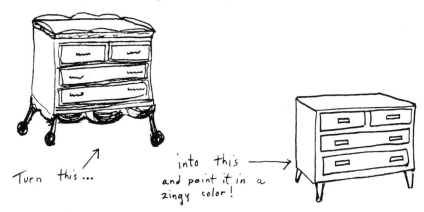

Turn this ...   into this —→ and paint it in a zingy color!

5. If there are protruding decorative wooden edges, you can usually lift them gently with a small chisel to remove. Remove table legs and cabinet legs if possible. Take drawers out of cabinets. Decide whether to saw down legs, replace them with new ones, set the piece flat on the floor with no legs or use the old ones again.

6. Strip off old finish. I use a heavy-duty paint and varnish remover and follow directions on the can, if many layers of paint or if a thick varnish must be stripped off. If the wood is

merely dirty, however, but the finish is not chipped or cracked, it need only be cleaned and prepared for refinishing. Use a liquid sandpaper preparation and apply it with a rag or with extra-fine steel wool following directions on the can.

7. If there are chips and cracks in the wood, they must be filled with a cellulose-fiber wood filler, applied according to directions, and then sanded. If the wood veneer has lifted in spots, you can literally press it down with an iron on the "cool" setting. A minute or two should be enough to melt the old glue and get the wood to hold.

8. To paint a solid color, use cans of spray enamel according to directions, using two or three light coats. Or use rollers on large flat surfaces or use brushes and cans of enamel. To stain a dark wood color, follow directions on the stain you select. Wax stains are rubbed on with a cloth, and then buffed; liquid stains are brushed on, then rubbed in with a cloth and allowed to dry. Paint drawers and any other removable parts separately. Do not replace these until piece is refinished and completely dry.

9. If you are neither staining nor enameling, but prefer the natural wood you have cleaned or uncovered, wipe it all over with a rag saturated in lemon oil. This prevents the drying out that can crack and warp wood, and it also restores the appearance of the wood after the pickling action of the varnish remover. Let the oil soak in well, then apply a second coat of oil and wipe with a clean dry rag. Wipe a second time to make sure no oily residue is left on the surface to collect dust. Clean periodically with lemon oil or furniture polish. Oak pieces take well to being rubbed with a paste-type floor wax.

10. For colored stains, antiqued finishes and other special effects, consult with your paint or hardware dealer. He knows his supplies and can give you tips on how to use them.

11. For a hard plastic finish that is resistant to staining and good to use for a table top or desk, get a polyurethane glaze and follow label directions. Or, for a protective finish, use two or three coats of varnish.

12. To perk up a large old piece a chest, paint or paste a picture on one of the drawers. Work out your design on paper first, then transfer to the wood. Use acrylics or enamels. Or select a picture from a greeting card, gift wrapping or wall-

paper. Cut it out carefully, trimming to fit your space, and position it. Glue in place. Border your painting or "appliqué" with a painted-on edging or with glued-on flat braid in gold or an appropriate color. Finish off entire piece with two or three coats of clear varnish.

13. Line drawers and the interiors of shelf cabinets with prepasted wallpaper, adhesive-backed vinyl, or fabric. A small all-over print is effective.

14. Have you considered a new top for your piece? A slab of marble, glass, butcher block, plastic laminate? Or tiles? Depending on the use you have for the piece, one of these might be more practical, as well as more effective, than the refinished wood.

Turn a Room into a Live-in Environment

"Environment" is the freshest and most significant new concept in furnishing. A forerunner of the environment was the conversation pit, a multilevel seating arrangement, frequently carpeted on all horizontal and vertical surfaces, that allowed people to drape, dangle or seat themselves either in clusters or in a larger circle. Focusing on people and their interactions made the outer boundaries and other furnishings of the room seem insignificant.

From there only a leap of the imagination was needed to conceive of a room that was furnished as a multifunctional single unit, virtually a sculpture, that would perform all the essential functions usually fulfilled by several pieces of conventional furniture. Because of the totality of such a unit in

relation to the individual who used and lived in it, it came to be known as an Environment.

You can create your own Environment, custom-designed by you for your needs. Standard unfinished-furniture units are your taking-off point. A little arithmetic and patience show you how to fit them together into your own work of live-in sculpture. Best of all, the units can be taken apart, to be recombined into a new Environment or to be moved into other, more traditional arrangements, whenever you feel the need for change.

Here's how to go about creating your own Environment.

1. Obtain the illustrated catalogue of units from an unfinished-furniture dealer or mail-order house. Be sure it lists the measurements of all pieces.

2. Decide which pieces shown in the catalogue you want to incorporate into your Environment. Start with the two or three

Sample Environment # 1

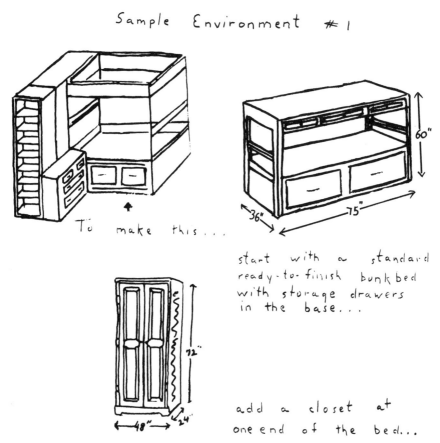

To make this . . .

start with a standard ready-to-finish bunk bed with storage drawers in the base . . .

add a closet at one end of the bed . . .

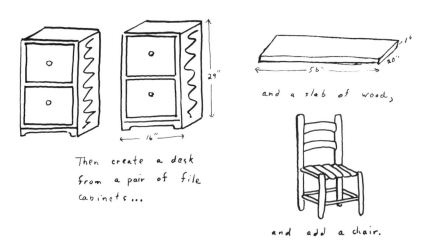

Then create a desk
from a pair of file
cabinets...

and a slab of wood,

and add a chair.

that are most important functionally to you. Note the dimensions of all the pieces you choose. The Sample Environment
illustrated began with a bed and a closet.

3. On graph paper, outline your room, letting 1 square equal
1 foot. Show all features of the room that must be contended
with, such as doors, closets, windows, beams and electrical
outlets.

4. On another piece of graph paper, mark to the same scale
shapes of furniture desired and cut out. Write on each cutout
which piece of furniture it is.

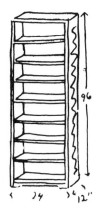

and   bookshelves...

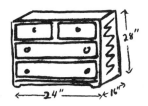

and   a   low   chest
to   double   as   a
night   table.

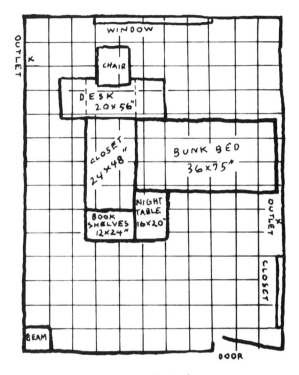

This is how it looks
as a floor plan for
a standard bedroom (11' by 14')

5. Now place your cutouts on your floor plan and move them around until they fit the way you'd like. When they do, staple or glue them in place. If you use a dab of rubber cement, you can pull them off and replace them easily. Bear in mind that desks and night tables should be close enough to electrical outlets so that lamp cords don't have to run across the floor.

6. When you've decided on the placement of your major pieces, start on the minor ones. Drawer chests and bookshelves come in all sizes and proportions, so you can almost always find one to fit any space.

7. Don't worry about the sides or backs of furniture pieces showing or jutting out. Clever use of paint, foil or fabric will turn these into design elements; cork panels will turn larger expanses into bulletin boards or display galleries.

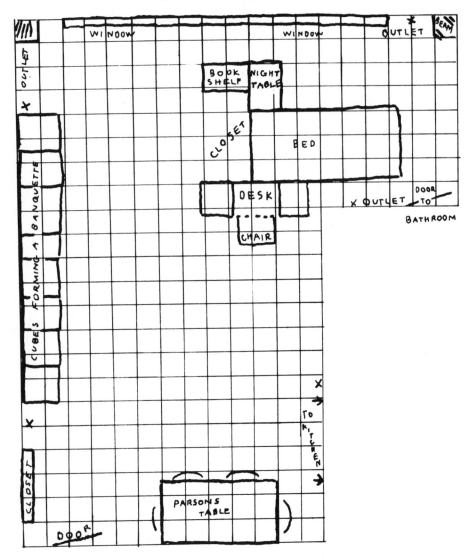

And this is one way to use it
to expand an L-shaped studio
apartment and disguise the
sleeping corner.

8. When your floor plan is set and glued together, start on the four "side plans" or projections. Use graph paper to sketch each side of your arrangement. Now you begin to take the height of each piece into consideration. If necessary, single-drawer or shelf units can be added to raise the height of any piece. There are sliding-door cabinets especially designed to fit on top of most closet units. Look through the catalogue again to get other ideas for new ways to use the unfinished-furniture units. Now is the time to think of your Environment in terms of the sculptural use of your space. Add a cabinet here, sub-tract one there, until your diagrams attract the eye from every angle.

9. When you've settled on what you need, order the pieces you want. Whether to place the pieces together, bolt them to-gether, or attach them with piano hinges so they swing open and closed along the side edges is up to you; so is the choice of whether to put casters under any pieces. If you explain your project to the furniture dealer, he may have some suggestions about this.

10. When your furniture arrives, get your paints and brushes and start to work! This is the fun part. You'll see your Environ-ment taking on a life of its own as you work on it.

11. Now that you have all your furniture in the center of the room, what can you do with the walls? Paint them a vivid color to match or contrast; cover with foil, or with wallpaper or felt or burlap. (See Chapter II for wall-coverings.)

One suggestion for finishing an Environment is to use a sophisticated version of common school colors such as blue and orange. Visualize this: marine blue carpeting on floor and wall (use do-it-yourself carpet squares); furniture painted in matching blue enamel with flashes of orange and mustard, per-haps used on drawer fronts or bookcase sides, and on the plastic laminate for the desk top. Accent with streaks of chrome: chrome drawer-pulls and other hardware, aluminum-foil tape outlining edges of furniture, chrome bullet lamps, and adhesive-backed foil covering an inexpensive wastebasket. Add large felt or vinyl cushions in orange and mustard to heap on the floor for informal seating; and an orange vinyl or enameled wood desk chair.

And these are the side plans...

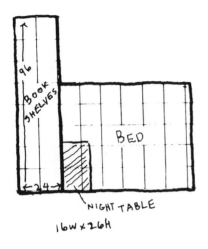

side view, bookshelf side

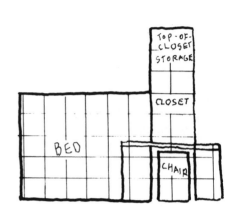

side view, showing desk
and side of closet

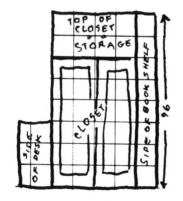

end view, showing
closet and sides of
desk and bookshelves

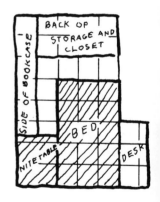

end view, from
foot of bed

Sample Environment #2

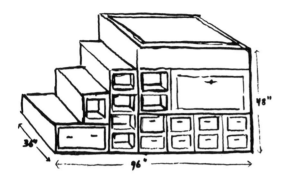

Climb up a flight
of storage units to
reach a platform bed.
It rests on chests of
drawers on one side...

and a combination of
a closet and chest
on the other.

Use this Environment
as an island in the
center of a room. The
back of it becomes a
picture gallery.

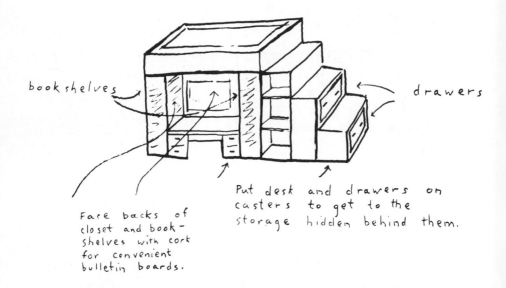

Add a desk in this variation:

book shelves

drawers

Face backs of closet and book-shelves with cork for convenient bulletin boards.

Put desk and drawers on casters to get to the storage hidden behind them.

Design an Environment to concentrate furniture in one part of a small room, leaving the rest of the space free for other activities. Both Sample Environments diagrammed here combine bed and storage, and could be used in a studio apartment or "bed-sitter" with plenty of room left over for seating and dining (or floor cushions and a low cocktail table). They could also function in a child's room, leaving the rest of the floor to be used as a play area.

∾ II ∾

Cover-ups

Or camouflage, if you prefer. Whatever you want to call it, what I'm talking about is the easiest possible way to make silk purses from sows' ears—in an interior decorating sense, of course. Do you have a blank window? A dull bed? A "dead" wall? Does it seem as though every room in your home has "the blahs"?

If so, Cover-ups are the answer. Every dead, dull, dingy blank *blah* can be turned into a smashing center-of-interest, *if* you treat it to the right Cover-up. Whether you use paint, fabric, plastic or paper—use *imagination*, think *zingy*, and get the doldrums out of your domain.

Cover-up a Window

Top it with a canopy valance. This is an easy and effective way to solve several decorating problems. In my little girl's room I used a canopy valance over a window looking out on a dark courtyard to scale down the high ceiling to the right proportions for a very tiny miss, to detract from the non-view, to brighten and unify a dull wall with a window that was both large and badly placed.

Nina's canopy is hot pink, to match the draperies, bedspread and some of the lacquer-finished furniture. Lighter pink ballfringe hangs from the scalloped bottom.

You can do just about anything you want with a canopy. Make it tailored, with simple braid around the edge and boxed-in corners. Navy with green braid or wine with red braid would be suitable for use in a boy's room or den. Sew multicolored fringe balls or the small pompons that you can buy by the yard here and there all over, or appliqué gay cotton or felt circles for balloons, stitching on yarn "strings." Make a canopy white and frilly, of sheer fabric with a lace edging; make it double width for extra-frilly fullness.

Use drapery fabric, heavy cotton, sailcloth, bedsheets (available in colorful designs and drip-dry fabrics); try a canopy made from a bath towel over a high, narrow bathroom window;

kitchen towels or tablecloths could be used in a kitchen or dining area (use more towels or the rest of the tablecloth to make matching cafe curtains for the lower part of the window).

The only trick to making a canopy is in the curtain rods. You need two. The canopy hangs from a regular rod attached by brackets to the wall. This rod usually has a 2-inch turn at

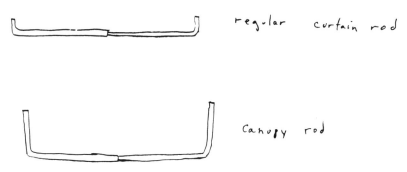

regular curtain rod

Canopy rod

each end, and is adjustable. But the flaring-out of the canopy is accomplished with a special canopy rod that slides through a casing near the bottom of the canopy and rests against the wall. Also adjustable in width, it has a 6- or 8-inch turn at each end, and rests against the wall but does not attach to it. If your window is very wide you will also need an extension section for each rod.

But the first thing you need is an accurate yardstick or carpenter's rule, and perhaps someone else to hold one end of it in place while you measure. Oh, yes, don't forget a pencil and paper—there's a bit of arithmetic to do on this one. But the sewing is easy, and the effect of the canopy makes it all worthwhile.

Here's how to plan and execute a Canopy Valance.

MATERIALS:
two curtain rods and brackets, as described above
fabric and twill tape, in amounts determined in steps 1
    through 7 below
trim (braid, fringe, etc.) as desired

HOW-TO:
1. Measure width to be covered by the canopy. The canopy may extend an inch or two beyond the window frame, or it

x and y indicate position of
curtain rod brackets

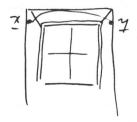

may fit right into it—as you choose. In either case, the position of the brackets is indicated by x and y. The distance (x-y) shown in the diagram is the *basic width* of your canopy.

2. To figure width at upper casing: add to basic width 2 times the turn at the end of the curtain rod, plus 1″ to allow for finishing the sides. (Thus, if the distance between brackets is 48″, and the curtain rod has a 2-inch turn, the upper casing width will be 53″—that is, 48″ + 4″ + 1″).

3. To figure width at lower casing: add to basic width 2 times the turn at the end of the canopy rod, plus 1″ to allow for finishing the sides. Thus, if the distance between brackets is 48″, and the canopy rod has a 6″ turn, the lower casing width will be 48″ + 12″ + 1″ or 61″.

4. Decide how deep you want your canopy, and then how deep you want the drop, the part that will hang below the canopy rod. You may want to try out several possibilities, using wrapping paper attached to your wall with masking tape to give you an idea. There are no hard and fast rules for finding these proportions; it's all a question of what looks good to you. Oddly enough, a wide canopy might look well if it is short, and a narrower canopy might be well proportioned with more depth. See sketches for ideas on proportion.

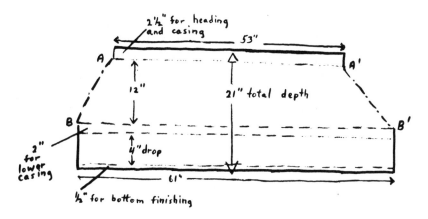

5. Now get a piece of paper and diagram your canopy, using the figures you arrived at in steps 1 through 4. See sample diagram, based on a basic width of 48", a depth of 12" between upper and lower casings and a 4-inch drop.

6. To figure the total depth: add 2½" for top heading and casing allowance, 2" for lower casing allowance, and ½" for finishing bottom, plus depth you have decided on, plus drop. (The casing is the part the rod goes through, of course; the heading is the very top just above the casing.) In the sample, the total depth is 21". (For sheer or lightweight fabrics, allow 3¼" at bottom for a 3-inch hem, and 2" extra in width to turn side edges twice in finishing.) Draw diagonal lines A-B and A¹-B¹ for sides of canopy as in sample diagram.

7. Now you know how much fabric you need. You will also need a 3" wide strip of fabric or 2" twill tape to make the inside part of the lower casing. This strip should be the length between *B* and *B¹* in the diagram, and 2½" wide after finishing the raw edges. And whatever trim you decide on should be that same length.

8. Cut out fabric, following your diagram. If fabric is patterned, make sure that the center of interest of the design will come in the center of the canopy. Be sure to buy enough fabric for piecing if necessary.

If you have to piece the fabric, either because your canopy is to be wider than the fabric width, or to get the design centered, be certain to add sections symmetrically at both ends.

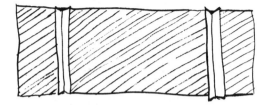

Sew added sections of fabric to each side of center section, and press seams open.

9. Now you are ready to do the actual sewing. This part goes fast. Finish side edges first: machine stitch along each side ⅜″ from edge; fold edge to wrong side on stitching line and stitch again ¼″ from fold. For lightweight or sheer fabrics, fold in once more and stitch close to outer fold to make a narrow hem.

10. Finish bottom edge in the same way.

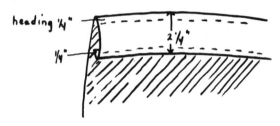

11. Stitch ¼″ along top edge, fold edge to wrong side on stitching line and stitch again at edged fold. Mark 2¼″ from top and fold to wrong side. Stitch ¼″ from fold to make heading.

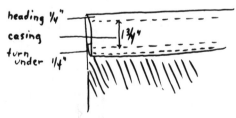

12. To make upper casing: with wrong side of canopy facing you, push loose flap of fabric at top up slightly toward heading, and stitch down 1¾″ from row of heading stitches. This will give enough fullness to the back of the casing so that the front will lie flat against the curtain rod.

13. To make lower casing: mark position of upper edge of casing on wrong side of canopy with chalk or pins. Pin one edge

of twill tape (or strip of fabric with edges turned under ¼"
and stitched down) in place over this marked line, and stitch
down. Push loose edge of tape gently toward first row of stitching and stitch along edge. There should be 1½" between rows
of stitching on right side of canopy, and the tape on the wrong
side of the canopy should buckle slightly.

14. Sew desired trimming along bottom edge and wherever
desired. Shape bottom edge in points or scallops, starting from
center and working symmetrically out to side edges.

15. Insert rods, attach brackets to wall and hang.

Or to Cover-up a window, "frame" it. Draperies and swags,
while elegant, often just don't seem appropriate with today's
clean-lined furnishings. They are expensive dust-catchers as
well. For a new finishing touch for the well-dressed window, try
one of these ideas:

1. If window has a molding around it, paint (with enamels
or acrylics) the molding and the inside of the window frame in
a bright color to pick up one of the colors in the room. Hang
simple cafe curtains to match, in a lighter shade of the same
color, or a print that features your color. Or decorate a window
shade to match (see ideas below).

2. If window has no molding, you have more flexibility. You
can add a molding, of course, by gluing and nailing down a
stock molding cut to size from the lumberyard, and then
paint it.

3. Or you can glue a broad colorful braid all around as a
frame. Use white glue. Miter neatly at corners. Trim bottom of
ordinary window shade with the same braid; or sew braid to
the tapes of Venetian blinds and also glue it to the top valance

and bottom bar of the blinds. Or use the same braid to trim cafe curtains or simple straight curtains.

4. Instead of broad braid, glue stripes of ribbon—red, white and blue, perhaps; or two shades of green.

5. Or cut a decorative motif from adhesive-backed burlap in the decorator color of your choice, and frame your window

with paper dolls standing on each other's heads, or with toy silhouettes, fleurs-de-lis or simple geometric shapes. Trim window shades with same cutout appliqués.

Cover-up a window with a "curtain" of yarn and tassels. Cut strands of rug yarn or twisted upholstery cord the length of the window plus 5", allowing two strands for each inch of width across the window. (For a window 25" wide and 48" high, cut fifty 53-inch-long strands.) Make a slipknot at one end of each strand. Buy tassels, or make them (for each tassel, cut 8 strands of rug yarn or upholstery cord 8" long, fold in half and tie together through the center with a short length of yarn or cord). Knot tassels to long strands at 10" intervals. Trim tassels and ends of knots. Slide slipknots over a cafe curtain rod and hang. Make sure the tassel at the bottom of each strand just touches the window sill or just covers the front, or apron, of the sill. Trim bottom ends of strands and tassels evenly.

Cover-up a window with striped draperies that need no lining and little sewing. This is particularly effective on very wide windows. The trick is to seam together long lengths of 36-inch wide colored cotton fabric—the kind of fabric that has no "wrong" side. Cut lengths to the height of your window plus

detail

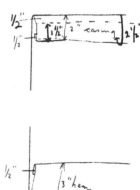

6″. Cut at least six lengths, or as many as necessary to add up to two to three times the window width, depending on the fullness desired. Sew lengths of fabric together just outside the selvage. Press seams open. Make 1″ hem at each outer edge. Make heading and casing by folding under ½″ at top, then 2″, pressing, and stitching close to bottom fold and ½″ from top fold. Make bottom hem by folding under ½″ and then 3″ and stitching first fold to right side of draperies. Add braid, fringe or other trim along hemline if desired. Each side of the draperies should have three or more stripes of fabric. Use harmonizing colors—three shades of green, or gold-orange-brown; or contrasting colors—pink-yellow-green or red-white-blue. This is an effective way to pick up the colors of a print fabric used elsewhere in the room.

Cover-up a Window Shade

For a custom-decorated window, and at a budget price, try one or more of these ways to disguise an old or ready-made shade.

Cover-up a window shade with glued-on trim. Simply attach ball-fringe, braid, rickrack, ribbon, or a wide border of fabric with white glue to an ordinary white or cream-colored shade. Add decorative trim to the bottom 12 or 18 inches only, to avoid having the trim disturbed by being wound around the roller when you pull the shade up. This is the easiest way to turn a plain old shade into just the right decorator accent that will coordinate your window with your room.

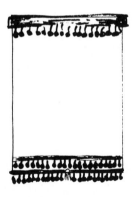

Cover-up a window shade with paint. Acrylic paint. Boldly brush a freehand design directly onto the shade, picking up colors from a printed fabric or other accessory in the room. Or lightly pencil a design traced from some other object onto the shade and paint it to match a bedspread or a wall-hanging.

Cover-up a window shade with dye. Create an entirely new design in the colors of your choice. First, prepare shade by dipping it into a bathtub-full of lukewarm water several times to remove the sizing. Hold shade by roller while dipping, but don't get roller mechanism wet. Don't drain the tub yet. Then stretch the wet shade out on top of several layers of newspaper on a floor or table. Wear rubber gloves. Use liquid dye in one or several colors. In a measuring cup mix ¼ cup dye to ¾ cup hot water. Dip an ordinary paintbrush into the dye and brush wavy lines across or down the shade at intervals. Wash brush thoroughly before changing colors. Repeat with second and third colors. Or saturate a sponge in dye and rub it over the shade in stripes or any other design that comes to mind. Rinse sponge thoroughly and repeat with another color. Let dye set for 15 minutes. Meanwhile, open drain of tub and let cold water run in. Immerse shade in tubful of cold water, dipping it up and down several times so that excess dye drains away. Completely change the water at least once. Rinse until water runs clear, or nearly so. Hang shade up in its window to dry, placing plenty of newspaper under it to catch the drips.

Important: choose a shady time of day; direct sunlight during the drying process might change the colors.

Cover-up a window shade with appliqués. Cut designs from adhesive-backed vinyl, wallpaper or fabric, and press or glue them onto shade. Glue on braid or other trim as a border.

Cover-up a window shade with a new look in shade-pulls. Try a drawer knob screwed into the bottom slat; a tassel, large pompon or two ball-fringe balls tied or stapled to the slat; or a cafe curtain rod suspended by upholstery cord from screw eyes screwed into bottom slat of shade.

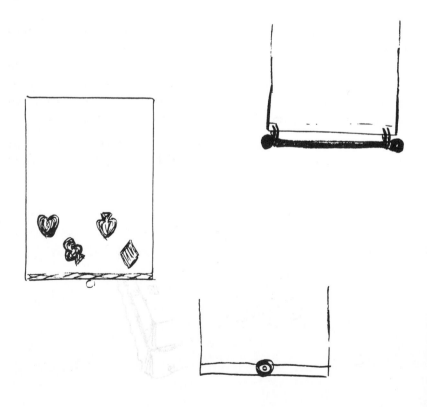

Cover-up a Bed

What do you spend fully one-third of your life in yet ignore for the other two-thirds, never use when you have guests, and is probably the clumsiest object in your home? That's right—your bed! Here are some things you can do with, to and for a bed to make it a more useful and/or attractive object to have around the house.

Cover-up a bed with dozens of throw pillows and turn it into a seating island that is the center of life and interest in your room. (See Chapter III for throw pillow ideas galore.) This is a good solution to the one-room or studio apartment problem of disguising a bed; but it is also a way to turn a bedroom into an all-day-long place for conversation and relaxation.

Cover-up a bed with a stunning two-level spread that begins with two decorator-designed flat bedsheets. Spread one sheet

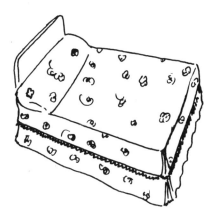

evenly over the boxspring to form an unruffled dust ruffle dipping down to the floor. And use the other as the bedspread. Not essential, but nice to add: a color-coordinated fringe all around the spread, the dust ruffle or both.

Cover-up a bed with a lace tablecloth, old quilt or any other extraordinary piece of fabric you have. So what if it is too small for your bed? Buy two flat bedsheets in a solid color that coordinates with your fabric or your room, and use them as above, one for a tailored dust ruffle, and the other across the top of the bed. Now center your lace or other fabric on the top-side sheet; the color will show through the lace as well as border it. Sew both layers together, taking long loose stitches, about an inch from the edges of the lace or other top fabric. To keep lace in place, you might want to sew across center of spread, too; just remember to keep your stitches invisible on top. I like a strong color with lace—deep blue or avocado, a soft but definite rose, or a deep gold. Happily, bedroom linens now come in all these great colors, and many others.

Cover-up a bed wall with a "headboard" made of felt and hung from a cafe curtain rod. Cut felt to the width of the bed and 2″ longer than the finished headboard. Fold over 2″ at top and stitch to make casing. Install cafe rod on the wall behind the bed at the desired height, having hardware at outer edges of bed with finials or decorative ends of rod extending beyond bed. Sew or glue appliquéd designs of your choice to the felt. Cut felt into strips and shape ends to points or scallops, alternating colors to coordinate with a spread if you like.

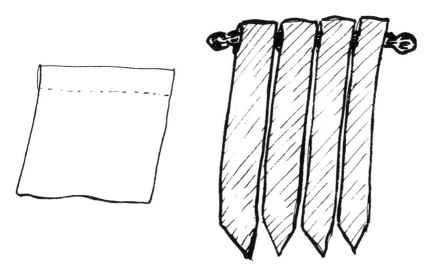

Cover-up a bed wall with a "headboard" that you hang like a picture on the wall behind the bed. Take a slab of clear ½" plywood as wide or wider than the bed and as high as you like. You also need white glue, a slab of foam rubber 1" or 2" thick,

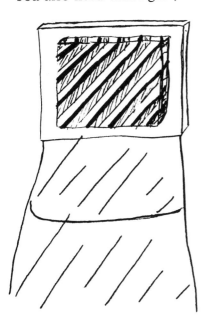

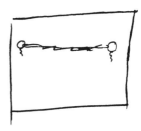

and 2″ less in each dimension than the plywood, and a piece of the fabric of your choice big enough to wrap around the foam rubber. Sandpaper the plywood, and enamel it in a bright color of your choice. Center foam rubber on wrong side of fabric, fold ends up neatly as for a gift wrapping and glue ends to wrong side of foam rubber. Spread wrong side of foam with glue and fasten to plywood. On back of plywood insert screw eyes and connect them with picture wire. Hang from two picture hooks on the wall. (See Chapter IV for more details on how to hang pictures.)

Idea! Coordinate this Cover-up with the bedspread-from-sheets one above. Open the seams of the matching pillowcase, iron to remove crease and use as the covering over the foam rubber. Enamel plywood in the color of the fringe or other trim used around spread.

Another idea! Use this plywood-and-covered-foam-rubber construction to make a headboard for a daybed and forget about bolsters. Make a single long headboard, or a pair of smaller ones. Toss throw pillows in contrasting colors against it.

Cover-up a bed with a canopy. The original bed canopies were devised several centuries ago to keep out "night vapours." Even though evening drafts are not a problem in our steam-heated homes today, the bed canopy has exciting decorative possibilities. Here are four easy ways to get the effect of a canopy over your bed, any bed . . . it doesn't even have to be a four-poster.

1. When I was about to hang the canopy valance over her window (see above), Nina, then four, thought of another use for it: "It would look pretty over a bed." And she was right. Hang a canopy valance over a bed or a crib, installing the curtain rod hardware low on the wall, the width of the bed apart.

2. Create a bed-with-a-view by gluing a length of fabric to the wall behind the bed and to the ceiling over it (use white glue or wallpaper paste). Let the front edge of the fabric hang straight down from the ceiling above the foot of the bed, and border it with fringe. Choose felt, striped awning fabric, or some other fabric that does not have a "wrong" side. The fabric width should at least equal the width of the bed. Coordinate color of this headboard-plus-canopy with the bedspread, of course. A floral-print spread of pinks, greens and whites could be topped with hot pink felt trimmed with dark green fringe.

3. A softer-looking version of this idea results from looping a long length of fabric over dowels or cafe curtain rods placed directly over the ends of the bed and suspended by rope from the ceiling. The secret of working this one out is the screw hooks, inserted in the ceiling, over which you hang a loop of rope, cord, ribbon or drapery tiebacks. Hang the dowel or rod from the bottom of the loop and drape the fabric through it (see diagram). Create a "tent" effect by letting the fabric droop slightly above the bed. Fabric ends, hemmed and/or trimmed with fringe, fall to the floor outside the head and foot of the bed. Trim front of tent-canopy with fringe, too, if you like.

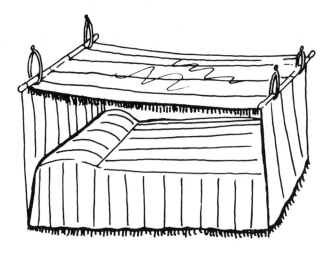

Again, choose fabric at least as wide as the bed, and with no "wrong" side. To determine the length of fabric needed: length of bed plus twice the distance from floor to ceiling. Since canopy will hang several inches below ceiling at each side, this will allow for bottom hems of about 2".

4. Surround a bed with a daintily elegant canopy made of Austrian curtains suspended from the ceiling above the bed. Available in stock sizes at most department store home-furnishings departments, Austrian curtains, with their graceful draping, can be raised and lowered to any level. Combine two Austrian curtains with a length of matching fabric draped over a rod as in #3 above. Or completely surround a bed, using one curtain at the head, one at the foot and one on each side. Or have any headboard you chose, and enclose the bed with Austrian curtains on three sides only. A matching spread would be lovely.

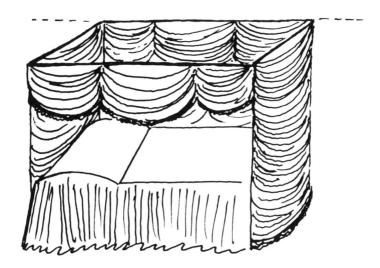

Cover-up a Wall

Cover-up a wall with paint. The least expensive and the fastest way to perk up a wall (or a door or a ceiling) is a fresh coat of paint. Please don't waste your elbow grease on a lifeless neutral color. Paint *bright* colors—a yellow that sings, clear blue, a deep bronze. Try bright red for a wall and a ceiling (if it is high). Paint all the woodwork a deep avocado. Paint a single door bright purple (a friend of mine did—and it is among the most interesting things in her expensively furnished home!). Paint a beam orange. And if you decide on white (perhaps to set off colorful paintings or furniture) make it a clear, pristine white, not one of those arty, graying off-whites.

Cover-up a wall with wallpaper or adhesive-backed vinyl. Choose a big, vivid design. Bold stripes, big flowers, or flowing, impressionistic splashes of color. No small, tidy patterns, please; they're too uptight. Don't choose dingy, pale, washed-out colors that have no *oomph*. Keep reminding yourself as you turn the pages of the sample books that you want to make a splashing, smashing *effect*. For extra zing, choose a wet look. The right wall-covering can set the color scheme and even the whole tone of your room.

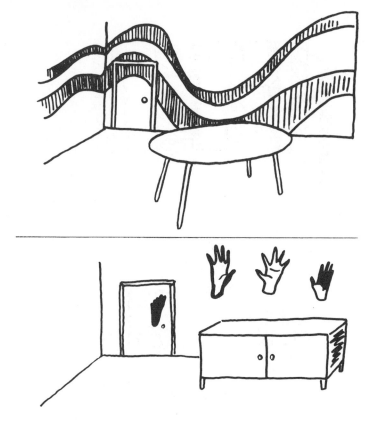

Cover-up a wall with a supergraphic. Think big. Imagine your problem wall with a broad three-band stripe of glaring colors cutting diagonally across it. Or with an enormous green footprint on it, or perhaps a path of footprints going across it. You can buy such things as a gigantic blue adhesive-backed hand to stick on your wall, or stripes and angles in various colors, also adhesive-backed, to combine—but they cost quite a bit of money. Why not dream up your own supergraphics and work them out with paint or adhesive-backed vinyl bought by the yard? Use a pencil, yardstick and a dinner plate to get your basic shapes up on the wall. Test them first by sketching and cutting on brown wrapping paper if you're leery. Or trace around your own hand or foot, shoe or shirt. If you will use paint, stick masking tape along your outline and you can paint away boldly. Pull the masking tape off before the paint dries completely to keep the fresh paint from chipping. Paint enor-

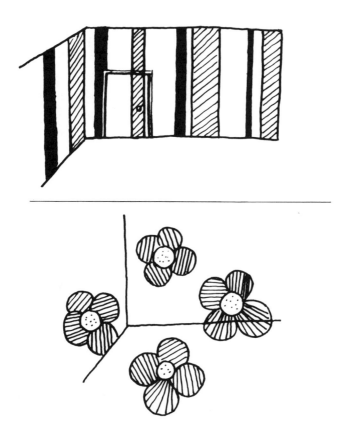

mous, fanciful flowers. Or bring a stripe across door, ceiling, two walls and even a window shade. Paint your supergraphic onto the floor, too. Use enamels or acrylics—both come in wonderful colors and take well to walls and floors.

Cover-up a wall with a collage. How about gluing wine and beer bottle labels helter-skelter on a dining-room wall? Or postage stamps (buy the large economy-size collector's pack) or playing cards on a den wall? Or whatever you come up with. Use white glue, work on a wall area of a square foot or two at a time, and finish off with a protective vinyl spray the next day, when glue is thoroughly dry.

Cover-up a wall with felt. Feature a wall covered in a bright felt—pumpkin orange, kelly green, raspberry. Perhaps a window wall, difficult to perk up with furniture or accessories, would come to life when highlighted in this way. Cover the window with a shade, blind or simple draperies, picking up the color of the felt as accent or trim on the window treatment. To get the felt up on the wall, use the kind of wallpaper paste used for fabric or vinyl wallcoverings or double-faced rug tape.

Cover-up a wall with dress fabric. Buy inexpensive dress fabric, such as a lightweight cotton, in a delicate or bright print, and glue it directly onto a wall. Paint the woodwork in a coordinating color. You can create an attractive effect if you attach molding to the wall horizontally about 3 feet

from the floor, and glue the fabric from the molding to the ceiling; paint the molding and wall below it in one of the colors in the fabric. A friend of mine did this in her daughter's room, on a wall that already had moldings on it. A white-and-green toile print went up above the moldings, and the moldings and remainder of the wall, as well as the rest of the woodwork in the room, were painted in an apple green to match. She covered a shade in the same fabric, and trimmed it with green fringe.

Cover-up a wall with carpeting. With a *rug.* A carpeted wall is an ideal way to personalize and humanize one of those open-plan contemporary apartments that invariably has the thinnest of walls separating it from the identical apartment next door. It is also a good way to modernize a large, rambling old white-elephant type of house. A carpeted wall can turn a large, open room into a cozy den. It adds warmth. It has amazing sound-deadening qualities. It can be cleaned quickly with a vacuum cleaner. It never needs repainting or rehanging.

Would you believe a room-size elevator with blue carpeting running up its walls? The Whitney Museum of American Art, on Madison Avenue, boasts what is probably the world's largest passenger elevator, spacious enough to transport the oversized constructions of many of today's artists. Riding in this elevator used to give one the feeling of being trapped in a cavernous chrome icebox. Recently redecorated with loopy carpeting covering its walls, it transports the museum visitor securely and cozily to the upstairs galleries.

To do it yourself, use squares of carpet that attach to floors or any other surface with special double-adhesive-backed carpet tape. Choose plush, shaggy or firm pile. Start at floor level and go up—as high as you like. Up to the ceiling if that's your preference. Or halfway up the wall; end with a border of wood molding, perhaps. Match your wall and floor coverings for a "where-does-the-floor-end-and-the-wall-begin" effect. Even better, carpet some furnishings, too. Make a banquette of a row of wood cubes, perhaps, carpeted all around to double for sitting and storage. Or the outer walls of an armoire or bookcase could be carpeted to blend into the wall. This is an excellent way to disguise an unfinished wood or inexpensive metal or fiberboard closet, or a beat-up old filing cabinet, or any other necessary but unattractive storage piece.

Cover-up a wall with mirrors. Mirrors are not just for looking at yourself. They can create wonderful effects when used well—enlarge a small space, bring a cityscape or a pastoral scene indoors, enhance the appearance of works of art. But when used badly, mirrors reflect only the "blahness" of a room.

I expanded a narrow corridor used for dining by placing mirrors on both walls low enough so that guests are seated both in front of and facing mirrors. Wherever they look, they see a glittering infinity of reflections, instead of being hemmed in by walls. And I stand sculptures in front of a mirror so that their total structure can be seen.

Put-them-up-yourself mirrored tiles make it possible for you to cover a whole wall or an area in almost no time, and at moderate cost. Follow directions with the tiles.

A mirror calls attention to what appears in it. Don't put mrirors where they will reflect nothing, or something of little interest. Place mirrors to reflect an outdoor view or a beautiful object in your home. Mirror one wall in a room and paper the others; the mirror will brighten and reflect the whole room.

If an entrance to your home faces a closet door (I wonder why so many do) or a hallway wall, cover the door or wall with mirrors. If the hall between bedrooms is a small cul-de-sac, mirror it. Or mirror the walls of a bathroom. Mirror tiles can also be effective when attached to cubes, built-in closets and the side walls of bookcases. But never hang a mirror as though it were a picture. I did, once—and hated the sight of the pair of oval, elegantly framed mirrors instantly. It was as though I were hanging empty frames, for all the effect those mirrors provided.

Cover-up a wall with foil, for a more subtle, more shimmering reflection. Use a foil-finished wallpaper, adhesive-backed foil, or glue on heavy-duty aluminum foil from the supermarket for a super-economical super-smashing effect. Do one wall in foil and the rest of the room in an all-over color-printed wallpaper. Or use a room of foil-covered walls to reflect brightly colored furnishings, expand a small room or set off an austere black-and-white color scheme with cool, elegant chic.

More Cover-ups

Cover-up a door with a trompe l'oeil painting that pretends to show what might be on the other side—a house, trees, a garden, a cloud-filled sky. The whole trick is to paint a realistic picture on the panels of the door. If you can't do it yourself, get an artist friend to contribute his talents while you contribute the idea. And if there is no artist handy, look for a wallpaper design that has the same effect, and buy only one roll or panel of it. Or cut realistic pictures from magazines or seed catalogues and combine them your way.

Cover-up pipes and beams with bright paint. How about orange and yellow to turn such eyesores as overhead water pipes, steam risers and gas meters to good advantage? Or red, white and blue? Instant pop art. For an elegant look, cover a ceiling or a floor-to-ceiling beam with wood-grain adhesive-backed vinyl, or glue wide braid, or velvet, felt or other fabric, to the beams.

Cover-up a switch-plate with paint, wallpaper, fabric or adhesive-backed vinyl. First, prepare the switch-plate for recovering. Remove it from wall (usually two screws hold it in place). Then clean it to remove grease and dirt; use detergent, or steel wool if necessary. If there is an accumulation of old paint on it and you have some paint remover handy, use it; if not, buy a new switch-plate, the least expensive variety, in the hardware store.

Cover with paint to contrast with your walls, to match the woodwork or a supergraphic or a painted beam or door. Use washable, bright acrylic or enamel.

To cover with fabric, wallpaper or adhesive-backed vinyl: trace outline of switch-plate on wrong side of covering material. Add ½" allowance all around. Cut out. Slash in corners and at center of pattern as indicated in diagram. Cut out holes

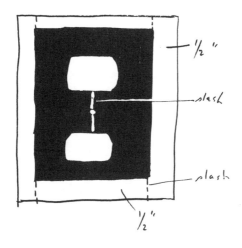

for switches. If using adhesive-backed vinyl, remove paper backing and place switch-plate face down on adhesive side. If using fabric or wallpaper, spread wrong side with white glue or wallpaper paste and place switch-plate face down. Turn margin to wrong side, folding long sides under first and then pressing shorter sides down. Use fingers to smooth covering down and press out paste or air bubbles. Make sure screw holes are accessible by opening covering ¼" at center slash. When pasted covering is dry, screw switch-plate back onto wall.

Cover-up a Floor

Cover-up a floor with a patchwork rug you make from carpeting remnants. These are pieces about 18" by 30" or 24" by 36" that are sold at most carpet stores for use as TV mats. Use white glue to secure your carpet patches to a backing of cotton canvas or duck. Choose patches of related color but different textures—for instance, blues ranging from pale through marine, or golds, rusts and browns, in shag, loop, velvet, carved pile and tweeds. Cut carpeting to shape with a carpet knife or sharp shears, working on the carpet backing along a metal straight-edge (trying not to clip off any extra pile).

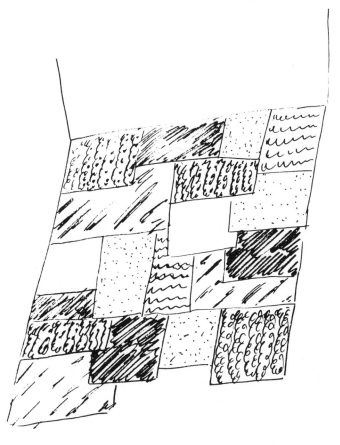

Cover-up a floor with a checkerboard in vinyl or linoleum tile. Plan a red and white checkerboard, and outline it in blue at the edges of the room. Or be different and match your color scheme with cream and brown, outlined in orange. Or whatever your color scheme is. Perfect for a playroom, child's room or den.

Cover-up a floor with an area rug cut in the design of your choice. Buy a cut-it-to-fit nylon carpet—the kind intended for use in bathrooms. Decide on your design, trace it on wrapping paper first and cut it out. Try it on your floor for size and shape. When the pattern is finalized, trace it onto the carpet backing and cut out, using sharp scissors. Outline your design with twisted braid or fringe, in a matching or contrasting color.

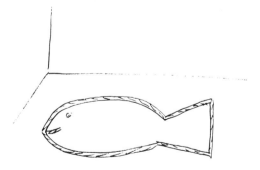

Designs for area rugs could include simplified bird, fish or dog shapes (to match a pet, perhaps), or playing-card symbols, zodiac signs or . . . whatever you come up with.

Cover-up a Seat

Cover-up a chair or sofa cushion with Instant Upholstery. Turn a foam rubber seat pad of any size into a handsome place to sit, with little or no sewing, for the quickest and least expensive way to dress up an inexpensive sofa or daybed. Cover wedge or square bolsters to match, and you have a smart new sofa. Best of all, you will have invested so little of your time and money in this Instant Upholstery that you will have no qualms at all about discarding it and replacing it with a new version in a year or two.

The trick of Instant Upholstery is to wrap the foam rubber up as though you were gift wrapping a package. Measure your covering fabric as though it were wrapping paper—you need enough to go completely around both sides of the seat cushion plus an inch or two for overlap. And each end should extend

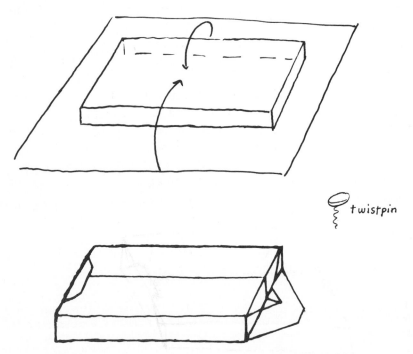

twistpin

beyond the pillow at least the combined measurement of the depth of the pillow plus 2". (It becomes clearer if you look at the diagram.)

Then, start wrapping. Probably you'll want the seam hidden on the underside of the cushion. So center the cushion top down on the wrong side of the fabric. Bring the sides of the fabric to the top, smoothing them out neatly so they overlap approximately at the center of the cushion. Now stick straight pins down through the overlapped layers of fabric right into the foam rubber, at intervals of an inch or two all the way across, and leave them there to hold the fabric in place while you continue wrapping. Fold in both corners at one end exactly as though wrapping a package, bring end up neatly and pin down into the foam rubber. Repeat for other end. Now, you have a neatly wrapped "gift" of foam rubber.

To fasten your handiwork more or less permanently, you can:

a) Use twist pins (available at the notions counter) to replace straight pins, following package directions.

b) Use an automatic buttonhole-attaching gadget (also to be found at the notions counter) and the regular shank button fasteners that come with it. The gadget punches the fastener through the fabric into the foam rubber, where it stays and holds. When you want to remove the fastener, simply cut off its T-shaped head.

c) Sew, using a cross-stitch and buttonhole twist or cord for extra strength; a curved upholsterer's needle might be helpful. Make your stitches large and decorative, to call attention to the construction of your cushion; or make them invisible.

If you choose decorative stitching, have the long sides of your fabric meet and overlap at the front upper corner instead of being concealed at the center of the wrong side.

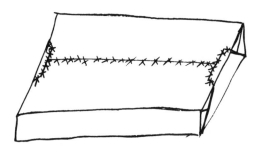

Or decorate your gift-wrapped upholstery with a sewn-on "ribbon" of braid running across it in both directions. Sew on a flat bow, too.

For fabrics, anything goes if it is closely woven, firm and not scratchy. After all, it is to be sat on. No burlap, for example. But do use mattress ticking, awning material, felt or denim. Polyester knits are good stretchy fabrics that go on easily and wear well. You might turn a woven Madras bed throw, a Scotch tartan, or a length of men's wear suiting into striking upholstery.

If you cut with pinking shears, you won't have a problem with raveling edges. But if the fabric of your choice tends to fray at the cut edges, allow an extra inch in each direction, turn under ½″ on each edge and stitch ¼″ from fold. Of course, the selvage edge of the fabric does not have to be hemmed in this way. So use it, if possible, for the long edges of your covering. And felt does not have to be hemmed at all.

Cover-up a Lampshade

Cover-up a lampshade with new trim. For a lampshade that's dull but still in perfectly good shape (and who doesn't have at least one of those?), get out your imagination, scissors, a container of white glue and scraps of fabric, assorted trimmings or colored paper. First check to make sure the basic shade is really worth working on. If it isn't, buy an inexpensive one in the five-and-ten, or look below for two quick ways to recover it.

Remove all old trimming, if any, from the shade; if it is stitched down, cut the stitching to remove. If trim is glued down you may have to dampen it with a sponge and wait a few minutes for the old glue to soften before you can gently pull it off.

Revive your shade with any of these ideas that are appropriate to the room in which you will use it:

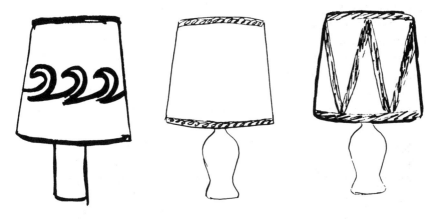

1. Glue gimp (upholstery braid) or grosgrain ribbon around top and bottom edges, folding it over to cover the wires to which the shade is attached at top and bottom. Use clothespins to hold gimp in place until glue dries.

2. Glue gimp or ribbon in a design on the center of the shade.

3. Glue the balls from ball-fringe helter-skelter over the shade; use the braid part to trim top and bottom.

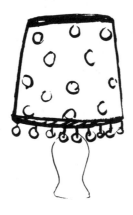

4. Glue felt or construction paper cutouts in suitable designs around shade. Use paper-doll or clown shapes for a child's room, playing-card symbols or silhouettes of chessmen in a game room.

5. Glue fringe to top and bottom instead of gimp.

6. Glue colored tissue-paper pieces overlapping each other; use white glue diluted with an equal amount of water and brush on thinly under and over patches of paper. Let dry. Then glue ribbon or braid at top and bottom. The colors will glow like stained glass when the lamp is lit. Use the right colors for your room, of course.

Cover-up a lampshade with fabric or wallpaper. If the old cardboard or other stiff material of the shade is still sturdy, but just not fresh, give it a new lease on life. Cover it with fabric—light- or medium-weight cotton, like gingham. Silk is best for letting light through, but a loosely woven heavier fabric can be effective, too. Or repeat the room's wall-covering.

Cut covering to the height of the old shade. The width will be the circumference of the shade plus 1″ for overlap. Use white glue diluted slightly with water.

Remove all trim from old shade. Brush diluted glue evenly over shade. Place new covering in position, starting from bottom and carefully smoothing it out to remove air bubbles. Trim overlap to ½″; brush with glue and press fabric or wallpaper in place. Use clothespins to hold until glue dries. Then trim in any of the ways suggested above.

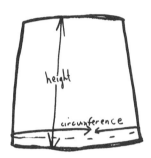 

If shade slopes sharply, cut covering two or three inches deeper than shade, and cut to the widest circumference plus 1″. Start positioning covering from center bottom, smoothing it upward and outward. The fabric can be stretched to the shape of the shade by smoothing and pulling it on the bias from center bottom up and out to the corners. Trim excess at top and bottom; trim overlap allowance to a straight ½″ seam, and to go straight up one side of shade. Glue overlap seam. Do not use a striped or other regularly arranged design for covering this shape shade.

Cover-up a lampshade with a new cardboard shade. Remove old shade carefully; it will become your pattern. For the new covering, choose a light, flexible firm paper or cardboard, such as oak tag, parchment paper or rice paper, all available in art supply stores. Cut to size required, following the dimensions of the old shade. Be sure to allow at least ½″ for overlap. (Don't attempt a cardboard replacement for a very curvy shade.)

Remove old tape wrapping the wire frame of the old shade, if any. If wire frame is damaged, rub it with steel wool and wipe clean. Rewrap top and bottom wires of frame, using cot-

ton bias twill or seam tape (*not* bias binding). Wrap tightly, overlapping tape slightly as you work, holding beginning and end with clothespins. Sew end of tape securely to beginning with small, invisible stitches.

Glue new covering to top and bottom of frame, and hold in place with clothespins until glue dries. Trim overlap to an even ½", and glue. Hold with clothespins until dry. Now trim or decorate as desired.

৵ III ৵

Everything You Always Wanted to Know About Throw Pillows...

My nomination for the most adaptable, useful decorative accent is the throw pillow. It can be frilly, feminine, romantic, tailored, practical, perky, elegant, cozy; it adds color to a monochromatic room; it pulls together a room with too much pattern and color in it; it creates an intimate effect even in a formal setting; brightens a dull corner; brings a contemporary note to a traditional background; and softens the starkness of a modern setting. Or it blends unobtrusively with the other furnishings. In short, it can create any effect you want it to.

Where Should Throw Pillows Be Thrown?

On a daybed, tossed in a heap against the bolster to make sitting more comfortable and inviting. On a sofa. On a bed. On an easy chair or a lounge chair. On a bench or window seat. On the floor. Almost anywhere.

Use throw pillows when you want to pick up and emphasize one of the colors in a printed fabric. When you are tired of a room's look and want to freshen it with a clear color accent. When the back of the sofa is just a bit too far from the front for comfortable seating. When a lounge chair seems to be an unbroken expanse of one color or fabric. *Any*time.

You can use one, two or a dozen—it's up to you. But never, never put one teeny-weeny pillow all by itself. If one is all you want, then be sure it's a great big noticeable one that makes a grand effect.

You may find that throw pillows are addictive: you can start with two, and just keep on adding more. I know one gal who got so carried away that she added two at a time to a guest-room daybed until there were so many pillows on the bed that no one could sit on it! And when she had to make the bed up for a guest, it took five whole minutes just to remove and stack the throw pillows. Dramatic action was needed to cure this extreme case of throw-pillow addiction. The lady in question moved to a smaller apartment, with no guest room. She did save her three favorite throw pillows, however, to toss on a lounge chair; but she hasn't gotten another one since.

Why Are Really Nice Throw Pillows So Expensive?

The high cost of labor, I suppose. I don't know. Inexpensive ones can be found at the dimestore, but the trouble is that they usually look exactly as though they came from the dimestore. (See the end of this chapter for ideas about what can be done to dress them up.)

Why Can't I Make One Myself?

Now you're talking! Of course you can. You can make stunning ones for just pennies, and in practically no time, too. And you can make really elegant ones, from luxury materials like leather and velvet, for only a little more money, and not necessarily more time. If you are a clever shopper, you will discover odds and ends of exciting fabrics that can be bought for a fraction of their original cost.

What Should a Throw Pillow Be Stuffed With?

You *can* use anything from old rags to absorbent cotton. Here is my list, in preferential order.

1. *Nylon stockings (and pantyhose)*—those with conspicuous runs, of course. They have the advantage of being, alas, usually available in quantity, at no additional cost. As you wear out your hose, launder them, cut into 4″ or 6″ lengths (don't even bother to measure; just cut) and store in a shoebox or shopping bag until you collect enough to stuff a pillow. Discard the elastic parts, if any. If, in addition, you use washable fabric and shrink-proof trim, you'll have wash-and-wear pillows. One of my favorites is nylon-stuffed, its cover crocheted in acrylic yarn and trimmed with acrylic fringe. It goes in the washing machine and dryer regularly. If you use nylon leftovers for pillow stuffing, you may need to make a pillow slip; see number 5 below.

2. *Old feather pillows.* Everybody usually acquires one or two of these, usually sooner than she'd like. When your pillows have gotten too flat even to give to guests, here's what to do.

tack corners
together

tack corners
together

For a rectangular throw pillow: hold pillow vertically by two corners and shake until all the feathers that are left in it tumble to the bottom. Then, fold top half over bottom half tack top corners to bottom corners. My pillow measured 21″ by 27″ when it was new, according to the label. But when I got finished shaking and folding it, I was able to push it into a 17″ by 17″ pillow form.

For a cylinder-shaped or bolster-type throw pillow: hold pillow horizontally by two corners and shake and roll until top edge is alongside bottom edge and you have a plump cylinder shape. Tack corners and both edges together.

If you have two old feather pillows, tack one on top of the other and cover with vinyl for a floor pillow.

3. *Store-bought pillow forms.* My five-and-ten carries foam rubber, or urethane foam, pillow forms. Usually several of the

following standard sizes are available: box-edge, 2½" deep; and knife-edge, 10", 12", 14", and 16" round and square. In addition, there are some special sizes designed for use as seat pads, but these could make pillows or be combined with other pillow forms for special effects: 15" by 15" by 1½"; 17" by 17" by 1½"; 17" by 17" by 2"; 18" by 18" by 3" and 22" by 36" by 2".

This useful material also comes by the pound in bags of shredded flakes (see number 5 below) and by the yard in sheets 1", 1½" and 2" thick.

What you find when you shop for pillow forms may be a matter of chance, depending on how well-stocked your local merchant is that day. Fortunately, foam rubber can be both cut and glued, so that even if all you can locate is 1" foam by the yard, you can cut it (with scissors, a single-edge razor blade, an electric knife or a saw). Measure first, of course, and mark with a ballpoint pen. Glue pieces together with rubber cement. In this way you can also build up cubes or pyramids or any special shape you dream up. Cut or shred leftovers and save to use for stuffing more pillows.

Sheet foam rubber can also be used to make a cylinder or bolster shape. Simply cut it to the width desired and roll, jelly-roll fashion, until your cylinder is as thick as you like. Cut off excess on an angle to make a neat edge. Fasten with rubber cement along inside of edge and also tie loosely with strong thin thread (dental floss or buttonhole twist) about 1" from each end and in a few places between. Be sure to tie loosely enough so that the foam isn't compressed out of shape.

Muslin-covered kapok-filled pillow forms can be bought in some stores. These are, of course, more expensive; and there is no way to change the size or shape.

4. *The insides of old throw pillows.* If you're lucky, you can reuse the pillow forms that gave your old, worn-out throw pillows their shapes. You have to be careful, though. One day, I was all set to do this, and had even cut my new fabric for the new pillows I was going to make, when I opened my old throw pillow to find that its insides were a mass of threads. Another time, I found a foam rubber interior that was shredding all by itself. (The newer foam rubber of the last few years is not supposed to do this.) So open a seam for an inch or two in order to analyze whether what lies within is worth recycling.

5. *Kapok, cotton batting, foam rubber flakes.* These have the minor disadvantage of needing a cover or slip made for them, unless the outer cover of the pillow is to be of a firmly woven fabric. However, it's easy enough to make a cover.

Cut two squares or rectangles of plain cotton fabric (muslin, an old sheet or even an old linen dishtowel will do), making each dimension 1″ larger than the finished pillow's corresponding dimension is to be. Place right sides together and sew com-

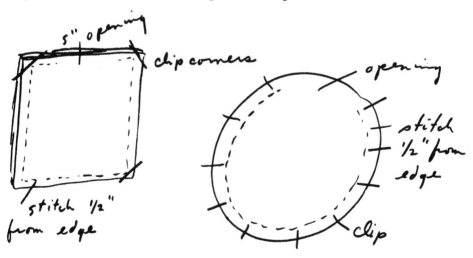

pletely around ½″ from edge, leaving a 5″ opening. Clip corners of rectangle, or clip every few inches around circle (clip means to cut neatly through from the outside edge just up to the stitching). Turn inside out, and stuff with shredded foam, cut-up nylon hose, or whatever. Pack stuffing in tightly; be sure to get it into corners and around edges. Use a long pencil or a fork to help. When your pillow form is well stuffed, sew up opening with small slipstitches close to edge.

What Can I Use to Cover a Throw Pillow?

Almost anything that will lie flat and can be stitched (or, in a pinch, glued). Almost any woven fabric (but not, I hope something like burlap, which sheds and is scratchy), and felts and vinyls. Here are a few quick-and-easy ideas; detailed instructions for making Eight Basic Fabulous Pillows are below.

1. Place two cotton or linen dinner napkins with their right sides together and sew around three sides, leaving at least a ½" seam and making the square of stitches ½" larger all around than the pillow form you will cover. For example, to cover a 14" square knife-edge pillow form, sew a 14½" square in 16" napkins, leaving a margin of ¾" on all sides. Clip corners, turn right side out, insert pillow form, turn under edges of

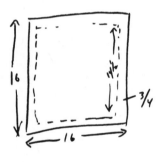
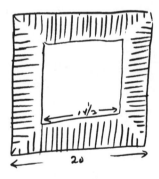

opening and slipstitch close to edge. Or, instead of napkins, use terry washcloths or fingertip towels—the rough texture looks great against slick vinyl upholstery, or on rattan furniture. Use smooth terry velour washcloths to make throw pillows for a child's room. Or simply cut 16" squares of any fabric of your choice.

2. Cut two pieces of felt or vinyl 20" by 20". Mark margin of 2¾" all around. Place with *wrong* sides together and sew three sides of a square 14½" by 14½". Insert 14" square knife-edge pillow form; sew up open edge close to edge of pillow form.

Cut through both layers of felt or vinyl every ¼″ to make self-fringe, graduating cuts at corners. Use sewing machine and matching thread for invisible stitches; or add decoration at the same time as you sew by hand-stitching with contrasting yarn, cord or embroidery floss. Use running or back stitches, or any decorative stitch you like.

3. Make this simple sew-around pillow of tweed or heavy linen, following directions in 2 above. Pull threads out at margin for self-fringe. For a crewel-embroidered version, see Pillow number 2 below.

4. Use yarn to blanket-stitch felt squares or circles together, or glue them together (use white glue). Cut felt 1½″ larger in each dimension than the pillow form. For a 14″ knife-edge pillow form, cut felt 15½″ by 15½″ square, or 15½″ in diameter. Stitched or glued seam allowance is ½″. This one is really quick. Trim as desired; glue on decorative fringe or purchased embroidered motifs.

5. Make one large afghan patch or crochet four smaller ones together, for each "face" of a crocheted pillow. With wrong sides together, work a row of single crochet around three sides;

insert pillow form and crochet up the fourth side. Keep on crocheting for a more prominent edging; add picots or any other fancy stitches you like. Trim with yarn tassels (see Chapter IX).

How Do You Get It All Together?

I've just shown you the easiest way: simply sew right around a knife-edge pillow. This makes a cover that cannot be removed.

To make a removable cover, insert snaps or a zipper instead of sewing the fourth side closed. Add trimming around the edges to conceal the opening.

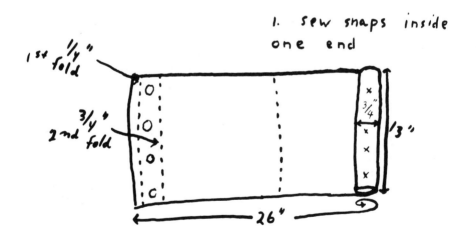

Easy Way to Make a Snap-Closed 12" Square Pillow Cover

1. sew snaps inside one end

2. sew snaps on outside of other end

3. close snaps; fold in half with right sides together; sew up ½" seams at each side. Unsnap and turn right side out.

snap closing

Box-edge pillows are more complicated. The Round Felt Pin-Together Pillow, number 4 below, is the easiest and quickest one I know. Pillow number 5, the Box-Edge Leather Square, is a handsome way to do it. But I don't think it's worth the fuss to sew up a rectangular box-edge pillow, when you get just as good an effect with much less fuss from the knife-edge style. And effect is what you're after.

Eight Basic but Fabulous Throw Pillows

PILLOW #1: SELF-FRINGED SUEDE SEW-AROUND

Luxury materials turn the simplest pillow into a knockout. Try making this suede variation of the sew-around style.

MATERIALS:
    2 pieces of suede 16″ square
    10″ knife-edge pillow form
    pins and/or rubber cement

HOW-TO:
    1. Sandwich pillow form between suede squares, centered. Stick pins through on both sides to hold in place. A dab of rubber cement might be helpful, too.
    2. Stitch around pillow, sewing close to pillow form. Be careful not to catch any foam rubber in your stitching. Use hand or machine stitches, use blending or contrasting colored thread.

3. Cut fringe ½" apart, with slashes ending ¼" from stitching.

Idea! Make it round, instead. Or make a pair.

PILLOW #2: CREWEL SEW-AROUND WITH SELF-FRINGE

MATERIALS
   ½ yard linen
   assorted crewel or finger yarns
   crewel needle
   1 sheet paper, pencil, dressmaker's carbon paper
   12" square knife-edge pillow form

HOW-TO:
   1. Cut two 18" squares of linen.
   2. Mark a 10" square on paper. Choose design (from any source: wallpaper motif, coloring book or one of the flower or other patterns in Chapter X). Use pencil and dressmaker's carbon paper to center design on paper. Then place carbon face down over one linen square, center paper pattern on cloth and trace design.
   3. Work design in yarn, using the basic embroidery stitches suggested in Chapter IX, or any stitches you know. Don't worry if the edges of the fabric ravel while you're working; you're going to pull out a lot more of them for the fringe.
   4. If work looks rumpled, block, following directions in Chapter IX. You can avoid excess rumpling of embroideries by using a hoop or by being very careful.

5. Place both fabric squares with their wrong sides together and center pillow form between them. Pin through fabric into foam to hold the "sandwich" steady.
6. Stitch completely around pillow close to pillow form. Make two rows of stitches adjacent to each other. If you sew by machine, use one of your crewel yarns to cover up the machine stitching decoratively. If you sew by hand, work two rows of running stitches with crewel yarn.
7. Now start pulling threads from the edges. Pull them out until there is only about ½" of woven fabric left beyond the stitching.

PILLOW #3: ANY-SHAPED PILLOW
WITH DECORATIVE EDGE

MATERIALS:
½ to 1 yard firmly woven fabric
assorted trimmings
  and/or contrasting fabric for appliqué
  and/or thread or yarn for embroidery
1½ to 2½ yards braid, fringe or other trim for edges
shredded foam rubber, kapok or other stuffing

HOW-TO:
1. Cut two pieces of fabric to shape desired, 1½" larger in every dimension than finished pillow is to be. To make a triangular pillow 14" by 14" by 14", cut two pieces of fabric 15½" by 15½" by 15½". To make a rectangular pillow 12" by 16", cut two pieces of fabric 13½" by 17½".
2. Embroider or appliqué desired design (see suggestions at end of this chapter, and designs in Chapter X for ideas) on right side of one piece of fabric. The flower on my triangular pillow and the fish on my rectangular pillow were appliquéd in contrasting colors and sewn to the main fabric with yarn in both the main and contrasting colors, using chain and running stitches and French knots.
3. Add up the dimensions of the sides of the pillow as cut to determine how much fringe is needed to go around.

The triangle would need 46½″ (3 times 15½″); better figure on 1½ yards. The rectangle would need 62″; get 2 yards. Use extra fringe in design, or save scraps for other projects.

4. Pin fringe to right side of top piece of fabric, so the base of fringe is ¼″ from outer edge of fabric and the fringy part faces toward center. Ease around corners. Baste or stay-stitch near base of fringe.

5. Place second piece of fabric over top piece with right sides together. Fringe should be sandwiched between them, with only the woven base showing around edges. Pin to hold; then sew around ½″ from edge. Fringe will be caught up in the stitches and firmly attached to pillow cover. Leave a 6″ opening.

6. Turn right sides out. Poke corners to get them straight. Push stuffing into pillow.

7. Slipstitch opening.

Idea #1: Make a Pillow-Doll: The basic shape is a vertical triangle. Round off the points. Sew seams as above, omitting fringed edge. Embroider features; use yarn and braid it for hair; tie with thick acrylic yarn hair-ties; sew on real buttons for front of dress, real lace for collar. To conceal seam, tack thick acrylic yarn around edges.

Idea #2: You may want to cover the pillow stuffing with a pillow slip before making the outside of the pillow. If you choose a loosely woven or thin fabric for the pillow covering, you will have to make a pillow slip.

Idea #3: If you are planning a pillow with a really tricky shape, get 1″ foam rubber by the yard and cut two pieces of

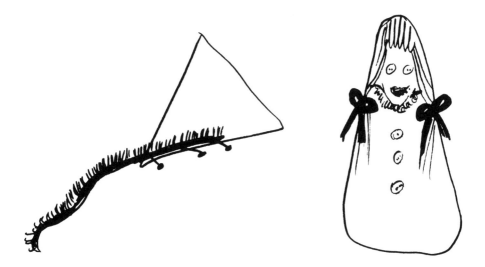

it in your pattern, using shears. Cut excess foam into small bits and sandwich it between large foam pieces for plumpness just before sewing up the pillow opening.

PILLOW #4: ROUND FELT PIN-TOGETHER

MATERIALS
    14″ round foam-rubber pillow form, 2½″ deep
    ½ yard wool felt, color A
    ¼ yard wool felt, color B
    knitting worsted, color B
    scraps of felt or other trim in contrasting colors
    white glue, needle, pins, pinking shears

HOW-TO:
    1. With pinking shears, cut two circles 15″ in diameter from color-A felt. (Use a large platter or pot lid as a pattern for the circle; or make a compass out of cord by tying two knots 7½″ apart; pin one knot to felt and tie pencil to cord at other knot; pivot pencil around to make circle.)

Note: If you don't have pinking shears, or for a different effect, cut felt circles with straight shears and work a ¼″ blanket-stitch edging around the outside of each circle.

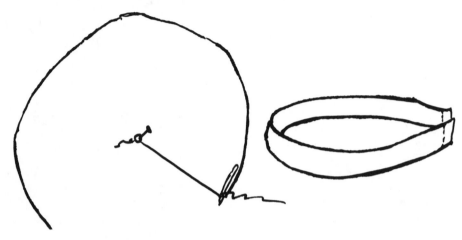

2. With straight shears cut boxing strip 44½" long and 3½" wide from color-B felt.

3. Place two short ends of boxing strip together and seam ½" from end. Turn right side out. Place around pillow form, with long edges extending ½" over edge of pillow form. Fold this allowance over and pin into foam rubber, evening out fullness of felt as you pin. Pin at both top and bottom.

4. Sandwich pillow form between felt circles, carefully centering them over and under foam "filling" so that there is ½" of felt sticking out all around. Pin felt circles into foam.

5. Use yarn and large running stitches (about ½" long) to sew top felt circle to pinned-under edge of boxing strip.

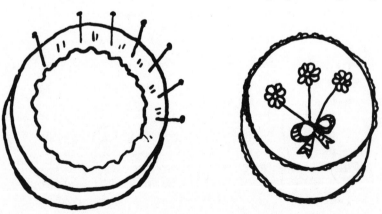

Stitches will be about ¾" from outer edge of circle. Remove pins as you sew. Repeat for bottom felt circle.

6. On the top of the pillow, use glue to appliqué design of felt geometric shapes or whatever you like. Or glue "flowers" of ball-fringe, using strips of yarn or felt for "stems."

Idea: You can sew decorations onto top and bottom felt circles before step 4. Sew bright buttons; machine stitch felt appliqués; embroider a simple outline design in yarn.

PILLOW #5: BOX-EDGE LEATHER SQUARE PILLOW

MATERIALS:
garment-quality split cowhide skin, about 4 sq. ft., color A
scraps, about 1 sq. ft., of contrasting color B
fine-point felt-tipped marker
rubber cement, sheet of paper
heavy scissors, one-edge razor blade or craft knife
metal straightedge
leather punch
9" square foam-rubber pillow form, 1½" deep

HOW-TO:
1. Use felt-tipped marker and metal ruler to mark color-A leather on wrong side, following the diagram. Outline two 10" panels and two 2" by 22" strips.
2. Use shears or razor blade or knife held along metal ruler to cut out marked sections. Round off corners of

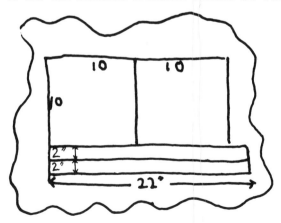

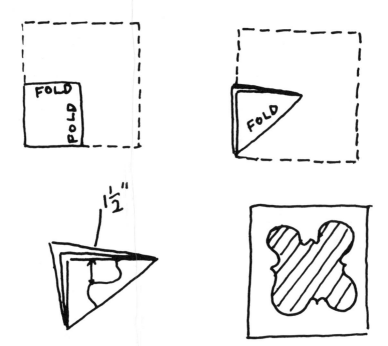

square panels slightly. Cut remainder of color-A skin in long strips about ¼″ wide for lacing.

3. To create symmetrical appliqué design: cut a 10″ square out of paper. Fold in quarters, then fold once more to form a triangle eight layers thick. Cut a free-form design into folded paper. Unfold to see your design. Anything goes, as long as there is a minimum paper margin of 1½″ all around the sides. If you don't like the first design you create, get another piece of paper and fold, cut and unfold again.

4. On wrong side of color-B leather, mark a 10″ square and cut out. Trace your appliqué design onto wrong side of this square, and cut it out. Glue design panel over one color-A panel with rubber cement. Press gently, making sure that center cut edges of design are securely attached to leather. Rub off excess rubber cement.

5. Mark panels and boxing strips for lacing holes. Holes should be ¼″ from edge and ½″ apart. There will be twenty holes on each side of panel, including corners.

6. Punch holes, using largest hole of leather punch. On appliquéd panel, punch through both layers of leather.
7. Cut one end of each lacing strip at an angle to form a point. Place one boxing strip along one edge of bottom panel, about two inches in from the left corner, with wrong sides together and holes matched up. Lace as though you were doing an overcasting stitch. Leave a 2″ end of lacing between pieces of leather. Bring point of lacing through hole in boxing strip away from you. Bring it over to the front and through both layers of leather from front to back. When you get to corner, work two stitches in same set of holes to turn corner. To join new piece of lacing, work old lacing through top hole, bring end of old lacing to wrong side and weave it back under four stitches, leaving a short end. Start new lacing on

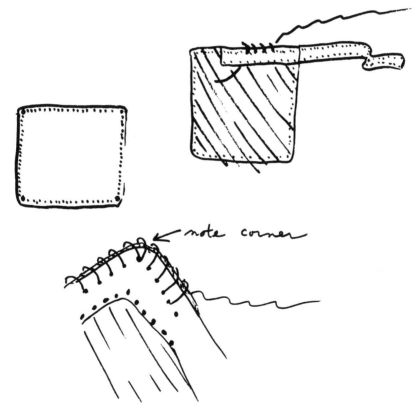

note corner

wrong side, leaving a 2″ end between pieces of leather. Work through bottom hole, then work next four stitches catching end of new lacing into them on wrong side. Glue loose ends inside with rubber cement later. When you have laced up to the last inch of the first boxing strip, join second boxing strip by overlapping them for 1 inch, with holes together, and lace through all layers.

8. Lace completely around one panel. End off and glue all lacing ends to inside. Also glue overlap of boxing strip.

9. Put top leather panel in place with corners corresponding, and lace along three sides. Lace all ends. Insert pillow form and continue lacing around fourth side until pillow is completely closed. If necessary to attach new lacing strip, poke ends between leather pieces to inside, and poke in a drop of glue, too. When finished, work lacing through last hole, cut end to 2″, brush with rubber cement and poke to inside of work. Rub off any rubber cement that gets on outside of pillow.

Idea #1: Buy two 5-foot skins and make two pillows, reversing colors.

Idea #2: Substitute felt or leather-like vinyl, and blanket-stitch edges with yarn or cord.

PILLOW #6: QUICK PATCHWORK CIRCLE

MATERIALS:

½ yard light cotton fabric for base (anything will do—a man's shirt, an old pillowcase, or unmatched leftovers)

assorted fabric scraps of related weight and texture (I used

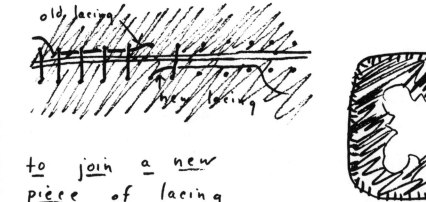

old lacing

new lacing

to join a new piece of lacing

6 old neckties; other possibilities are pieces cut off to shorten dress hems, odds and ends of upholstery fabric, swatches of fabric samples, or any sewing-basket odds and ends)

pins; needle and sewing thread

felt-tipped marker

embroidery needle; embroidery floss or twist

1 yard fringe or other trim for edge

shredded foam, nylon stockings, or 12″ knife-edge round pillow form

How-to:

1. Cut fabric into two pieces about 14″ square. On each trace a circle 12″ in diameter (a large dinner plate or a skillet lid is a good pattern). Use felt-tipped marker so that circe can be seen on both sides of fabric.

2. Prepare patchwork fabric. If you are using neckties remove linings and interlinings, and cut into irregularly shaped pieces about 2″ by 3″. For other fabrics, remove loose threads and cut similarly.

3. The time-saving feature of this patchwork is that you sew the patches directly onto the base of your work, using decorative topstitching as you go. No more tedious seaming and pressing with this method; lining, patches and embroidery are all worked on together. Here's how: Start approximately at the center of one of the circles you have drawn. Take one patch and fold one side of it

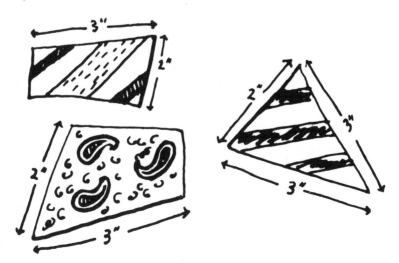

under about ¼". Use needle and thread to baste patch onto cotton base, working close to all raw edges only. Take second patch, fold one edge under and place it over the first patch so that the folded edge covers a raw edge. Pin this folded edge down. Baste raw edges of second patch. Continue working in this way until you patches have covered a good bit of the base fabric. Tuck a raw edge of one patch under the folded edge of the first patch and pin.

4. After a 4- or 5-inch area is covered, begin embroidering. Work a row of small blanket-, cross- or chain stitches around each patch, being sure to stitch through folded edges and secure them to the base. Vary stitches and colors of threads for special effects. (I used three shades of red, ranging from orange to wine, on patches featuring mostly red stripes against blues, blacks, golds; and finished pillow off with red fringe.)

5. Continue adding patches and embroidering edges until patchwork extends about ½" beyond the circle you have drawn. Work other cotton piece similarly.

6. To finish pillow: work a row of machine stitches or hand backstitches along circle; follow marks on wrong side of cloth. Trim cloth ½" beyond stitching; it's all right if you cut into ends of patches.

7. Pin fringe to right side of one patchwork circle, having base of fringe ¼″ inside outer edge and fringe part pointing toward center. Overlap fringe by about an inch to join ends; cut off excess. Baste near edge.
8. Place circles with right sides together, fringe sandwiched between. Seam together on marked circle, leaving a 5″ opening. Turn right side out, insert pillow stuffing and slipstitch opening closed.

Idea: Believe it or not, the silk of neckties makes an elegant pillow. Assorted tweed or knit patterns would also be striking. Or try calico and gingham patches, or a group of plaids. Suit the fringe trim to the fabric.

PILLOW #7: BRAID-TRIMMED CYLINDER

MATERIALS:

cylindrical pillow form (or make your own from an old feather pillow or a slab of foam-rubber by-the-yard; see above)

fabric to cover, probably about ½ yard

varied braids, ribbons, yarn and/or other trim

2 pompons or buttons

needle; buttonhole twist or other strong thread

HOW-TO:

1. Measure the length, circumference and diameter of your pillow form. (I rolled an 18″ by 27″ by 1½″ foam rubber slab into a "jelly roll" 18″ long, 7″ in diameter and 17″ in circumference.)

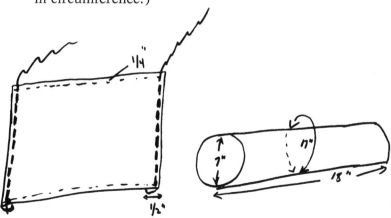

2. Cut fabric to measurements determined as follows: length = length of cylinder + ½ diameter + 1½"; width =circumference of cylinder + 1½"
(My "jelly roll" required fabric 22½" by 18½".)
3. Stay-stitch all around fabric ¼" from edge to prevent raveling.
4. Turn each short end under ½". With buttonhole twist, sew running stitches ¼" from fold. Do not end off, but leave a 10" end of thread for gathering later on.
5. Arrange braid or other trim on fabric, and sew in place. Do not put trim over part of fabric that will cover ends of cylinder.
6. Fold fabric lengthwise with right sides together. Sew side seam ½" from edge. Turn cover right side out.
7. Slip pillow form into cover and center it. Pull up threads at each end and gather; fasten securely.
8. Sew on pompon or button at each end to cover space between gathers.

Idea #1: Use the thick acrylic yarn sold as hair-ties and gift wrap. Make tassels for the ends.

Idea # 2: Make this out of felt or vinyl, eliminating the stay-stitching and seam allowances, and sew a visible seam with cord or yarn in criss-cross lacing style. If there is a good contrast of color and texture between lacing and fabric, this might be all

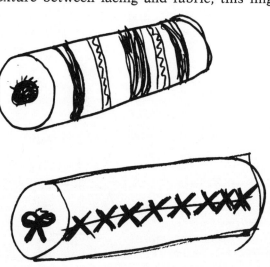

the decoration a cylinder pillow needs. Instead of a pompon, tie up ends of gathering yarn in a knot or bow.

PILLOW #8: "PRESTO-POINT" SQUARE

The elegance of needlepoint, a design of your own, and bulky yarn work up inexpensively and quickly into the most effective pillow of them all.

MATERIALS:
 single-thread rug canvas, 5 mesh to the inch
 bulky knitting worsted
 large-eyed tapestry needle
 masking tape
 tracing or carbon paper, pencil
 waterproof felt-tipped marking pens in black and various
   colors
 shredded foam rubber, kapok or other stuffing

HOW-TO:
1. Find a very simple design that you love. Find it in a coloring book, on upholstery fabric or wallpaper; on wrapping paper; on a ceramic tile, adapt a drawing made by a child. Ideally, you are looking for a simple pattern with large areas, using only about half a dozen colors or even fewer. A stylized flower or a geometric pattern such as a checkerboard or concentric squares would be ideal. See chapter 10 for more ideas.
2. Trace your chosen design onto tracing paper. If necessary, rearrange the elements a little. You might want to group flowers closer together, for example, or make a leaf larger. Outline the outer edge of your pillow around your design; if your pillow is to be 12″ by 12″, draw a 12″ square around your design.
3. You will need enough rug canvas to make up your finished pillow plus 2″ in each dimension. To make a 12″ square pillow, get a 16″ by 16″ piece of canvas. Bind edges with masking tape to prevent fraying.
4. To get your design onto canvas, place your copy of it under the canvas and pin or tape in place. Design will show through the mesh. Decide on the colors that you

will need. Use felt-tipped markers in those colors (or close to them) to outline parts of the design. Don't bother filling them in; all you need is the outline, and your needle and yarn will do the rest.

5. Start doing the actual needlework. Use lengths of yarn no longer than 24″. No knotting allowed; work ends under stitches for an inch or two on the wrong side. Use *half cross-stitch* for main elements of design (see diagrams of stitches in Chapter IX). To fill in the background, try the *slanted gobelin stitch*, which covers more territory at a time and works up even more quickly. Or try any of the other stitches shown if they seem appropriate to your design.

6. When entire design is finished, it must be blocked. Follow instructions in Chapter IX for finishing needlepoint.

7. To make felt pillow cover: cut two felt squares 1½″ larger in each dimension than finished design. Place right sides together and sew around ½″ from edge, leaving a 6″ opening. Trim corners, turn right side out, stuff and slipstitch opening closed.

8. Trim needlework ½″ beyond stitching. Turn canvas margin to wrong side; slipstitch invisibly to felt pillow. If desired, tack an edging of yarn or cording completely around pillow to conceal slipstitching.

Idea #1: Use rug yarn, instead of bulky knitting worsted. Or use velvet, instead of felt.

Idea #2: Use needlepoint canvas, 10 mesh to the inch, and knitting worsted. This goes somewhat more slowly. Stitches are smaller, and you can work a more complex design.

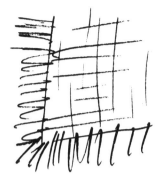 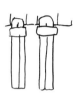

Idea #3: Make a pillow completely of your needlework, using two squares of rug canvas. Block as in step 7; omit step 8; turn margins of canvas to wrong side and tack in place. Place canvas squares with wrong sides together and sew by overcasting with yarn through outside threads of the canvas mesh. Sew around three sides; insert knife-edge pillow form in correct size and sew up fourth side. To add fringe: cut yarn into 6″ lengths. Take one strand at a time, fold in half, and use crochet hook to pull fold partway through two matching corner meshes. Bring cut ends of strand through this loop and pull tightly to form knot. Continue knotting strands in every other pair of meshes around pillow.

The Greatest Throw Pillow Dress-ups Ever

Sew or glue thick acrylic yarn in day-glo colors to outline a gigantic, stylized flower (or any other simple shape); tack border of same yarn all around edge of pillow, and make tassels

(see Chapter IX) of same yarn for corners. For a little girl's room, outline paper-doll shapes with yarn; for a little boy's room, outline a sailboat, car, airplane; use coloring-book designs for ideas.

Appliqué felt paper-doll shapes across top and bottom of pillow; tack acrylic yarn border around all edges. Or use felt scraps to duplicate any coloring-book design. Felt appliqué goes on quickly with white glue; or embroider on with cross-, blanket-, running- or chain stitches in colorful cord or yarn. Design highlights can be accented by using strands of yarn for hair, flower stems, or around doll clothes; glue on clusters of ball-fringe balls for flower centers, hats, sails; sew on button features.

Use a printed upholstery fabric to make a simple pillow cover, first embroidering over a portion of the printed design to add emphasis and textural interest. Use any stitches that the design itself may suggest: cross-stitches might accent a check or plaid; lazy daisy for small flowers, satin stitch for other design areas. Run concentric rows of chainstitch inside paisley motifs, or simply outline a paisley with chain stitches. To edge pillow, use matching cording or ball-fringe, or use yarn in one of the highlighted colors to make corner tassels.

From upholstery fabric printed with larger motifs, cut one

unit out, leaving about ¼" margin around it. Turn margin to wrong side and center it on throw pillow of coordinating color. Pin in place. With embroidery floss appliqué motif to pillow, using outline or chain stitches to go completely around cut design. Around edge of pillow tack cording or other trim to match appliqué colors.

Use wide braid or ribbon to

a) Cover a pillow front completely: sew on as many horizontal stripes of braid as needed to fit across.

b) Form a square within a square or a rectangle within a rectangle: miter corners neatly, conceal joining place of braid under one corner.

c) Make one single effective stripe down the center of a pillow.

d) Create an off-center criss-cross.

Use ball-fringe to

a) Edge a pillow completely.

b) Make a bunch of four or five balls gathered at corners, instead of tassels.

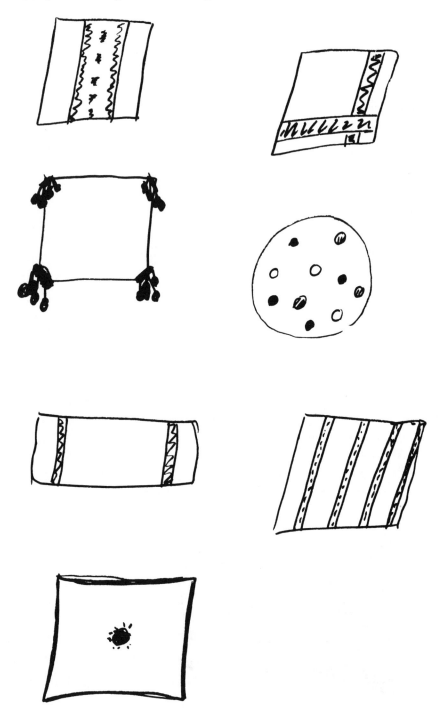

c) Tack individually in a multicolored scattering on a round pillow, or in neat rows on a square pillow.

d) Make concentric squares or circles, starting from the outside of a pillow and working toward the center; alternate two or three colors (black-white, red-white-blue) or use two or three shades of one color (red, orange, yellow).

Use narrow braid or ribbon to

a) Border two short edges of rectangular or cylindrical pillows.

b) Add textural interest and emphasis to one color over one line of a plaid.

c) Create a stripe.

Attach a matched pair of buttons through the center of a pillow; tack on cording border in color to match.

Sew a lace ruffle completely around pillow. To make lacy flowers: sew gathers at base of small strips of lace and pull up

tightly to form a circle. Then glue in place. Glue a small felt circle or a ball from ball-fringe to center and pin in place on pillow; add flower stems of soutache braid or narrow ribbon. Use pins until you get the arrangement you like; then use white glue to attach to pillow top.

Weave lengths of 2″ wide ribbon in different colors to cover pillow top completely. Cut lengths 2″ longer than pillow, turn each ribbon strip under ½″ and tack at both side edges and at top. Weave loose ribbons over and under. At bottom, fold excess ribbon to wrong side and tack to pillow seam.

❧ IV ❧

Hang-ups

Nature abhors a vacuum, and I abhor an empty wall. Whenever I see one, I return its blank stare. Then I start imagining all the things that could have been done to give it, and its room, *personality.*

As bad as an empty wall is one with something dull and uninteresting on it, a whatever-it-is hanging there just to fill space. How awful to live with uninteresting things! If something is to be put up on such a prominent place as a wall, let it be something worth looking at.

The first thing most people think of when trying to decide what to put on a wall is art. But fine art is expensive—too expensive for most of us to cover our walls with. And there are so many other things to buy, to collect, and to create yourself. In this chapter and the next are suggestions of new things to hang, where to find or how to make them, and new ideas for how to hang them.

What to Hang Up: the End of the Empty Wall

A room is surrounded by its walls. Defined by them. Closed in by them. Or expanded by them.

Wherever we look in a room, we see walls and what is on them. Every wall is too important to hang just any-old-thing on.

We have to look at whatever we put up there. And we have to like whatever we see. After all, we will be living with it.

Never hang anything just because it i*s pretty.* You can get very tired of a picture of flowers, if you bought it only because you liked the colors of the flowers. Fresh ones have more variety and interest, even as they wilt.

Only put on your walls something that is exciting to look at —something that will please you anew every time you pass by it. Something that you will look at, and live with, in pleasure, day in and day out.

The room I work in is a small one, but its walls are covered with things I love. There is not a dull or merely pretty thing on them! I have three Mexican rugs, a bright ceramic platter from Morocco, two carved masks from Liberia, a tiny print of an eighteenth-century London street scene, three prints of Hudson River views and one of the New York waterfront; and lucite shelves with small Mexican ceramic jugs and African sculptures. On the wall over my kitchen table are French cheese plates, Mexican and English tiles, and a cowbell. On other walls I have mirrors in interesting tin or carved wood frames, pages from a seventeenth-century songbook, and a fragment of embroidered fabric from North Africa. You can see that I practice what I preach. As this partial inventory of my walls demonstrates, there is almost no end to what can be put on one.

Many people plan to buy a magnificent painting for their most prominent wall—someday. Fine. But until someday comes, is that wall just going to stare at you? And what about all the other walls that surround your rooms?

I say put something exciting on your walls right now. You can always remove it later, when you buy that museum-quality work of art. A little spackle, a dab of paint, and your wall will be as good as new. So start looking at your walls with new eyes, thinking of what you can do with them to make your rooms more beautiful, more interesting to look at and live in.

I'll bet anything that at this very minute you have plenty of treasured belongings hidden away in closets and drawers— things that could be brought out of hiding and placed where you and your family and friends could enjoy them all the time: *on the walls.* What about . . .

Photographs. Instead of keeping a pile of snapshots in a scrapbook or drawer, or placing a few framed ones on a table top or mantel, why not select eight or ten and have them enlarged to enormous, even poster-sized, proportions? An empty wall is an ideal location for a family or pet portrait gallery, or house and garden exhibit, or travelogue, or display of whatever your favorite photos are. The wall above a table or a chest of drawers is a good photo gallery, too. Get slabs of plywood in the exact sizes of your photo blow-ups; sand and shellac the edges, and attach screw eyes and picture wire to the back. Brush white glue over the plywood and slide your "posters" into position.

Maps. Have you a collection of road maps marked with the routes of your vacation tours? Or of *National Geographic* maps? Or street plans of cities you have lived in or visited? Or maps clipped from newspapers to commemorate major events? These could be mounted on plywood as is, in the same way as the photo blow-ups. Or the maps could be photostated and enlarged to poster size. Or, instead of mounting on plywood, glue maps directly on the wall; and build a "frame" of wood molding around each, painted in a brightly contrasting enamel.

Fabric. That's right, a piece of cloth. But a beautiful, colorful one. An heirloom quilt or needlepoint. A designer scarf. A remnant of dress or upholstery fabric. Something from a thrift shop—old lace, perhaps. Even a pillowcase, but it must be a smashing one. Glue the fabric of your choice to white mat board (buy in art store) cut to allow a 2" or 3" margin all around; and use a narrow white wooden frame. Or buy a large wood frame in the five-and-ten and enamel it white; glue white linen

or burlap to the cardboard backing that comes with the frame and glue your fabric in place on it. Of course, if your fabric is predominantly white, beige or another pale color, you would want to set it off against a contrasting backing; think blue, black, orange, brown, with frame to match. If your fabric is large and heavy—a hand-crocheted bedspread or an embroidered and fringed piano shawl—mount it as a wall-hanging (see Chapter V) instead of in a frame.

Gift-wrap. Find a beautiful gift-wrapping paper, and frame it in the same way as the fabric. Or mount it on a plywood slab, in the same way as the photo blow-ups; brush with polymer gloss medium or spray with clear vinyl for durability and sheen. Enamel edges of plywood in a contrasting color. Hang several different gift-wraps in coordinated colors.

Shopping bags. Did you ever see a stunning shopping bag? Some of the recently designed ones have been quite imaginative, beautiful and/or whimsical. If you see one you like, frame it! Smooth it flat. Measure it. Buy a plywood slab a few inches

larger all around, so there will be an attractive margin. Sand and shellac plywood. Glue or tack your shopping bag on it. Spray with clear vinyl gloss, or coat with polymer medium. Hang with screw eyes and wire. Instant pop art.

These five ideas were just to get your imagination started. You could display an 1890's gown or a 1920's dress; postage stamps; photostats of newspaper front pages; horoscopes; even newspaper advertisements that strike your fancy. Select from a ten-year accumulation of *Time* magazine covers. Or theater programs. Imagine a collection of automobile advertisements going back thirty years. Or sheet music or picture-postcards of the 1940's. Or whatever your special interest is.

A Gallery Is Where You Make It Happen

Any vertical surface can become the location of a gallery. Even a closet door or a bathroom wall will gain importance when used for display. It's almost impossible to run out of wall space, for you can always go up—right to the ceiling. Any wall that isn't doing something, any wall that isn't interesting to look at—that's the place to start.

Have you a long, narrow hallway, with no room for anything? Don't turn the light down low and forget it. Hang things along one or both side walls, and run spotlights near the ceiling at intervals to highlight your gallery collection. Or install mirrors, large and small, in a multitude of shapes and sizes, along both walls right up to the ceiling; they will reflect your lighting and

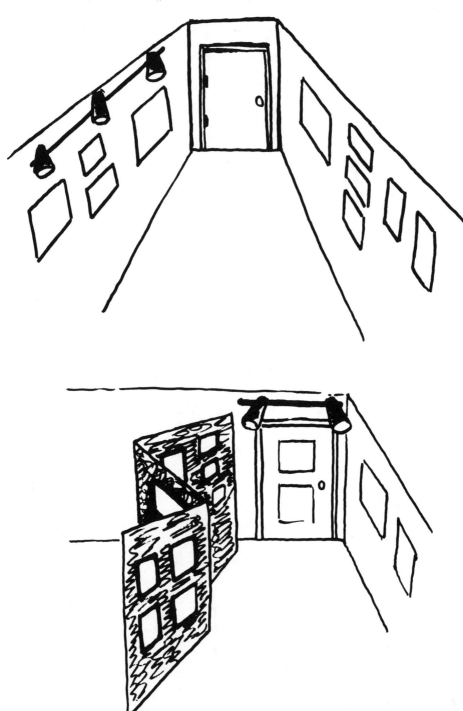

each other, adding brightness and expanding the size of the hallway in a most effective optical illusion.

Have you no hallway at all? Just a door and a wall? Then hang things on the door and the wall, treating them together as a gallery unit. Or get an inexpensive burlap screen and stand it at one side of the door to create an entrance-gallery.

Lots of cabinet doors but no wall in the kitchen? Discover what fine display areas cabinet doors and refrigerator sides can be. From cookbooks and magazines, cut out herb and spice charts, favorite recipes, measurement and equivalent charts, food and cookware advertisements—even a calorie chart. Glue to plywood, or to a plastic platter or tray, and hang. Or glue directly to your walls or cabinet doors, using white glue. Brush with polymer gloss medium or cover with transparent adhesive-backed vinyl for a wipe-clean, splatter-free surface. Border with colored tape. When you tire of the display, pull everything off and start over.

Now go through your home and make a list of all the walls you want to hang things on. Check out every single wall in the place—even in the bathroom (how about that wall above the towel rack or hamper?). You should have uncovered several potential gallery locations.

Arranging a Wall Arrangement

The most important factor to consider when planning what to put on a wall and where to put it, is what looks right to *you*. The three keys to an effective wall arrangement are *height, proportion* and *balance*.

First, *height*. Pictures should be hung at, or near, eye level. In a living or dining room, where the viewer will most often be sitting down, eye level comes down quite low—to about 42" from the floor. Figure on hanging pictures with their bottom edges from 3" to 8" above a sofa, chair or mantel. If you are planning an over-the-sofa grouping of several pictures or objects, you might have the bases of the lowest ones only an inch above the sofa back. The idea is to keep even the uppermost items in such a grouping within comfortable viewing range.

Similarly, in a bedroom you might start a grouping only an inch or two above the headboard, or over a tall dresser. However, figure on hanging things 12" above a low chest or dresser.

In a hallway, however, where whatever is on your walls will be viewed by standees only, eye level will begin at about 48" to 52" off the floor.

How high is up? That depends on what you are hanging and where you are standing. The top of a large picture, rug or other fabric can conceivably reach almost as high as the ceiling. *If* it can be comfortably viewed from a distance, such as across a sizable room; and/or *if* the design is striking but not detailed —okay. But if you would be constantly craning your neck and straining your eyes to see what's at the top, it's a "no-no." Never hang small items with their bottom edges higher than the top of your head, or between 65" and 70" from the floor, unless you want either a pain in the neck or not to look at them at all.

Next, *proportion*. Have you ever seen a small painting hanging all by its lonesome on a large wall? Even the most beautiful work of art could become a sore thumb if it is out of proportion to its surroundings. When you have a single painting or other object to hang, choose a wall area that is in good proportion to it.

Don't isolate a small object on a big wall. Either place it on a small wall or wall area, or feature it in combination with other objects on a large wall area.

Similarly, don't hang a large painting on a small wall or wall area. It will make the whole room look cluttered and smaller.

No !

And last, *balance*, which may be formal and symmetrical; but most likely will be informal and asymmetrical. Balance takes into consideration not only the pictures that will hang there but everything that your eye sees when you look at a wall—sofa, lamps, plants, bookshelves or whatever.

To achieve formal balance, arrange your objects so that what is at the left of center duplicates in size, shape and position what is at the right. Obviously. to work out a symmetrical arrangement, you will need objects in pairs.

Probably you will opt for an informal arrangement. For one thing, you probably have more unpaired than paired objects.

Yes!

Formal Balance

Informal Balance

For another, perfect symmetry, while the most obvious way to achieve balance, can also be extremely dull. Symmetry is most effective when the objects featured are particularly striking.

In an informal arrangement, there is greater flexibility. Several small objects can be hung together to balance a large object. Or several pictures may be grouped to balance a lamp, a bookshelf or a plant. If the things to be hung are of different sizes and shapes, this is your only choice.

Combining both formal and informal elements in the same arrangement can be extremely effective. On my mantel, for instance, an old French clock is centered between two tall brass candleholders. The outermost objects in this arrangement, however, are unpaired: at the right a small pre-Columbian ceramic pot and on the left two African carved-wood figures. Above the mantel a painting is centered; on its right two smaller paintings are hung vertically. They are balanced, on the left, by an old wooden barometer.

Informal Balance

Combination Balance

Combination Balance

Across the room is another combination arrangement. The furniture—sofa, end tables, brass oil lamps—is arranged symmetrically. But on the wall above, five antique maps are hung on the right, while they are balanced on the left with a shelf supporting three African carved figures.

For me, these arrangements work. The symmetry of some pairs of objects heightens the effectiveness of the asymmetrical groups. If, as is quite likely, you have some objects paired and several that are unique, this might be your solution too.

It is not necessary for the bottoms of the lowest row of pictures to be aligned; this all depends on the balance as your eye sees it.

Make a wall plan to help you figure it all out. You'll need two or more pieces of graph paper, some marking pens and a pencil and scissors. Measure your wall, and round off the measurements to the nearest half-foot and draw it in place.

Now spread out all the objects you want to hang. Measure each, round off to the nearest half-foot, and draw each on the second sheet of graph paper. Use colored marking pens to iden-

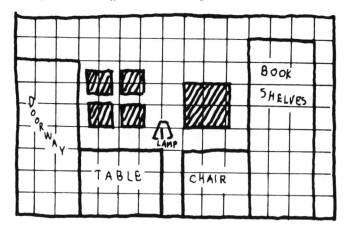

Wall Plans

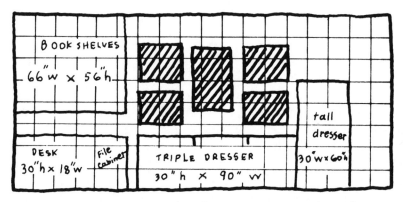

tify each shape and make them easy to work with. Cut out these small shapes and place them on your wall plan. Move them around until you think you have an arrangement that will work.

To test it, spread your things out on a floor, a bed or a table, in the arrangement you have chosen. Still like it? Fine. Want to make some changes? Go ahead. Think about it for a while, and shift things around some more.

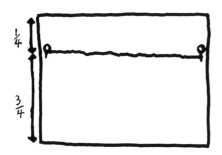

screw eyes are inserted
¼ of the distance down
the back of the frame

wire is looped
through screw
eye and twisted
around itself
several times

When you have it, go back to your wall plan and glue your "pictures" in position on it to serve as a guide while you hang the real ones.

How to Hang Up

With picture hooks, of course. (No nails, or any other makeshift solution; use only hardware designed for the job of hanging pictures.)

For hanging pictures and other things painlessly, try these suggestions:

Check the screw eyes that hold the picture wire. They should be inserted straight into the wooden part of the frame back, and the wood should not be dry and crumbly around them. If they are insecure, remove them and insert in another spot, making sure that you measure evenly down from the top of the frame. Place screw eyes ¼ of the way down the back of the frame.

Check the wire on the back of the picture to make sure it is not worn out. If it is, change it. Make sure it is neither too slack nor too tight—it should have the slightest bit of "give" but not be loose enough to lower your picture when it is hung.

Use the right size hook for the job. They come in sizes according to the loads they have to bear—usually 5, 10, 20, 30, 40 and 50 pounds. Don't try to hang a bantam-weight with an elephant.

Two hooks instead of one will hang even a large picture so that it won't ever lose its balance. Step by step, here's how:

1. Position your picture against the wall. With a pencil, lightly mark all four corners on the wall. Mark the position of the screw eyes at each side.

2. Put the picture aside, and check to make sure your positioning of it was level. The foolproof way is to use a carpenter's leveler to line up the screw-eye markings. (But I usually use just my eye, and frequently wind up rehanging the picture and swearing I'll get a leveler "next time.")

3. Mark 1″ in from each screw-eye marking. At last, this is where the picture hooks will go. Gently wash off all other pencil markings.

4. Criss-cross two small pieces of transparent tape over the hook marks to prevent plaster cracking.

5. Place picture hook and nail in position and hammer firmly.

6. Slip picture wire in place over hooks.

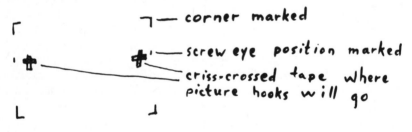

How to prepare a wall before hanging a picture

An alternate method of hanging flat things like decorative ceramic tiles and mirrored squares uses double-faced mounting tape (Magic Mounts). Here's how:

1. Again, use pencil to lightly mark, corners only, of object held in position against wall.

2. Cut 1″ lengths of tape, or use as many precut sections as recommended on the package for the size and weight of object you are hanging. For a 12″ square mirror, for example, I use

five 1″ tape sections—one in each corner and one in the center.

3. Place tape in position on back of object following package directions.

4. Remove paper backing from tape and press object gently but firmly into marked position against wall.

5. If object is slightly warped or wall uneven, use a double layer of tape to fill in. (But if wall is very uneven, or object is very warped, what you hang is likely to come crashing down. As it will, also, if your wall consists largely of plaster that is about to come loose. So check your wall first.)

The Frame-up: Frames and Mats to Make Yourself

Every picture that's worth hanging deserves the right frame.

Never count on an elaborate frame to enhance a dull picture. All it will do is emphasize the picture's faults.

When in doubt, choose the simpler of two frames.

A narrow frame is never wrong; a wide one very well may be.

When a complicated framing problem comes up—what to do with something that has unusual proportions, is round or oval or perhaps three-dimensional—consult a professional framemaker or art supply dealer.

When in doubt about mats, choose white, off-white or natural. For a special effect, choose a colored mat, and perhaps a frame of a darker shades of the same color. Imagine, for instance, an olive mat with a dark green enameled frame; or a mustard-gold mat with a walnut-stained frame. A simple gold, silver or black frame will go with almost any color mat.

A good frame need not be expensive. In the last few years a handsome frame has become available in the form of components that you put together yourself. These brushed aluminum units are sold in pairs that range in size from 8″ to 40″; buy two sets and you're ready to go. Glass, mat and backing cut to size are inexpensive; so that a minimal outlay will result in an extremely handsome frame—the very frame, in fact, that was originally developed at the request of the Museum of Modern Art in New York.

To restore an antique carved frame (at least, this is what I did with an old gilt frame I found at a very attractive price in a thrift shop):

1. Get a small can of spackle (moist plaster compound) from a paint or hardware store. Use fingers and toothpicks to fit the spackle into cracks, to shape the tip of a leaf or petal that has broken off, or to round off the dents of time and mishandling. Let spackle dry thoroughly—the label on the can will give you an idea of how long this should take.

2. Use paint that simulates gold leaf, antique gold, antique bronze or whatever finish is required; available in small cans or jars in hardware and paint stores and even in the five-and-ten. Use a fine brush with very little paint on it. Paint with short brush strokes and an almost dry brush across the mended portion of the frame. If the short brush strokes don't blend the new paint into the old as well as you'd like, dip the corner of a soft piece of cloth (an old handkerchief or cheesecloth) in the paint, and rub frame gently with it.

If the back of a frame is a mess, cut a new piece of paper—brown wrapping paper to fit. Remove screw eyes and picture wire. After everything else is back in place in the frame, glue the new paper backing to the wooden back edge of the frame. Replace screw eyes and picture wire.

The do-it-yourselfer has other frame possibilities for creativity, too.

Start with a slab of ½" plywood cut to the size you require.

1. Sand all edges. Paint, varnish or shellac in the color of your choice. (Rub in bright acrylic paint with your fingers and let dry—beautiful!)

2. On the wrong side, measure ¼ of the way down from the top and mark for screw eyes ½" in from each side edge. Insert screw eyes and string picture wire between them, twisting it around itself at each end.

3. If you get a plywood slab cut to the exact measurements of what you are displaying, only the plywood edge as seen from an angle will be your frame. But if you have the plywood cut to allow a 2" or 3" margin (or more, or less, as you choose) all around, the plywood becomes frame and mat in one.

4. For a more decorative variation, add a wood molding around the edges. Or hammer in colored upholstery tacks or brass or black tacks for an original and effective border.

5. For a special effect, cover plywood slab with burlap, felt

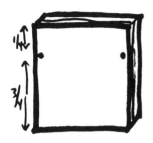

Back of plywood slab
marked for scren eyes

Needlepoint Sampler
mounted on plywood
against wide margins

Upholstery tacks create
contrasting border on
plywood slab frame

or other fabric, or wallpaper, adhesive-backed vinyl or foil, or wrapping paper coated with shellac.

To cover a plywood slab with fabric or foil: cut covering material 2″ or 3″ larger all around than the plywood. Spread an even layer of glue over one surface of wood. Place covering material wrong side up on table, and press glued wood surface down in center of fabric or foil. Turn right side up and smooth with fingers, working excess glue to outer edges. Place right side down on table again, and spread glue over end sections of covering material. Fold up, making neat corners as for gift wrapping. Smooth foil or fabric with fingers against end edges

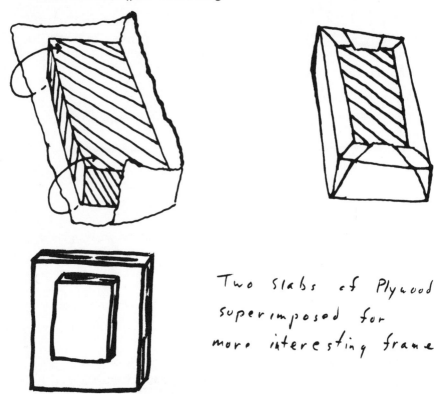

Two slabs of Plywood superimposed for more interesting frame

of wood. Next spread glue over side sections of covering material, and press up against side edges of wood. Spread more glue and smooth remaining foil or fabric in place on wrong side of wood, folding corners neatly. Let dry. Cut a piece of felt to the exact size of the wood, and glue over bottom to cover.

6. Still other framing effects can be achieved with ¼" or ¾" plywood, or by superimposing two slabs of plywood so that the bottom one, painted in a contrasting color, shows all around.

Start with an inexpensive wood frame from the five-and-ten.
1. Stain or enamel the frame.
2. Paint the mat that came with it. Or discard the mat and cover the cardboard backing with burlap or velvet. Or cover the frame with acrylic yarn in a bright color, spreading white glue or polymer gel medium on the frame first. I have done white frames with pink mats, orange frames with natural burlap backings, hot pink acrylic yarn frames with white velvet backings.

3. Try matching frames and mats: marine blue, or flag red. Or a shiny white enamel frame with a black mat. Or combine light and dark green, or a rich brown walnut frame with a burlap backing.

Cover any simple frame with lightweight fabric: linen, gingham, denim. All you need, besides the fabric, are scissors and white glue. Use leftover upholstery fabric, or match curtains or bed linen.

1. Remove glass, mat and backing from frame and set aside. Place frame right side down on the wrong side of the fabric.

2. Cut out fabric about 2″ larger all around than frame. Spread glue along one edge of fabric and fold it neatly over corresponding side of frame. Tuck in corner for mitered edge, as though gift-wrapping a package. Continue around other sides of frame.

3. Trim off excess fabric neatly on inner edge of back of frame, using additional glue if necessary to hold in place.

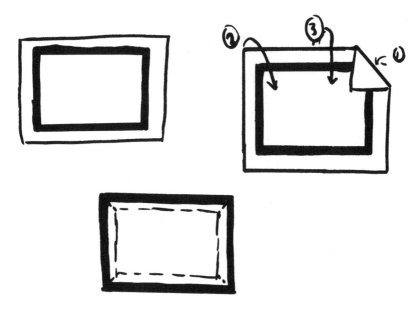

4. Slash fabric in center of frame to each corner. Trim off about 1″ from inner edge of frame. Working with each flap in turn, cover with glue and fold over to wrong side of frame, using fingers to tamp it carefully in place.

5. This same method of covering a frame will work with adhesive-backed vinyl or foil. If mat, glass and backing are to be fitted back into frame, only a lightweight covering can be used.

6. If you are framing something that won't need glass, you can cover the frame with a heavier fabric such as felt, burlap or velvet. But thick materials like these would take up too much space along the edges, and the glass and mat would no longer fit.

Cover any mat with fabric or adhesive-backed vinyl.

1. Cut covering material to length and width of mat plus 2″ each (to cover a mat whose outer dimensions are 8″ by 10″, cut covering material 10″ by 12″).

2. Cut rectangle from the center of covering material, leaving a 1″ turn-under allowance. Slash from inside to inner corners of mat. Cut out 1″ squares at each outer corner.

3. Spread wrong side of fabric lightly with white glue, or peel off paper backing from adhesive-backed vinyl. Place mat on glued or adhesive surface and press down. Fold inner and outer

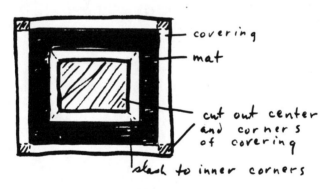

covering
mat
cut out center
and corners
of covering
slash to inner corners

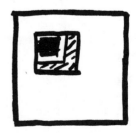

edge allowances over and press down on wrong side of mat. If glued, let dry.

4. Try covering a mat with newspaper, colored tissue paper or any patterned paper. Suit your mat to the picture it will hold.

Idea! Mount it off center. Get the added effectiveness of asymmetry right into your framing by mounting with uneven margins. This can be done against plywood slab frames, or against burlap or other backings. Just be sure there is strong contrast of color and/or texture when you mount off center.

Mounting Sculpture—Too Much Fun to Be Left to Professionals

When we acquired our first sculpture—an African figure about 20 inches tall—I stayed awake nights trying to visualize the right kind of display for it. It needed, I decided, a pedestal high enough to stand on the floor. But, since the carving would be in the living room, the pedestal should not be so high that the figure would be above the eye level of someone sitting down. We did not want a stand so elaborate or large that it would call attention to itself instead of to the figure on it.

I spent a day making the rounds of galleries to get some ideas —and learned that a pedestal custom-made to my specifications of height and width would cost from $50 to $100. Since I preferred to put that amount of money toward the purchase of a second piece of African art, I decided that my next steps would take me in the direction of the nearest thrift shop. Several junk shops later, I came upon exactly what I was looking for.

It was a pedestal of just the right height and proportions for the job. Under its coat of dust I could make out the peeling brown paint that proclaimed its origin perhaps a hundred years earlier as a staircase post in a now torn-down or remodeled New York brownstone. But to me it was a treasure— and at a cost of only two dollars! I remember putting it into the back of the stroller and trudging to a paint store, where another couple of dollars purchased some strong paint remover and two broad brushes.

At home, I go to work. First, I spread newspaper on the kitchen table and floor. Then I put the post in the laundry tub and scrubbed it down with detergent and water. Gingerly I applied some of the thick, acrid-smelling paint remover to one patch of brown paint, waiting according to the label instructions, and was delighted to find the brown paint blistering up and turning a sickly orange. After a second application of remover, I had the pleasure of scraping off a thick layer of gook and uncovering wood.

Now that I knew it would work, I stood my treasure up on the table and brushed the smelly chemical all over it. Some two hours after I had brought the post home, it had been stripped naked. Triumphantly, I carried it into the living room and set my African figure in place. My pedestal was just right! But its old wood was in less than pristine condition and two coats of white paint (left over from the living room walls) were necessary before it could be put to its intended use.

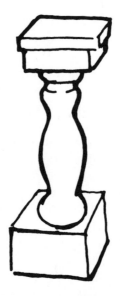

Since then our collection of African sculpture has been considerably expanded, and so has our accumulation of home-designed and home-created bases—all of them inexpensive and made up of easy-to-find materials.

We went along for quite a while with kindergarten blocks filched from our children's toy chest. They were washed with detergent, rinsed and dried; painted with mahogany enamel; then padded on the bottom with adhesive-backed felt.

The very special requirements of a larger sculpture— a helmet mask from Nigeria—led us to order a 15" by 18" by 2" butcher

2 nails to
support mask

Butcher block
plus
kindergarten block

kindergarten blocks
become bases for
sculptures.

block at the same time we were having a table top made; when he learned why we needed the extra piece, the dealer gave us another piece of almost the same size that he had lying around. That was fortunate, for we soon acquired a Liberian mask that was displayed perfectly when we stood a triangular block upright on this thick slab, and added two nails to support the mask's chin.

We decided to go after a new effect and try clear lucite bases. We found a plastics store where lucite sheets were cut to order; a base consisted of five squares that I could join together with a jar of special adhesive and a paint brush. Then we noticed the variety of inexpensive lucite picture frames being sold in department stores and photo shops, and we devised ways in which these could be converted into stands for small sculptures. A two-piece picture frame, separated into a rectangular block of lucite and a U-shaped section, could become two mountings. Or the lucite rectangles from two of these in different sizes could be combined for one larger mounting. A 4″ picture cube with five sides was designed to hold five photos in place by means of a cardboard or foam rubber inner core. By removing the inside, we had a crystal-clear mounting.

An even smaller cube, 1½″, was designed to hold passport-sized photos or postage stamps. Since it consisted of two U-shaped sections that clamp together, we separated them to get a pair of bases for tiny objects.

And in an Oriental imports shop we discovered lucite cubes and boxes in various sizes and colors, ranging in size from 1″ by 1″ by 1″ at 20 cents to 8″ by 15″ by 5″ for nine dollars. All of these sizes we have used—the smallest ones are perfect for displaying shells, coins and pebbles.

Next to the staircase post, our most unusual pedestal was made from a cork wastebasket, stained a shade darker with liquid shoe polish and turned upside down to support a tall Nigerian housepost.

How to Attach Sculpture to a Base

If possible, sculpture and nature objects should be attached so that they can be removed without damaging either the

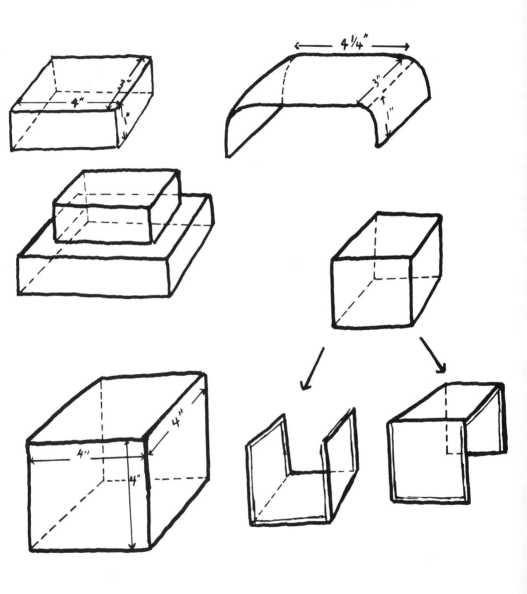

Lucite picture frames become bases for small sculptures.

object or its stand. Try these methods, in the order in which they are given:

1. Use a wad of clay-like weather-stripping material (such as Mortite) or florists' clay to hold irregularly shaped sculptures in place.

2. A blob of polymer gel medium or white glue will hold most wood, lucite or nature objects in place, and might work with other materials as well.

3. A square of double-faced mounting tape (Magic Mounts) might work.

4. If all else fails, you will have to resort to a contact cement or—last choice—epoxy cement. With a gentle touch and a knife you might if necessary be able to separate two things glued together with contact cement (I use a smooth-edged steak knife). But the epoxy is virtually permanent, and can't be removed without causing some damage to whatever is on one or the other side of it.

5. Where the mounting surface of an object is badly eroded, or uneven for other reasons, you may want to build up the worn areas with Epoxy Marine Compound. This material comes in a choice of light, dark and wood tones; it is available in boat supply and some hardware stores. With it, you can build up the bottom of an object and at the same time attach it permanently to a base; it will stick to almost any material.

Investing in the Real Thing

Whether you have fifty or five thousand dollars in your art purchase fund, you'll get greater pleasure out of what you buy if you learn all there is to know about it. If you're buying art for love, you'll love it more if you find out as much as you can about the period, style, subject, artist, medium.

And if you're buying art as an investment, study your chosen period, style and artist as carefully as you'd study the prospectus and performance record of any stock you were considering. But, unless you are one of those rare individuals who gets esthetic pleasure out of contemplating a stock certificate, be sure that you love to look at whatever work of art you decide to buy.

If you "like modern art but don't know the first thing about it"—stop, look and study before you buy. This advice holds for earlier periods, too. Within the work of every art period there are many individual styles and artists. Window-shop in museums and galleries; read some of the available books dealing with your chosen period and/or artist; attend lectures at your local museum. Know what you like and what you want before you buy.

Among the things to investigate, particularly if you are about to purchase work by a not-yet-famous contemporary, are gallery exhibits that have included your artist; museums that hang his work; prices paid at auction by other collectors for his works. Your gallery dealer should be able to give you much of this information. The periodicals in an art-museum library will be of help too.

A fine work of art need not be an oil painting. Instead, choose a print or drawing by a noted artist of the past or the present. A graphic will always be lovely, and always keep its value. But a copy of a masterpiece—even if you buy it from the museum that owns the original, even if its surface has been treated to look like oil on canvas—is a lifeless, as well as valueless, shadow.

If you are ready to invest in works of art, an original sculpture of table-top size is as good a place to start as an original graphic. Many contemporary sculptors have their works produced in limited editions, just as a print is. And a gallery is just as likely to have one of these, and in about the same price range, as to have etchings.

Also in the small-sculpture category are such works of "primitive" art as pre-Columbian heads or figures, some African masks or small figures, and even Hopi Indian katchina dolls. All of these are easy to display (see ideas for mounting smal sculptures earlier in this chapter), exciting to live with and fun to collect.

The original work by the Hopi Indian, African, or ancient Mexican artists should not be confused with "airport art," the mass-produced craft items offered for sale to the tourist. Of course, one can certainly find works of art while traveling. But the stay-at-home searching for small-scale works of art can come up with many exciting finds. It is wise for the beginner to buy only from a reliable source—a recognized gallery, a museum sales desk, or a dealer who may be recommended by a museum staff member.

Don't be surprised if your first purchase of a work of primitive art leads quickly to a second, and then to the third. This kind of thing can be contagious. I know, for it has happened to us.

❧ V ❧

Art Hang-ups

Until you save up enough money to buy the work of art of your dreams, you can put something you create yourself on the wall or the coffee table. You'll find dozens of ideas in this chapter.

But first, let's be absolutely honest with each other. What you will be creating, what I have been creating—these are not Art. In *their* art, painters such as Picasso, Mondrian and Jackson Pollack were making statements about what painting is. They were expanding horizons, discovering something new about line and shape and color and proportion.

What *we* are doing is making effective, colorful, dramatic designs. And most of them are designs that we wouldn't be able to imagine were we not familiar with the work of the twentieth century's great painters.

There's nothing at all wrong with our making these designs and installing them on our walls. But, since you and I are not creative geniuses using art materials to make an original statement, our creations are not Art.

Now that we understand each other, let's get to work and have fun making some great-looking things to put up on your walls.

"Found Art"

#1: THE PAINTSPLOTCH

This, with apologies to Rorschach and his followers, is a decorative, sophisticated version of an inkblot.

MATERIALS:
   acrylic paints in two or more colors
   one or more brushes (optional)
   polymer medium or mat medium
   water
   paper for painting (canvas-textured paper, available in pads at art stores, is my preference) in the dimensions of your choice

How-to:
1. Fold paper in half vertically or horizontally, as desired. Open. Splash some water on paper and spread with fingers to cover.

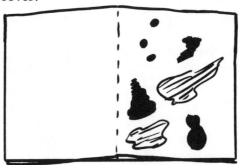

2. Dilute paint slightly, to consistency of thick cream. Dribble or blob paint on wet paper, anywhere. Use at least two colors. Have them meet, or keep them separate.
3. Fold paper in half again along previously made fold-lines. Rub fingers or whole hand over outside half of paper. You will feel the blobs of paint moving under your fingers. Spread paint well, to cover as much of paper as possible.
4. Open and observe the progress of your Paintsplotch. Does it need a few more blobs of yellow there? How

about a streak of red along the side? Whatever it needs, add it on. Fold and rub-spread again.

5. Open and observe again. Perhaps you want to add some brushwork now; go ahead. Fold again or not, as you like.

6. When the paper is colored to your satisfaction, let dry. Brush with polymer medium for a glossy protective

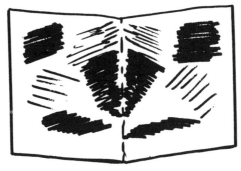

"The Paint Splotch"

finish, or with mat medium for a dull protective finish, or with a blend of both mediums to achieve a light gloss finish. Frame as you like—I prefer a polished aluminum do-it-yourself sectional frame.

And that's all there is to it—you can finish it in an hour. Experiment; the materials are so inexpensive that you can make several Paintsplotches until you get one you like well enough to hang. The design possibilities are literally infinite. Try folding paper at different angles, or try making several folds in one painting. A few tubes of paint and a pad of paper will go a long way.

Combine different paint textures and different rubbing techniques as well as different colors. You'll find that if you put the paint on thickly the resulting texture is very different from the one that results when the paints are thinned. Your Paintsplotch may come out looking like a cloud or a butterfly, or simply as an indefinable shape. Don't hesitate to use a brush to enhance the design that you see emerging.

Idea! For a really enormous Paintsplotch, use heavy wrapping paper and make folds in several places. Mount on plywood or masonite to hang.

#2: ON A PAINTSTRING

MATERIALS:

acrylic or tempera paint, in two or three colors

several pieces of string (any thickness, from bakery string to package twine, but it should be a fairly flexible, not a stiff, kind of string)

wrapping paper

canvas-textured paper, good quality drawing paper, or plywood

polymer medium (optional)

HOW-TO:

1. Thin paint to cream-like consistency. Color should be strong though, and not watery. Work a sample on a piece of wrapping paper to get the idea. Holding one piece of string in the center, dip both ends in paint and drag them across paper. Back and forth, criss and cross . . . Let dry. Try another color, another piece of string. Hold string by both ends this time, and dip center loop in paint and drag across paper. Practice while humming a lullaby, or while listening to a rock record. After a few minutes of practice, you'll have an idea of the many ways in which you can handle the string, and the many kinds of designs you can produce.
2. Now you're ready to work on your Paintstring. Paint background paper or wood in color desired. Try spread-

On A Paintstring

ing acrylic paint on plywood with your fingers for a
clear color effect with wood grain showing through.
Let background dry.

3. Do your thing with string—whatever design you liked
   the feel and appearance of during your practice session.
   Let each color dry before going on to the next; if you
   use acrylic paint this will take only a minute or two.
4. That's it. It's done whenever you think it is. Brush with
   polymer medium for a glossy protective finish if you
   like. And mount and hang as you like.

Idea! Try white-painted string across a black background.
Another idea! Try multicolors across a white unpainted background. (I used rust and midnight blue stringwork on white.)

#3: STRING THING

MATERIALS:

at least 2 yards string or yarn, white and/or colors
dye or acrylic paint (optional)
polymer gel medium or white glue
cardboard, cork, glass or wood panel in size desired

HOW-TO:

1. If desired, dye string or color it by soaking in acrylic
   paint diluted with water; let dry.
2. If desired, paint background panel. (Cork and glass
   are not painted, of course.)
3. Spread a thick layer of polymer gel medium or white
   glue over background or, if background is large, over
   a part of it.
4. Use fingers to tamp string down into gel or glue, making
   curves and swirls as desired. Don't hesitate to cut string
   anywhere; or to tuck a new string into the gel and
   swirl it into the design.
5. If gel gets too dry, spread on more. Add string in a
   second or third color if you like.
6. You can probably come up with a great design once
   you get the knack of it. But if you are hesitant, sketch
   with pencil on paper and then trace your design onto
   the background and follow it with string.

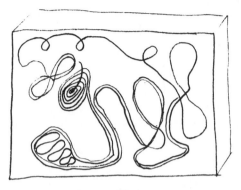

String Thing

7. Finish by covering string and all with another layer of gel. It dries hard and glossy, and will keep your design in place. Or dilute white glue (about 1 part water to 2 parts glue) and use it as a protective finish.

#4: OPWORK

Op art, a style that arrived on the scene during the sixties, is so named from the optical effects of its coloring and precision drawing. In many examples, the colors and design seem to change as the viewer shifts his position. Here is a now-you-see-it-now-you-don't painting for you to produce.

MATERIALS:
  corrugated cardboard
  acrylic paints in several colors plus white
  ruler and pencil
  fixative spray
  patience
  and a steady hand

HOW-TO:
1. Prepare cardboard by pinching ribs of cardboard between your fingers so that a sharp vertical crease is formed in front of each rib. Cover with a light coat of white paint. Crease and paint a practice piece of cardboard, too.
2. Work out your design. The center creases are the dividing line. You will be painting a different design to the

left of the rib creases from the one on the right. Perhaps your design can be circles on the right face, and triangles on the left; or a swirling, curved pattern on one side and a pattern of sharp-cornered squares on the other.

3. To transfer design to cardboard, brush ribs gently to one side. Use pencil and ruler to sketch in design outline. Then gently brush ribs of cardboard to other side,

Opwork

and sketch in other design. Make circles by pressing ribs to one side and tracing lightly with a pencil around coins of various sizes. For the opposite face, cut triangles from stiff cardboard to use as a pattern and trace around them. Paint the circles in black on white, the triangles in yellow on green. Or whatever design and colors appeal to you.

4. Paint design slowly and carefully. Acrylic paints are easy to control, and dry quickly so that there is little danger of colors running where they meet. Brush ribs gently first toward one side and then toward the other. After both sides of design have been painted and are completely dry, brush ribs gently back to center.

5. Spray with fixative. Mount by gluing or tacking to plywood or masonite cut to same size. Or glue to burlap-covered board with 2″ or 3″ margin all around.

Idea! Instead of a pattern, your design could simply be colors. Use shades of different colors on each side of rib creases: paint three or five ribs in each of several shades of blue, and their opposite sides in shades of yellows and oranges. Or combine pink-to-reds with lavender-to-purples.

#5: THREE FROM TISSUE PAPER

These art hang-ups derive their brilliant color effects from layers and layers of tissue paper bonded to each other. The method couldn't be simpler. Here's how:

1. Cut tissue paper to the shapes desired.

2. For the bonding agent use polymer medium or diluted white glue (1 part water to 2 parts glue). The glue mixture takes longer to dry.

3. Place one piece of tissue paper down over the background. Brush the *top* of the tissue paper with bonding agent. Place another piece of tissue paper down, overlapping the first in part or completely as your design requires. Again, brush *top* of tissue paper with medium or glue.

4. Continue until your chosen design is built up, always brushing bonding agent on top of the last tissue-paper piece put in place. Let dry.

5. For a glossy protective finish, brush one or two coats of the bonding agent over the entire work.

6. You may want to experiment to see the different color effects you can achieve. Try bonding scraps of tissue paper on a heavy white paper or cardboard background until you work out the color effects you want. You will find that a yellow bonded over a brown has a different appearance from brown bonded over yellow; that dark colors like red and green may run when you brush the bonding agent over them, and provide a new color effect. Or you might try crinkling paper up for still another effect.

a) "Stained-Glass" Picture

MATERIALS:
  polymer medium and/or white glue
  carbon paper and pencil
  brush
  cardboard
  scissors
  tissue paper in several colors
  black felt-tipped marking pen

plywood covered with burlap or foil, or a posterboard or mat board backing to be framed (see chapter 4) for background

How-to:
1. Choose a design or picture. It should have simple shapes. Coloring-book pictures or folk art designs are just right; look in chapter 10 for other ideas.
2. Use carbon paper to trace picture on cardboard.
3. Cut out picture; cut on all lines so that you have a separate cardboard piece for each section of picture.

4. Using a cardboard section as a pattern, cut three or four layers of tissue paper in color desired. Bond several layers to cardboard pattern. Let dry. Trim edges if necessary.
5. Repeat for other portions of the design.
6. To make narrow strips, as for flower stems, brush a rectangular piece of tissue paper lightly with bonding agent and roll between fingers into ropelike strips.
7. Blacken rough edges of cardboard shapes with marking pen.
8. Assemble design pieces on backing and glue into place. Outline each design section with marking pen.

b) "Two Times"

This modular design was contrived by cutting tissue paper into strips whose dimensions were all 2″ or a multiple of 2″. The same trick could be worked with 3 or any other number.

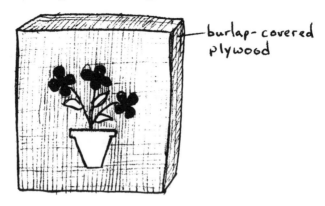

burlap-covered
plywood

"Stained-Glass" Picture

MATERIALS:
   white posterboard
   tissue paper in three or more colors
   polymer medium or diluted white glue
   ruler, pencil
   black felt-tipped marker (or other color if desired)

HOW-TO:
1. Choose your colors. (I used light yellow, dark yellow, green, red, brown, black, from a package of multicolored tissue papers.)
2. Place several layers of tissue paper together, holding with clips if necessary. Mark off and cut into pieces measuring 2″ by 2″, 2″ by 4″, 4″ by 4″, 2″ by 6″. If you're working on a large background, go on up the multiplication table: 2″ by 8″, 4″ by 8″, 8″ by 8″.
3. Mark design area (a multiple of two, of course, in both length and width) using ruler and pencil on posterboard. Starting at upper left hand corner, place any cut piece of paper down neatly along pencilled line and brush bonding agent over it. Continue to place pieces of colored paper down, sometimes overlapping, sometimes adjacent, but always keeping the "Two Times" square or rectangular relationships, until entire design area is filled with several layers of tissue paper. Let dry.
4. Outline every square or rectangle with black marker.

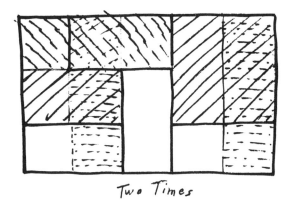

Two Times

5. Finish with a protective coat of polymer medium or diluted white glue. Frame as you like.

c) Tissue Montage "As You Like It"

This is really a free-form adaptation of the two previous projects in tissue-paper technique. In photography, a montage is an arrangement that involves both superimposing and juxtaposing two or more images on film. Here, we'll do the same thing with different shapes and colors of translucent tissue paper.

MATERIALS:
>   colored tissue paper, bonding agent, brush and scissors as before
>   white posterboard, or any other color; or aluminum foil (straight from the kitchen) regular or heavy weight, or waxed paper, or wrapping paper, or just about anything else you can think of to try for a background

How-to:
1. Cut tissue paper into any shapes of any size you like.
2. Bond them to your background as you like it, here, there and all about. Over, under, overlapping, adjacent . . .
3. Keep going, layer after layer, building up different effects as you go. You may have six layers in one place and next to it an area where the background shows untouched. It's up to you.

4. Finish with a final coat of polymer or diluted glue.

Idea! How about bonding scraps of fabric or newspaper into your design? Simply place down and brush bonding agent over them; then place tissue-paper layer over and brush with bonding agent to seal in place.

#6: COLLAGE, COLLAGE

And that idea leads directly to collages of all sorts. A collage (from a French word meaning paste or glue) is a unified design made by pasting a variety of different materials onto a background. The materials for collage are virtually endless, and may range from lace to lollipop sticks. A collage depends for its effectiveness on the contrast in appearance and textures of its materials. It may be organized around a unifying theme or idea.

MATERIALS FOR COLLAGE:

greeting cards, fabric and trimming scraps, odds and ends of string, lace, colored papers of all sorts, including tissue and gift wrap, stationery, business and income tax forms, invitations, book jackets, magazine and newspaper clippings, ice cream and lollipop sticks, plain and corrugated cardboard, package labels, buttons, theater tickets, paper clips, yarns, old photographs, dress patterns, and anything else relatively flat that can be glued to a background that you can think of. A quick tour of your home, including wastebaskets, will probably turn up a multitude of possibly useful items. You might file possibilities in large coffee cans, under such labels as "fabric for collage" and "paper for collage" so that when you are ready to get to work you'll have a large assortment of materials from which to choose.

EQUIPMENT FOR COLLAGE:

scissors, white glue (for most materials) or contact cement (for almost anything else), posterboard for background (or cardboard—you can even cut up and use the sides of a heavy cardboard carton), felt-tipped marking pens or crayons in assorted colors (optional).

HOW-TO:

1. Assemble the materials that suit your idea or theme;

decide on the background and the size your collage is to be.

2. Paint the background if your design idea calls for it.

3. Place the most important of the assembled materials on the background. Move them around; partly cover one up with another; turn them at angles; twist and bend them. If necessary, cut or tear into special shapes or smaller sections of pieces.

4. When you are absolutely sure of where you want to place something, glue it down. Keep on placing materials down and changing their positions, gluing whenever your composition seems to be doing the right thing. You may find that your design needs fewer things than you at first intended.

5. If you like, add outlines or other markings of crayon or felt-tipped markers to emphasize a design element.

6. Finish by spraying with fixative to preserve your collage. And that's all there is to it.

7. You can design a collage to commemorate an event, reflect a decorative scheme or suit a personality. Here are some suggestions:

a) *Wedding-gift collage* from invitation, bits of fabric left over from bride's dress and veil, garter, bright penny, place card, matchbook cover and/or cake box from reception.

b) *Hobby collage* for stamp or coin collectors from newspaper clippings, advertisements, catalogue pages, and even specimens.

c) *Collage for model railroad or auto buffs* from appropriate magazine or newspaper articles or advertisements, package parts and "furniture" for model set-ups.

d) *Memory collage* of fabrics snipped from favorite dresses, photographs, lock of hair.

e) *Kitchen collage* of food-package labels, recipes, plastic sandwich bags, dried beans, macaroni, paper napkins.

f) *First-apartment collage* from scraps of upholstery and drapery fabric, paint samples, wallpaper, carpet and linoleum swatches.

g) *Color collage* built around a single color or color combination: reds, blues, pinks, black-and-white. How many different greens can you find in your collage material collection?

#7: ASSEMBLAGE

I'm not sure what the official distinctions are, if any, between *collage* and *assemblage*. For me, when a collage has been built up to a noticeably three-dimensional effect, it has become an assemblage. The techniques for making an assemblage are essentially the same: gluing materials in a unified arrangement to a background. But the background must be more substantial than posterboard to suport the heavier weight of many materials; and in some cases hammer and tacks or nails can replace glue (see Assemblage Ideas *a* and *b* below).

A finished assemblage can be framed, or the back of its plywood background can be covered with felt and hung directly on a wall from picture wire twisted around screw eyes.

MATERIALS FOR ASSEMBLAGES:

strips of plastic, scraps of wood, hardware odds and ends, rope, leather, cork, sand, shell, steel wool, broken glass and china, sponges, styrofoam, can tops, tab-opening can tabs and rings, mirrors, plastic containers, wire and wire mesh, pencils, rulers, hair pins and safety pins, thread spools, zippers, parts of a broken clock or radio, drinking straws, small boxes, odds and ends of used clothes such as gloves, belts, socks. If your household is anything like mine, you've probably got the makings for a dozen assemblages at hand or under foot this very minute.

EQUIPMENT FOR ASSEMBLAGES:

choose from scissors, pliers, tin shears, razor blade or craft knife for preparing materials. Choose glue according to materials it must fasten: white glue or polymer gel medium will hold most objects to most backgrounds, but it is a good idea to keep contact cement or liquid solder on hand for metal parts. Backgrounds for assemblages should be sturdy like plywood or masonite, although heavy cardboard will do if the materials are not too bulky. Enamel or acrylic paint, foil or burlap can be used to finish or cover background. Other optional equipment might include felt-tipped marking pens and/or acrylic paints.

How-to:

1. Decide on the materials for your assemblage. Decide on the background material and size. An effective assemblage can be as small as 5" by 8", but the larger your background the more expressive and free-ranging your work can be. For a first attempt, work on a ½" plywood or masonite slab about 18" by 18".
2. Finish the background as you like it. Cover plywood with foil to reflect the materials that will be glued on it. Or get a clear color effect by rubbing wood with acrylic paint. Paint or spray with enamel, or cover with felt, burlap or other textured fabric. Or you may decide to involve the wood grain or masonite texture in your assemblage and leave it untouched. Cover back of background with felt.
3. Place the most important of your materials on the background. When you are satisfied with the positioning, start gluing. Use a lot of glue, especially if you are working on a masonite background, because it will be absorbed. Use scissors, pliers or what you will to shape your materials. Fray ends of fabric or string for a different effect.
4. Continue placing materials, shifting their positions and gluing them in place. Saturate some cloth with glue and bunch it up into a fist-size ball; or saturate string or yarn and wad it up into a ball. When the glue dries the fabric or string-ball will harden in place.
5. Add black or colors with acrylic paint or marking pens for emphasis.
6. Finish by spraying with fixative for protective surface if desired.

Assemblage ideas:

The first three of these ideas for assemblages put a limited variety of materials to extremely effective use. For the last— anything goes!

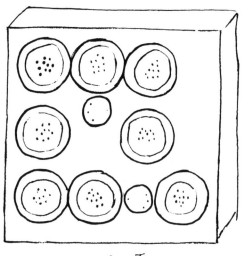

Can Top

a) *CanTop.* Save tops and bottoms of cans. Clean them; rub to a dull gloss with steel wool if desired. Get plywood in shape and size of your choice. Sand edges. Paint top and edges of plywood with dull black enamel (my preference), or with silver gray, or bright yellow or orange. Arrange can tops in any composition you like; rearrange until you are satisfied. Try eight large can tops with one smaller one, or all silvery can tops with one brass-colored one. Or whatever idea your can tops suggest to you. Use hammer and brass or steel tacks to fasten metal circles to plywood, hammering a cluster of tacks in center of circles, or a few around edges. The tacks add to the effect. Or, for a different effect, glue with contact cement, or use strong double-faced mounting tape to attach circles invisibly to background.

b) *TabTab.* Save tabs from tab-top cans. Add one or a few can tops. Hammer and tacks, as above; plywood background, as above. Paint or cover plywood as you like. Arrange can tops on background first, and tack into place. Then arrange tabs and attach, using one tack hammered smartly into the narrow end of each tab. Use pliers to curl up the broad end of each tab. I did my TabTab against a plywood background

Tab Tab

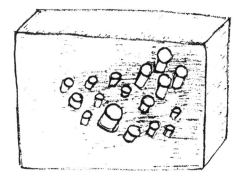

Ice Caps

rubbed with bright yellow acrylic, and used steel tacks. But it would look great done with brass or copper tacks into a foil-covered background, too.

c) *Ice Caps.* The inspiration for this assemblage was a work I admired in a gallery. It was composed of small lucite cubes attached to a gleaming polished aluminum surface in a seemingly random pattern, where they looked like so many ice cubes permanently frozen to a mirror. My duplication cost under two dollars. I covered a plywood slab with heavy aluminum foil. I bought, in the nearest five-and-ten, several packages of furniture tips, all white—(these are soft, rubbery caps designed to fit under furniture legs to prevent marking up floors, and they come in white, black and gray). I bought three different sizes, but mostly the smallest—and I arranged them on my shiny foil surface, attaching them with a blob of white glue squeezed around the inside. After an hour or two, my assemblage was ready to hang!

d) *Free Association.* Look over your accumulation of junk—oops! pardon me, *materials.* And simply pick out whatever you like. Or start with just one thing, be it a handkerchief, an old washcloth or a leather glove, a piece of a broken dinner plate or—whatever. Then keep adding, one idea at a time, as they occur to you. *Or,* spread an accumulation of materials out on the table in front of you. Close your eyes and run your fingers over them, stopping when the *feel* of something excites you. Put it aside to use, and continue feeling for materials to incorporate into your work. *Or,* browse in a hardware or dimestore and buy up to two or three dollars' worth of stuff that appeals to you—dishtowels, nuts and bolts, dog collar, children's toys, measuring cups and spoons or whatever. Go home, spread it all out in front of you and go to work.

"Found Sculpture"

If you're searching for something new and different to highlight a room, think sculpture! Here are some great ideas for sculptural things you discover or put together—things to stand on the floor, hang from a wall or sit on a mantel or coffee table.

#1: A FRAGMENT

A fragment of a building, that is. A building, decades old, in the process of being razed. All those lovely doors, moldings, mantels, archways, and carved stone decorations going to waste. Once you start keeping an eye out for this sort of thing, there's no telling what you'll come up with. The Brooklyn Museum in New York has a Sculpture Garden filled with wonderful stone decorations captured just in the nick of time from buildings scheduled for demolition.

To find a fragment of your own: (1) Become aware of buildings in your community that are due to be wrecked. Scout around and see if there's anything you want. Then, wait for the wrecking crew to arrive on the scene. Try to arrange with the foreman or one of the workers to save your treasure for you; you'll pay him a few dollars for the service, of course. Or (2), prowl the premises, carefully, after a day's work, and see what you can find. Or (3), in some communities, wrecking companies sell whatever building elements they can salvage. At one such "junkyard," we have come upon such wonders as leaded-glass panels, chipped marble cupids, an old cast iron radiator encrusted with glass "jewels" and adorned with decorative scrollwork, among other things.

What to do with a fragment: Probably any fragment you locate will be grimy and in nearly deplorable condition. What wouldn't be, after being exposed to the elements for countless decades? But gentle scrubbing with a soft brush and liquid dishwashing detergent should uncover its true loveliness.

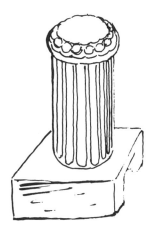

1. Place large fragments in the bathtub, on a foam rubber pad or an old tub mat to prevent them from scratching the tub. If the stone is very dirty, run the shower on it for a few minutes. Then brush with detergent. Rinse thoroughly, and stand on a thick wad of newspaper to dry.

2. If your fragment is metal, dry carefully with an old towel to prevent rusting. To remove old rust, use a commercial rust solvent (from the hardware or paint store) but follow directions carefully, so as not to remove any fragile, corroded metal. Brush with a rust-preventing preparation, or restore original finish with wrought-iron-black enamel or other paint intended especially for use on metal surfaces.

3. If repairs are necessary, use epoxy cement. But damaged old iron or stone has a charm of its own, so don't try to achieve a brand-new appearance in a seventy-year-old carving.

4. Depending on their size and shape, building fragments can be displayed either standing, resting on a shelf or mounted on a base. Epoxy marine compound (from hardware or boat supply store) will be required to hold stone or cast iron to a base. A suitable base for a stone fragment might be another building element, such as a large masonry brick.

#2: THE SUPERSCULPTURE

Have your carpenter make up two 30″ or 36″ squares of brightly colored Formica as though they were table tops, with

matched Formica sides or aprons about 2″ deep. Hang them—at angles—with screw eyes and wire.

Budget version: Or you can have 1″ plywood cut into squares. Sand thoroughly and enamel brightly. For higher gloss, varnish or spray with clear vinyl. For high gloss plus interesting texture, use a 1″ wide paint brush to coat thickly with polymer gel medium. Or rub bright acrylic paint into wood using a sponge or your fingers; then spray or coat with gel medium.

Bonus: Whenever you tire of the Supersculpture, take it off the wall and remove the screw eyes and picture wire. Attach chrome or brass legs and use together as bunching tables or separately as cocktail or lamp tables.

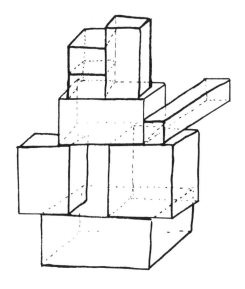

#3: LUCITE CONSTRUCTION

A novelty-store display of small clear plastic boxes ranging from small (for 25 cents) down to teeny (for 10 cents) gave me a sudden vision of a crystal tower. I filled my hands with the boxes and bought about two dozen, in glowingly transparent shades of yellow, blue, red, black and clear.

At home, I spread them out on my desk, separating some of the lids from their containers, and began stacking them like so many miniature jeweled blocks. An all-black tower, a yellow-and-blue tower, and two others sprouted in front of me. A little glue made my table-top sculptures permanent.

If you cannot find similar boxes for sale, you can still duplicate this effect. Save clear plastic pill containers, food containers, disposable glasses and photograph display cubes. Once you start looking for clear plastic containers, you'll be surprised at how many things you buy that are packed in them; and at how many kinds of plastic containers you can discover in any five-and-ten.

Glue note: white glue, cement for plastic models, polymer medium and polymer gel medium can all be used to bond plastic to plastic. These become transparent when dry; some model cements leave a textured surface wherever the glue has touched. My prefernce is to use polymer gel medium, which dried quickly and clearly. A little goes a long way; and the thicker texture of the gel helps keep the plastic pieces in some tricky positions until the bond is secure.

#4: CARDBOARD TUBE CONSTRUCTION

Save cardboard mailing tubes, and the tubes from paper toweling, wax paper, foil, etc. In a few weeks you'll probably have a shopping-bag full.

1. Stand the tubes up on a table before you, and start arranging them so that they touch each other. The tubes will probably be of different heights and create an interesting effect —a forest of plumber's pipe, perhaps. For more variety, cut the tubes down to size; use scissors, razor blade, craft knife or electric carving knife.

2. When you have an arrangement you like, glue three or four of the tubes together (with white glue, preferably), keeping them standing up. Let dry, and then add another three or

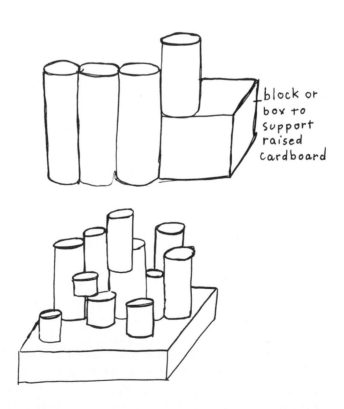

block or box to support raised cardboard

four. This time you might want to raise one or two; if so, put something underneath to support them while the glue is drying; a box, a book or a block could be used as a support. Continue adding tubes and gluing until you have the effect you want. Let dry thoroughly, overnight if possible.

3. Spray with enamel in the color of your choice; my preference is silver. When paint is dry, spray with a second coat or with clear vinyl or both.

4. To mount: Spray-paint a plywood slab to match or contrast, glue felt to the bottom, and glue your tube construction in place on top.

#5: SCRAP WOOD CONSTRUCTION

Would you believe that a structure handsome enough to grace any coffee table could be produced from odds and ends of wood by someone with no woodworking skills or equipment? I made one, and you can, too.

Start by accumulating wood scraps. Ask a carpenter or at a lumber yard (perhaps they'll let you poke around in their scrap barrel), collect ice cream sticks and toothpicks, beg or buy some blocks.

MATERIALS:
    wood scraps
    a plywood slab for the base
    a piece of felt the same size as the plywood
    sandpaper
    white glue
    paint, varnish or shellac, and a brush or two

HOW-TO:
1. Prepare the base for your construction by sanding the plywood slab. Cut felt to fit bottom and glue in place.
2. Now start building your sculpture. It's almost like building with blocks. Select two or three pieces of wood in shapes that appeal to you and arrange them on your base. Stack them on top of one another at crazy angles; lay them across one another; or place several next to each other in a repetitious row. Glue and let dry.
3. Add on more wood scraps, and more, until you're satisfied. If you want to, sandpaper some. Break those that are thin, like toothpicks and sticks. Depending on

Scrap Wood Construction

the size and shape of the wood scraps you use, your construction may be light and airy, or solid and chunky, or it may combine both effects.

4. After glue has dried, paint as you like. You may decide to simply spray with clear vinyl, or with a wood-toned enamel. Or you may decide to paint your construction in three or more bright colors. Use enamel or acrylics.

5. Finish with shellac, clear vinyl spray or varnish.

#6: HARDWARE CONSTRUCTION

This construction is built up from the odds and ends that accumulate in every tool box: nuts, bolts, gears, old keys and the like. If your accumulation is not inspired, a dollar or two spent at the nearest hardware store will get you started. The list of metal junk you can incorporate into sculpture includes: old clock parts, springs, old tools, spoons, knives and forks, hooks, cotter pins, wire, used fuses, paper clips, hinges, locks and lock parts, and nails and bolts or every size and variety.

MATERIALS:
  assortment of metal junk
  plywood slab for base
  a piece of felt the same size as the plywood
  epoxy cement, liquid solder or contact cement
  toothpicks
  fine steel wool (optional)
  needle-nose pliers (optional)
  hammer
  metal-colored enamels (optional)

HOW-TO:
  1. Prepare plywood base by sanding, painting if desired, and gluing felt to bottom.
  2. Start arranging your hardware. It's sort of like making a collage in three dimensions. You might start by hammering a few long nails into the base at different angles. Then build up other parts against and on top of them. Pieces of metal can lean against each other, lie atop each other or bend (use pliers) to fit around each other.

Hardware Construction

using hex nuts, old fuse,
spring, screw eye, and
assorted nails, bolts and
other hardware

Brighten metal by rubbing with steel wool, if desired. Position your pieces carefully, and hold in place (pliers help here, too) while applying cement to contact points with toothpicks. Let dry. Add more metal pieces to your construction; glue and let dry.

3. If desired, brush with a metal plating or finishing enamel such as copper, brass or antique gold. Or color some, but not all, components. Or spray with wrought-iron-black enamel, using masking tape to protect base and any parts you do not wish to color.

❧ VI ❧

And More Hang-ups

Hang a Wall-Hanging

If you have a Mexican rug or an Early American patchwork quilt, a fringed and embroidered piano shawl or an heirloom crocheted bedspread, put it on the wall! A fabric hanging is a striking decorative effect, and a practical one as well. Fabric is easy to keep clean, and it cuts down on noise and vibrations while adding a warm, intimate note to a room.

Surprisingly, many delicate fabrics take well to self-service automatic-type dry cleaning. If you take a delicate fabric to a service dry cleaner, be sure to specify "no pressing"; the heat of the iron, not to mention the carelessness of most pressers, can be fatal to antique fabrics. If necessary, you can touch up crumpled spots by using a hand iron on the warm setting over a lightweight press cloth.

If macramé is your thing, make a wall-hanging to show off your skill. Cover a whole wall with your knots, or make a long narrow hanging. Use a brass decorator cafe curtain rod to hang your work from. Do your knotting right on the wall—construct your own design as you go and leave the unfinished bundles of cord hanging in place while your work is in progress.

How to Hang a Wall-Hanging

By far the easiest way to hang any fabric anywhere is with curtain rods. You have an enormous choice, ranging from standard rods and slim brass cafe-style rods, to wider decorator cafe rods in wood tones or colors. You can slip the rod into a casing at the top of the wall-hanging; or you can sew cafe curtain rings to the top of the hanging. Even easier to use are the kind of cafe rings that clip onto the top of the fabric. The mounting brackets suitable for whatever kind of rod you are using can be installed directly on the wall.

When making a wall-hanging, you will have to add to the measurements a top casing allowance of 2″ to accommodate most curtain rods. Fold fabric to wrong side and stitch down near edge. A casing to accommodate one of the wider rods, of course, will have to be proportionately deeper. For fabrics that fray or ravel, add another ¼″ to turn under before making the casing.

A wall-hanging will hang better, in most cases, if its bottom is weighted in some way. An easy way to do this is to provide another casing at the bottom, and slip a second rod or a wood dowel through. Lead weights can also be sewn to the wrong

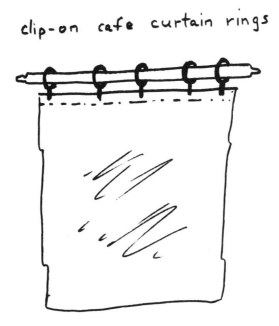

clip-on cafe curtain rings

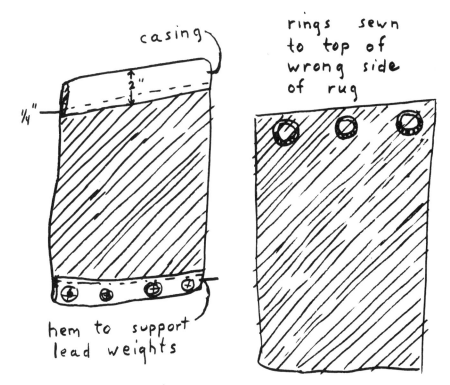

side of a hanging at the bottom; in this case a hem allowance of 1½" should be added.

When hanging a heavy fabric, such as a rug or a quilt, sew rings to wrong side of hanging just below the top edge. Leave the top half of ring free. Space rings evenly across fabric at intervals, so fabric will not sag when hung. Suspend each ring from a picture hook nailed into the wall, spaced to correspond. Weights are not needed for a hanging of this sort.

Another way to hang fabric is by tacking it to a slab of ½" plywood as long as the top horizontal measurement of the hanging, and 3" wide. Sand wood smooth and shellac or paint edges. Cover back with felt to prevent scratching wall. Tack (use decorative upholstery tacks in a color to blend) or staple top of fabric to top of plywood. Hang with screw eyes and picture wire.

Small fabric hangings can be displayed by gluing or tacking to plywood, or by tacking to cork.

Make a Wall-Hanging

#1: HANG A BANNER

A felt banner of your own design can be the most effective of wall-hangings. Best of all, it can be made, quickly and inexpensively, in any size and shape your wall may need. It is the ideal way to decorate a forgotten corner or a "dead" wall area.

Our banner, long, narrow and vertical, brightly conceals a "sore thumb," seldom-used door. On it are arranged seven Mexican flower and animal designs (see Chapter X for these), patterned after some of the folk art objects in the room. Narrow brass cafe curtain rods at top and bottom hold it in place. Concoct your own smashing banner right now.

MATERIALS:
    cafe curtain rod (or rods) and mounting brackets
    felt in background color, cut to the size you want
    felt square and scraps in contrasting colors (felt squares
        are sold at most notions counters; two or three are
        probably all you'll need for even a large banner)
    assorted buttons, yarn, sequins, braid, ribbon, bits of ball-
        fringe and other trimmings
    white glue

How-to:

1. Decide where you need a banner, and what size it should be. Experiment with wrapping paper and masking tape until you find the best size and proportions for your wall area. Be sure to add casing allowances large enough for your curtain rods at top and bottom.

2. Decide on background color and buy enough felt. Gather together or buy the scraps and pieces to use for your designs.

3. Cut felt background to size desired. Fold casing allowances to wrong side and stitch close to edge of fabric.

4. Decide on the design or designs to put on your banner.

Hang A Banner...

... almost any shape will do

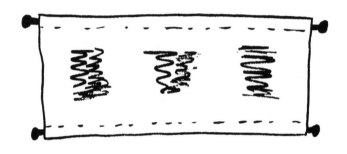

make a long, horizontal one
to hang over a bed or table

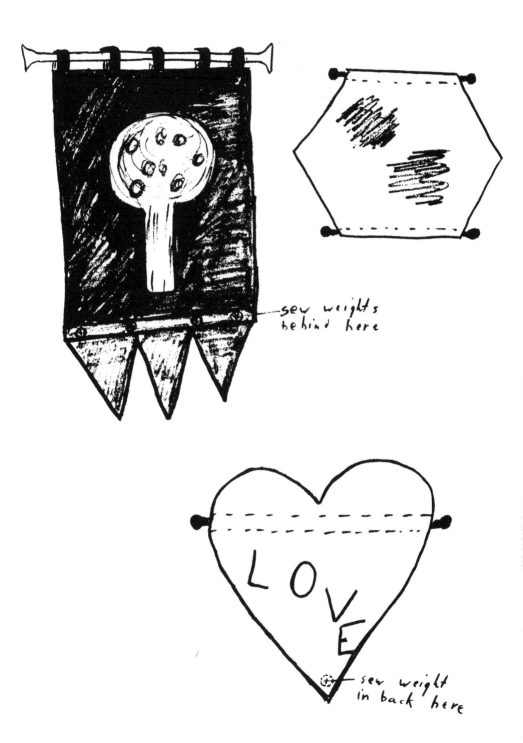

sew weights
behind here

sew weight
in back here

Let something in the room where your banner will hang suggest a design idea to you. Or see chapter 10 for some of my favorites. Trace design on scrap paper and arrange on felt background. Move pieces around until you decide how many design elements you want, and where you want to place them. Try larger or smaller cutouts if necessary.

5. Use the paper cutout patterns to outline your chosen design on colored felt scraps or squares, and cut out. Arrange the felt pieces on the banner. They will stick lightly by themselves; or you can pin them in place while you try out your banner on its wall.

6. When you are sure you have the arrangement you want, cut design details from small felt scraps, yarn, trimmings, etc. Use a few drops of white glue to attach details to larger felt cutouts, and then to glue cutouts in place on banner.

7. Attach brackets for curtain rods to wall, slip rods through casings, and hang your banner high.

#2: OPEN-WEAVE HANGING

MATERIALS:

burlap for background
cafe curtain rod or rods and mounting brackets
dowels, twine, yarn, other materials (optional—see below)

HOW-TO:

1. Cut burlap to size desired, including casing allowances. Sew casings for top and bottom rods.

2. Pull crosswise threads from burlap, leaving only lengthwise threads, in several places. Save pulled-out strands.

3. Tie some groups of lengthwise threads in bunches, using burlap strands or contrasting yarn. Leave some groups of thread straight.

4. Or you can weave in other threads, yarn, strips of fabric, straw, other fibers, going over and under several burlap threads. *Or* cut through some threads. *Or* weave in narrow rods of plastic, wood, straws, to add textural interest as well as to increase stability. Try knitting needles (double-pointed, either silvery or colored plas-

tic). Try wooden or plastic rods from children's construction toys. *Or* knot on such eye-catching odds and ends as marbles, shiny new pennies, bits of colored lucite, small boxes, rocks or shells—just tie them up in knots, using the burlap strands you have pulled from the background, or any other cord. *Or* sew on buttons, beads, bits of styrofoam, balsa wood, and anything else you can pull a needle and thread through.

Idea! Instead of a bottom casing, make knotted fringe by pulling out crosswise threads for 4″ to 8″ and knotting together clumps of about 10 fringe strands. Knot in some large wooden beads if you have them.

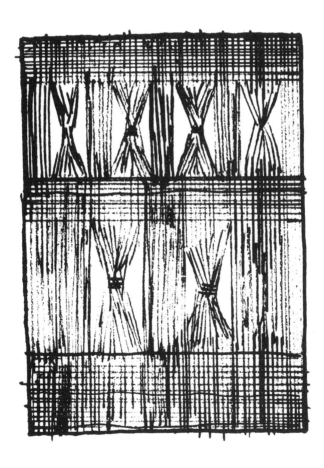

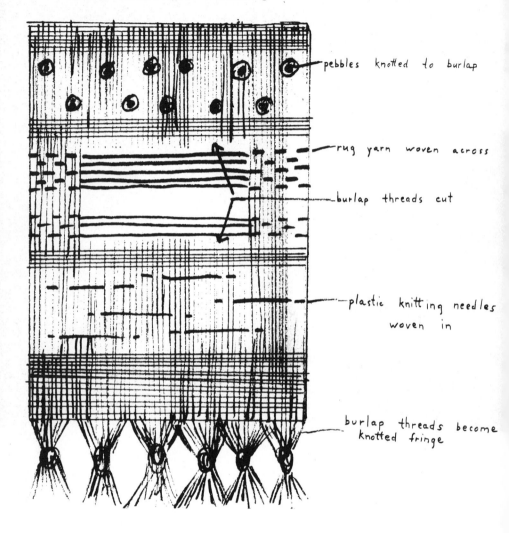

pebbles knotted to burlap

rug yarn woven across

burlap threads cut

plastic knitting needles
woven in

burlap threads become
knotted fringe

#3: EMBROIDERED HANGING "WAVES"

Using a variety of colors and only the simplest embroidery stitch results in a striking, unique wall-hanging.

MATERIALS:

a coarsely woven fabric such as linen or burlap in a neutral color, in any size you like

embroidery floss or cord, or needlepoint or any 2- or 3-ply yarn, in three or more colors

Mirrors are placed low on the opposite walls of the narrow corridor we use for dining. Instead of feeling hemmed in by a room less than six feet across, seated guests see an open-ended series of reflections. Mexican tiles and tinware, and old English prints, are also on the walls.

Right, from top: mount dried leaves on aluminum foil by covering with pink tissue paper and brushing generously with polymer medium; two Paintsplotches; and two Paintstring designs. Below: First Apartment Collage; and tissue paper design Two Times (all, Chapter IV).

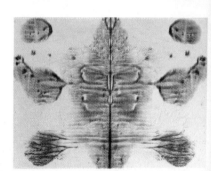

In the foreground of this view of our living room are the two chairside
tables made from old sewing machine drawers topped with Mexican
tiles (Chapter I). The symmetrical arrangement of these tables and
the chairs, and of the candleholders on the mantel, are offset by the
assymmetry of the other objects in the room (combination balance,
Chapter IV). The two small African sculptures on the left end of the
mantel are mounted on Kindergarten blocks.

Above: cardboard tube construction. Top left: lucite construction. Center left: scrap wood construction on burlap-covered base. Below, hardware construction (all, Chapter V).

The lucky find of a Chinese red bedspread determined the color scheme of our bedroom redecoration. The "armoire" in the corner was designed from two stock ready-to-finish wood units, enameled to match. On the wall over the bed an embroidered fabric fragment from North Africa is flanked by carvings from Ghana and the Ivory Coast.

Top and center right: papier mache creates a bud vase and a pad-and-pencil caddy, both acrylic painted. Bottom left: a cigar box covered with foil is a sewing box. Bottom right: a make-up caddy from pill containers, acrylic painted (all, Chapter XI). Below: three String Things (Chapter V).

In my daughter's room are, from left: banner with Mexican flower and animal designs in felt applique (Chapter VI); throw pillows including a cylinder, Nina's own needlepoint picture, and embroidered Lazy Daisy design; picture frames above bed are dimestore variety, painted; another dimestore frame disguised with acrylic yarn and a corduroy-covered mat stands on chest displaying a bead necklace and bracelet; and at the upper right is a corner of the canopy valance (Chapter II).

Above: Tie Dye Sampler wall hanging (Chapter VI). Left: embroideries for wall hangings or throw pillows are (top) Starflower and (center) Bull's Eye (Chapter X). Below left, patchwork throw pillow made from discarded neckties (Chapter III) and needlepoint pillow in Panes design (Chapter X).

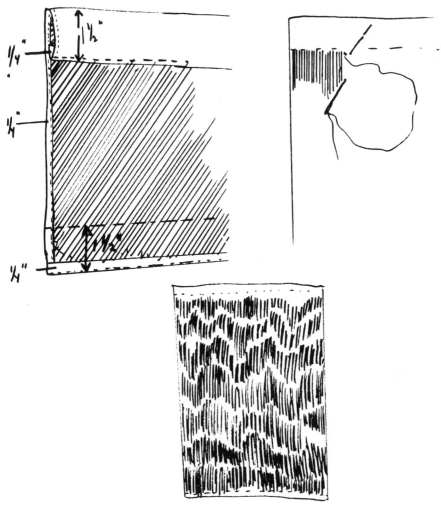

needle
curtain rod or rods and mounting brackets

How-to:

1. Prepare fabric for hanging. Machine stitch ¼″ from vertical edges, fold to wrong side on line of stitching and stitch again. Machine stitch ¼″ from horizontal edges, turn to wrong side on stitching and turn again 1½″ from first fold or whatever distance is required to make casing for the rod you have chosen. Stitch close to first fold.

2. Start embroidery by pulling needle up at left side of

work about ½″ to 1″ below casing. Put needle down through fabric just under casing. Bring needle up through fabric again right next to first stitch. Continue making straight stitches across top of fabric, varying length of stitches to create a wavy design. Change to a new color for second row, and straight stitch across, always putting needle down through fabric just below bottom of previous row, so that the wave pattern is continuous. Continue making wavy rows until fabric is covered; the bottom row should just meet the bottom casing.

#4: TIE-DYE SAMPLER

This first tie-dye wall-hanging is actually a sampler of three basic dyeing knots. You make it from handkerchiefs or dinner napkins, quick-as-a-wink, and almost as inexpensively.

MATERIALS:

3 linen handkerchiefs, linen napkins, or squares of cotton or linen fabric in white, beige, gray or other light or neutral color
liquid or powdered dye in a color to contrast with fabric
standard tie-dye equipment: rubber bands, enamel or glass container, rubber gloves, wooden spoon
yarn and yarn needle

HOW-TO:

1. Fold first piece of fabric in half and make several *rosette knots* through both layers of fabric, scattering them a few inches apart. Make a large *donut knot* in center of second piece of fabric. Fold third piece of fabric in half and then in accordion pleats; fasten with rubber bands at 1″ intervals to make *stripes*. (See chapter 9 for instructions and diagrams of tie-dye knotting techniques.)

2. Prepare dye bath using 4 tablespoons (¼ bottle) liquid dye or ½ package powdered dye and 2 quarts very hot water. Place knotted fabric pieces in dye bath and leave for 10 or 15 minutes, stirring occasionally with wooden spoon to make sure dye penetrates all parts of fabric.

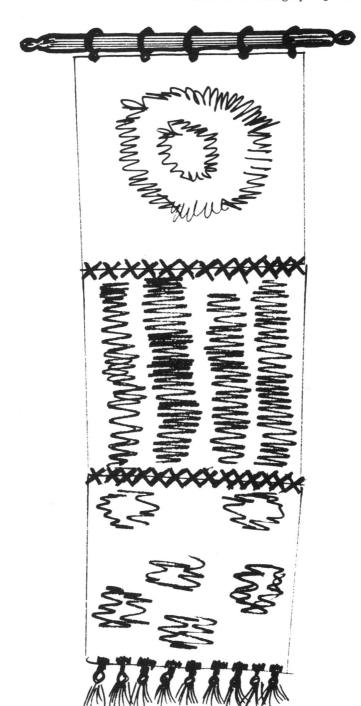

Cross-Stitched Open Seam

1. Start with knot under fabric, bring needle up at 1, down at 2 and up at 3. Continue putting needle down at 4 and up at 5. First cross-stitch made.

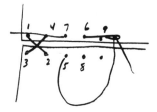

2. Start second cross-stitch: needle goes down at 6, up at 7, down at 8 and up at 9.

Sewn-On Tassels

1. Cut a strand of yarn 1 yard long. Fold in half, thread through needle. Pull quadrupled thread through fabric and cut across all threads ½" from needle.

2. Gather together all threads and knot, pushing knot up until it is just below the edge of the cloth.

3. Rinse thoroughly in cold water until water runs clear. Remove rubber bands and rinse again. Iron while still slightly damp.

4. Using yarn and making stitches ½″ wide, join fabric pieces with cross-stitched open seam (see diagram).

5. Finish with sewn-on tassels along bottom (see diagram) spacing at approximately 1″ intervals. To make the spacing come out even, work corner fringes first, then do one in the center, and space others evenly between.

6. Hang from cafe curtain rod using clip-type cafe rings.

Idea! Hang it in the dining area. Dye a tablecloth to match (try striping the entire cloth, or combining donut and rosette knots at random). Or tie-dye six or more napkins and sew together with cross-stitched open seam to make a table runner; fringe ends. Or tie-dye a set of placemats and napkins to match, varying knotting techniques within the set.

#5: TIE-DYE "SUNBURST"

Add two more knotting techniques to your tie-dye repertoire with this larger hanging.

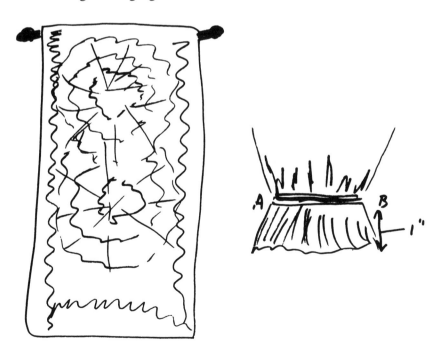

MATERIALS:

> plain cotton or linen fabric, about 18″ by 36″ (or less or more, depending on what you have; tear up an old sheet, cut the back out of an old shirt and square off, slit the seams of an old pillowcase, or buy a half-yard of muslin)
> liquid or powdered dye in the color of your choice
> dyeing equipment as in previous project

HOW-TO:

1. Knot fabric in sunbursts and stripes: make one sunburst in top third of fabric, another just below center of fabric. Gather up fabric in uneven accordion folds about 1″ from bottom (A to B on diagram) and fasten with rubber bands. Gather similarly along vertical sides about 1″ from edge.
2. Prepare dye bath, using 2 quarts simmering water and ½ package powered or ¼ bottle liquid dye.
3. Immerse tied fabric and stir. Leave in dye bath 15 to 20 minutes, stirring occasionally, or until color is a shade deeper than you want it to be.
4. Remove fabric, squeeze out excess dye, and rinse in plenty of cold water until water runs clear.
5. Remove rubber bands and admire your design.
6. Iron while still damp, and hang from cafe curtain rods.

Idea! After removing rubber bands, immerse entire fabric in a dye bath of a lighter contrasting color. (My hanging was first dyed in dark brown; then tinted and dipped briefly in gold.)

Another idea! Dip entire untied fabric in dye of one color; rinse thoroughly. Then tie and dye in contrasting color. Try pink followed by purple, or yellow followed by olive green.

Still another idea! Now that you have a good working vocabulary of tie-dye knots, design your own wall-hanging, using a single size white bedsheet. Use ¾ bottle liquid dye or 1½ packages powdered dye, in a gallon of water or enough to cover sheet. The large hem of the sheet becomes a casing big enough to slip over a wide decorator cafe rod.

Hang a Room-Divider

Need a new wall? You might—to partition a wide room or separate an area, or to camouflage on old wall that's in a state of disrepair. Then hang a "wall" of fabric as a room divider that's inexpensive, quick-and-easy to install, and so portable that it can be dismantled in minutes. Here are two easy ways to do it:

1. Install a ceiling drapery rod in the desired length, using special mounting brackets. Stitch a 2″ wide strip of interfacing fabric into a 2½″ top casing on your fabric. Insert drapery hooks invisibly into wrong side of casing, and hang from rod.

Use a traverse rod for a room divider that can be removed by pulling to one side as needed. A tie-dyed sheet is ideal for using in this way; so is a reversible fabric such as a Rya rug. If necessary, weight the bottom of your fabric by stitching chain or lead weights into bottom casing of fabric. If necessary to sew weights on the outside of a fabric-hanging that does not have a bottom casing, stitch a length of braid or ribbon over hem as camouflage.

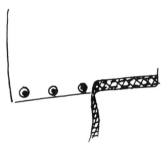

2. Get a 2″ by 4″ of clear pine or other unwarped wood in length required. Screw hooks into this wood bar at intervals as required. Paint bar to match or contrast with ceiling. Nail bar into ceiling with 3″ masonry nails. Sew rings to top of fabric at intervals to correspond with hooks on ceiling bar.

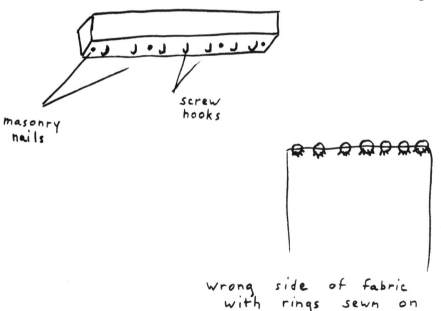

screw
hooks

masonry
nails

wrong side of fabric
with rings sewn on

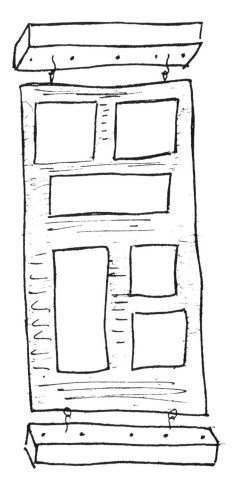

Hang a Picture Gallery

Idea! Hang a long, narrow strip of burlap to use as an art gallery or bulletin board. Pin or glue posters, photos, decorative fabric or what you like to the burlap. If you sew rings to the bottom of the burlap, too, and nail a bar with hooks into the floor directly beneath the ceiling bar, your two-way gallery will be held as tautly as any permanent wall.

Another idea! Use this method to hang a planter or a group of planters. Try it in the bathroom, or in front of a window.

Hang A Planter

The Art of Nature

Collections of objects from the world of nature are no longer to be found only in the sagging pockets of schoolchildren. Increasingly, sophisticated adults are discovering that in shells, rocks, driftwood, and pressed leaves and flowers, some of the purity and serenity of the natural environment can be captured and transplanted to the man-made environments of our homes. Along any shore, a parade of stooped-over beachcombers of all sizes and ages can be seen gathering the fragile, lovely treasures washed ashore. A new gadget that has proved its popularity in recent years is the rock polisher or tumbler, which turns stones into burnished *objets d'art* at the flick of a switch. And for those who can't gather their own, urban boutiques have sprung up to sell rocks and shells, mounted for shelf or table-top display, at a price.

But to me, ninety-nine and forty-four one-hundredths of the pleasure of owning one of nature's treasures is in collecting, preserving and mounting it myself. Whether your find is a spray of wild flowers or a basket of shells and coral, you can prepare it for exhibition as a decorative accessory in your home. Most of my ideas on this subject have developed out of necessity—the necessity of keeping the accumulations of my pack-rat children out from under my feet. City-dwellers though we are, just turn us loose on a beach, a country lane or a park, and our fists and pockets are sure to bulge with finds.

Driftwood. Clean your specimen thoroughly by brushing gently to remove all loose sand, dirt and other particles. Wash gently in lukewarm water and liquid dish detergent, using a sponge or a soft paintbrush or old toothbrust to clean out crevices. Rinse gently but thoroughly and place on a wad of newspaper to dry, changing the position of the wood two or three times so that all of it dries out.

Driftwood mounted on lucite base

Now comes the fun part: mounting. You have to decide whether your driftwood can stand by itself, or whether it needs to be treated as a sculpture and given a base to enhance its appearance (and protect your furniture). Any of the suggestions for mounting sculpture in Chapter IV will work for driftwood (or for rocks or shells, too). I particularly like the contrast of driftwood mounted on a lucite base—the wood seems to float into the room. Use white glue to hold the wood in place. If desired, spray with a clear, non-shiny fixative for protection.

Shells. Rinse off sand and any other foreign matter. Let dry. A single spectacular specimen can be displayed alone mounted as a sculpture. But plan a group arrangement if you have many smaller shells to exhibit. Several shells could be combined as a sculptural grouping on a lucite or wood base. If you want to hang up your shells, the Shell Mosaic and the Shadow Box (instructions below) are ideal.

Shells mounted on a slab of redwood

However you decide to show shells, they will be both protected and enhanced by brushing with polymer medium or spraying with a clear vinyl.

Rocks. Again, wash thoroughly and let dry. If you have a tumbler, polish your specimen in it according to directions.

A Rock on a Block

Mount rocks, polished or rough, as table-top sculptures. Or create a mosaic-like design of small, flatter rocks, as in the Shell Mosaic (instructions below). If you like, brush rocks with polymer medium to bring out their subtle colors and protect their surfaces.

If you are a macramé addict, knot small stones into your work. On a wall-hanging, contrast polished white stones with dark jute cord, or flecked gray-and-black stones with white nylon cord. Knot stones into the ties of a belt or the pendant of a necklace.

Flowers, Leaves. Small flowers and branches can be easily dried and preserved using little more than newspaper or an old telephone directory. Simply arrange your cuttings on top of a thick wad of paper and cover with another thick wad. Over all, place a few large-size magazines or a piece of carpeting (the kind of carpet remnant sold as a doormat or TV mat is perfect). If you press plants in the phone book, no additional pressure is necessary. A week of this treatment should be just enough for most small sprigs. For glossy leaves, wipe with a liquid wax furniture polish before pressing. Spray dried flowers with a non-shine fixative (or hair lacquer!) for longer life.

Pressed plants can be displayed in vases. Or, display them in a frame so they last longer. Remove glass and mat from a picture frame and discard mat. Cover backing cardboard as desired (see Chapter IV) and arrange dried plants on it. Dribble the slightest bit of white glue only where necessary to hold your arrangement in place; let dry. Replace glass in frame, and insert backing. Close up frame.

To preserve large branches of greenery, let them soak in a solution of ½ cup glycerine to 1½ cups water for two weeks

Wild flowers and ferns
tied with a red velvet ribbon
and glued to a red-and-white
gingham-covered backing set
in a lacquered red frame

to a month. First wash the leaves and stems gently; then brush each leaf with some of the glycerine solution. Crush or slit the end of the branch so the solution can penetrate it. Leaves should become firm and strong; but their colors may change somewhat as a result of this process, depending on the plant. Display these in large jars or vases; they will last and last.

SHADOW BOX DISPLAY CASE

For shells, small rocks, weathered wood branches and dried plants.

How-to:

1. Take a cigar box, necktie box, shoebox lid, or any rectangular box or lid from 1″ to 2½″ deep.
2. Cover it inside and out with adhesive-backed foil, wood-patterned vinyl, or burlap; or with enamel, tempera or acrylic paint. Or any combination of these or any other finishes you can think of.
3. For a gleaming finish, paint or spray with shellac, clear vinyl, clear varnish or polymer medium.
4. Prepare box for hanging by cutting "keyholes" in the back, about ⅓ of the way down from the top, using a sharp scissors or a razor blade or craft knife. If a box is of wood, insert small screw eyes, and connect with picture wire later.
5. Measure around bottom of box or lid, and cut a slab of foam rubber or cork to fit tightly into box. Tint light-colored cork with brown liquid shoe polish, if desired. Tint foam rubber by dissolving a few drops of liquid dye or food coloring in a cupful of hot water, and squeezing through (wear rubber gloves!). Experiment with this; interesting mottled effects come from squeezing food coloring or dye directly onto dampened foam, and then squeezing and rolling foam so that color penetrates unevenly. Let dry.
6. Arrange shells, rocks or whatever on cork or foam until you get an arrangement you like. Use white glue to attach objects. Hang when dry.
7. To prepare a shadow box to stand on a shelf, glue lead weights across bottom of box. Cover with felt for a surface that will not scratch up your furniture.

cut "keyholes" in back
of box for hanging ——

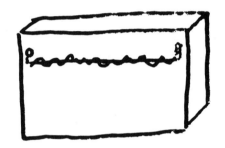

or insert 2 small screw
eyes and connect with picture wire

SHELL AND/OR PEBBLE MOSAIC

MATERIALS:
    white glue or polymer gel medium
    one or two paint brushes or cotton swabs
    vinyl spray or polymer medium
    shells and/or pebbles—a cupful or more
    the clear plastic top of a closet shoe box
    a skewer
    leather thong, yarn, or other decorative cord

HOW-TO:
    1. Select the three or four most dramatic—the largest,
       most brightly colored—specimens to be featured, and

pur slab of foam rubber

inside box ...

and glue
shells, pebbles or other
small nature objects in place

arrange them in or near the center of the inside of the
shoebox lid. When you have an arrangement you like,
remove one shell or pebble at a time and brush its
flattest side with gel medium or white glue. Try to get
thick blobs of glue along the inner edges or at whatever the "contact points"—where the shell will rest on
the plastic—will be. Also coat the plastic, and press the
specimen in place.

2. Repeat for all major shells or pebbles.
3. Working over one section of the lid at a time, brush lid
   thickly with glue or gel medium and press smaller
   shells into place, swabbing them with glue at the contact points if necessary. You will find that by moving
   them around a bit, and even overlapping some, they
   will fit very closely together, giving a mosaic appearance. Let dry thoroughly; both white glue and gel medium will dry to a glossy transparency.

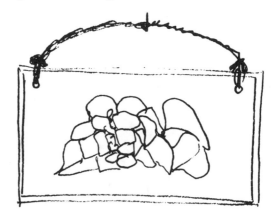

4. Brush all over with polymer medium, or spray with clear vinyl.
5. To prepare for hanging: heat point of skewer over stove and use to poke holes in plastic. Heat skewer and work around inside hole to widen it until it is large enough for a picture hook to slip through, or for a leather thong or other decorative cord to go through. Mosaic can also be displayed by standing on its side on a lucite base, attached with glue.

Stow-aways
and Stash-its

Storage Space and How to Find It

In the last few years, certain axioms of modern life have
been developed by people given to analyzing The Way We Live
Today. The first of these axioms to come to my attention was,
"If anything *can* go wrong, it *will.*" In the years since I first
heard this one, I've had occasion to recall it so often that I've
developed my own corollary to it: "—and at the worst possible
time." How else could I account for the fact that the dishwash-
er floods just before dinner guests are expected, that the oven
refuses to regulate properly whenever a quiche is deposited inside and that the thread in the sewing-machine bobbin always
develops a spasm of snapping just when I am hurriedly putting
the finishing touches to a garment that must be worn that
evening?

Along the same lines, I've noticed that work inevitably expands to fill the time available for it, with a large part of any
job still to be done when the deadline has come and gone. Or
that people are bound to rise to their own level of mediocrity
—and then teach their lack of skill to the refrigerator de-

liverymen who tore huge gashes in the newly laid linoleum, or the electrician who came to install a new appliance but couldn't read the wiring diagram.

One of my own perennial problems provided the inspiration for this axiom: *"Things* expand to fill the space available to store them in, with some things still left over." These inevitable, unstorable leftovers I have taken to calling "hard-core undeployables," and alas! every room in my apartment has its share. No matter how often I resolve to put each and every one of these objects in a place—*any* place—I wind up with something, or usually quite a few things, that won't tuck in anywhere.

But I have to admit that in all the years I've been trying to deploy these undeployables, I've developed some great storage ideas. Unfortunately, I haven't gotten around to using all of them yet, but I will. I'll get those things out of the way *tomorrow* . . . or next week . . . or next year!

As a consequence of this never-ending contest between too many things and too little space to store them in, I've come to define storage space as something there's never enough of. And I've learned to look for it *everywhere.*

Is there a 4½-inch gap between washing machine and sink? The perfect place to tuck a folding stepladder. The foot-wide space between the refrigerator and the window holds a rack of old newspapers as well as a bag of gerbil litter. Hidden behind a filing cabinet in an unexpected recess in a wall, I accumulate castoffs for Goodwill Industries in one of their enormous bags. (When I can see the top of the bag standing as high as my files, I know it's time to phone the Goodwill pickup truck.)

This filing cabinet itself illustrates my favorite solution to the storage problem. It is a stock piece of ready-to-finish furniture set on casters for easy maneuvering. And in the 10-inch space between it and the wall, a ready-to-finish bookshelf unit, also on casters, holds the sewing machine and several telephone directories. I finished both pieces in black enamel and added brass hardware and teak plastic laminate tops to match my desk. It was a triumphal occasion when I devised this solution for those former undeployables, sewing machine and phone books.

Put it on Wheels

There's no end to what you can put casters under—everything from a cube to a closet. Until you've tried it, you can't imagine how much more useful a Stash-it (storage unit) can be when it moves easily about. Try some of these:

Put a bookshelf on casters, cover the back of it with cork panels and use as a portable bulletin board for reading lists, study plans, sewing patterns, work diagrams.

If you can, fit a bookshelf on casters into an unused niche in a kitchen; store cannisters, pots and pans, mixing bowls, even dinnerware and flatware. Tack most-used recipes (the ones you always put in such a good place to keep them from

the kids and the pets that when you want them in a hurry you can't find them) on the cork-covered back. Or mount peg-board on the back or end and hang utensils from it.

Turn a shelf unit of counter-top height into a handy portable baking center by attaching the kind of casters that can be adjusted to a stationary position. Attach a pastry board to the top and store equipment used only for baking, including cookbooks and electric mixer if space allows, on the shelves. A pegboard rack on the back can hold spatulas, wooden spoons, measuring cups and forks, rolling pin and other necessities.

The kind of bookcase unit that has adjustable shelves can be turned on its back, with casters beneath it, and used for underbed storage. Use one or two of the shelves to divide the space for convenient organization of whatever you plan to keep inside (you may have to glue them in place). Add one or two drawer-pulls to the side so the unit is easy to pull out of its hiding place for cleaning under the bed.

A row of cubes on casters can provide toy storage for such bulky items as blocks and rag dolls and pull toys. Easy for a

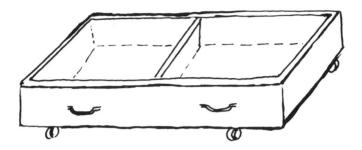

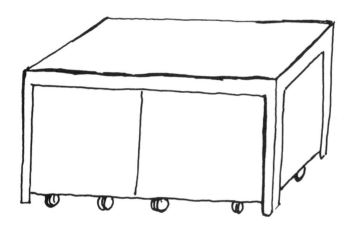

little one to push or pull to a play area, this is also easy for him to fill once play is over. The cubes can be topped with vinyl cushions for seating, or they can fit under a Parsons table that provides additional play space. Two standard 15″ cubes will fit under an 18″ by 18″ by 36″ table.

Use cubes on casters to store gardening supplies; arrange them under a Parsons table that serves as a plant stand.

Casters under small chests of drawers let a night table double as a coffee table in a convertible guest room-den, or in a "bed-sitter," as the English call what we know as a studio or one-room apartment.

A single cube on casters can hold magazines or a telephone and phone directories inside and double as a portable side, lamp, coffee or night table, or TV stand, as needed. Or stow records or tapes inside, and put the stereo turntable on top, for a compact music center.

A handy kitchen-to-dining room server consists of one cube bolted on top of another, with special gourmet serving equipment inside. The top surface becomes a serving area. This is where to keep your fondue equipment; or your wok, chopsticks and Japanese tea set, if you're into Oriental cuisine. Put a gallery around the top edges to keep things from being pushed off. Nail or glue wood molding strips, cut to the length of each side, around top. Paint molding to match or contrast.

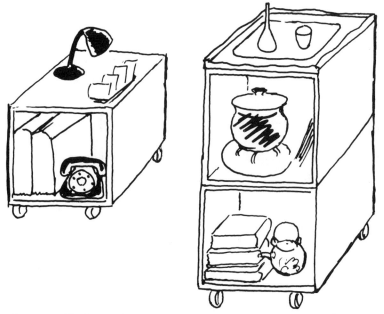

Make a roll-about bar by bolting two cubes side by side beneath a drop-lid desk unit; casters under it all, of course. A gallery around the top would be useful here, too.

Put a ready-to-finish closet on casters for instant rearranging of a multipurpose room. Covering the sides and back of one of these large things with cork panels turns a clumsy piece of furniture into an "instant art gallery." Or cover with posters.

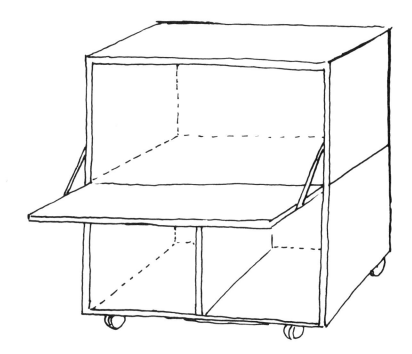

Bolt two bookcases back-to-back, put on casters, and swivel for double storage of books in the same space you had before. Or bolt four bookcases side-to-back-to-back-to-side for quadruple storage. Use extra casters if your put-together is extra large.

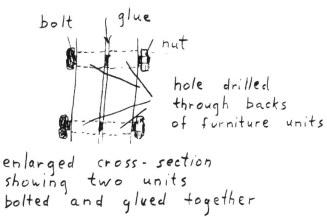

bolt glue

nut

hole drilled through backs of furniture units

enlarged cross- section showing two units bolted and glued together

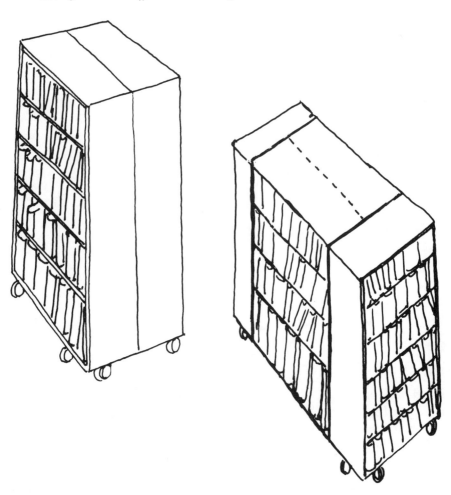

Here are some ideas for how to put together and finish your piece-on-wheels.

1. Casters come in beautiful metal finishes, ranging from brushed satin chrome to antique bronze, from shiny brass to wrought-iron black. If your piece needs other hardware—drawer-pulls, hinges, latches—get them to match.

2. Casters are attached by screwing the caster plate into the bottom of the unit. Choose the size of your casters according to the size and weight of the finished piece. Your hardware dealer can advise you. A bookcase will need larger casters than a coffee table; but you might want the decorative effect of the larger casters on the coffee table.

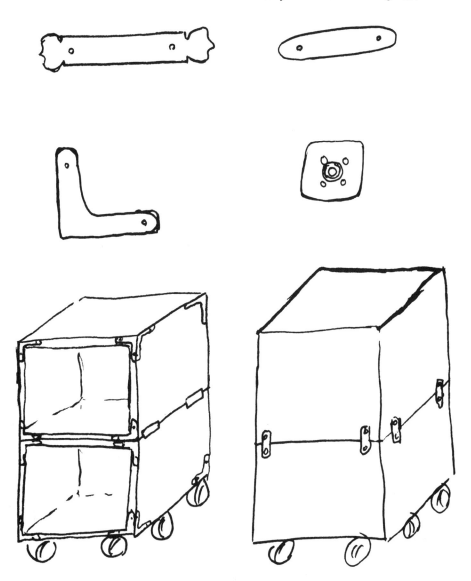

3. Always check to make sure there is a sturdy enough wood base to attach the casters to. Cubes or small chests of drawers are probably all right as they are. But if the casters will have to bear a heavy weight, as under a file cabinet or closet, or if you are attaching them to the thin plywood back of a bookcase to turn it into an underbed storage unit, you will probably have to add a supporting slab of wood across each corner first.

Glue and nail it into the bottom of your piece of furniture before screwing in the caster plates.

4. Paint with semi-gloss or gloss enamel for a bright, easy-to-keep-clean finish. Or cover with adhesive-backed anything—burlap, vinyl, foil. Or paste on wallpaper, or cloth (burlap, felt, gingham, tweed), and glue soutache braid around edges.

5. If your piece consists of different units bolted together, or different areas such as drawers and doors, paint in bright contrasts. For instance, the roll-about bar might be done in red, white and blue, or orange, green and yellow. A three-drawer chest might have red drawers against a silvery chrome cabinet, or purple on white.

6. If your unit consists of pieces bolted together, holes must be drilled through both units so they can be attached securely. Glue over the facing wood surfaces will add sturdiness.

7. Or, turn a liability into an asset by using hardware on the outside to attach two pieces. Brass or wrought-iron plates and angles come in a variety of styles for just this purpose. Match the hardware to the metal of your casters.

Up the Bathroom Walls

Although it didn't seem so at the time, in retrospect it is quite fortunate that my apartment came equipped with some very quirky storage ideas of its own. In the bathroom, for instance, there was no medicine cabinet over the large old-fashioned pedestal washbasin. Instead, set into the opposite wall, a small cabinet hung above my head. The mirror in the partly unhinged door showed its age most unattractively. My solution was, first, to remove the door of this antique and cover the entire unit and its shelves with adhesive-backed vinyl, for on-view storage of talc, colognes, hairsprays and the like; and second, to buy the largest medicine cabinet I could find and install in in the proper location.

Even with these bonus shelves, however, things overflow onto the window sill. We seem to keep more paraphernalia in our bathrooms than we used to; and at the same time, most bathrooms are smaller than ever. The only place to go is UP, on the walls above the towel racks and tub.

Such accessories as tissue holders and electric toothbrushes can be hung directly on the wall, just above eye level but still within easy reach. And small shelf units can also fit into even minimal bathroom wall space. Two- and three-shelf cases and tension-pole storage units are available in every hardware and housewares store, in colors that correlate with towels and other bathroom furnishings.

But it would be great, if you can find the space, to install a wall system in the bathroom. Most of these have uprights or standards (the poles from which the shelves are hung attach directly to the wall) in half length, so they might just fit from the tile line to the ceiling. If the wall system has a planter, by all means add it on at the top. (Plants thrive in the "john," but finding a place to put them is a problem. Hanging baskets or pots can be suspended from hooks in the ceiling, if there is enough head room. Or clay pots could stand on a single red-wood shelf set high on one wall.) And of course you'll want the magazine rack at the bottom. A bullet-type light fixture, or a heat lamp, can be attached to one of the shelves. So can towel rings, at the ends of the shelves, for guest or face towels.

If your sink is the type that stands on legs, you probably glare at the space going to waste underneath the basin. You can, of course, have a cabinet made to fit. But it is less expensive to get whatever unit of ready-to-finish furniture will fit—bookcase, cube, or night table—put it on casters and cover with wallpaper or paint to match the bathroom walls or tiles or towels. Then you'll have a good place to hide tissues, towels, soap and such, making room on the linen closet shelves for other things; or to keep cleaning supplies handy.

A Kitchen Should Look Like a Kitchen

A kitchen should look like a kitchen. It should not be as spic and span as a hospital or as cute as a honeymoon cottage. It is probably the most "lived-in" room in the house, and it should look like the busy place it is.

Have you ever peered into a restaurant kitchen at the array of pots and utensils, hanging and stacked in gleaming rows? Even the tiniest apartment-sized kitchen can easily be given this handsome, ready-to-go-to-work look. And fortunately, this easy way to decorate a kitchen expands its storage facilities at the same time. Again, ceilings and walls are the places to use for visible, stunning kitchen storage.

Kitchen equipment, whether it is a mellowed antique, a recent but well-worn item or something new and colorful, has a functional beauty all its own. The best way to stretch kitchen storage is to buy beautiful pots and utensils. Then you'll be happy to display them on open shelves or racks. At the same time, valuable cabinet space is freed to hold less attractive essentials.

(Handsome cookware is a time-saver, too, taking your cuisine from stove to table or buffet without its having to be transferred to an extra serving dish.)

Accumulate interesting older items as you find them. But for good buys in new cookware, wait for semi-annual housewares sales in August and February, and add at least one beautiful gourmet cook-and-serve item a year. In no time you'll have an impressive collection—and be able to make it the focal point of your kitchen decorating scheme.

Create a "Kitchen Sculpture"

You are about to plan a three-dimensional assemblage, a functional "sculpture" to give your kitchen distinction.

Take inventory of every inch of non-functioning space. This includes that narrow patch of wall separating two cabinets, the wall behind the table, the wall areas around the window, the inner frame of the window, the top of the refrigerator and of the cabinets, the wall behind the stove, the outside of the cabinet doors, and the ceiling. And any other nooks and crannies that may be peculiar to *your* kitchen.

Decide which area you want to make the focal point of your decorating. This is where your assemblage will be constructed. Now decide whether your chosen space can hold a shelf or shelves, or whether you will have to hang your assemblage directly on the wall. Perhaps you can combine the two, with an arrangement of one or more shelves plus wall-hung utensils.

Or perhaps you have overhead space, but no wall space, to spare. Consider basing your assemblage on a ceiling-hung rack.

Now spread out your most attractive kitchenwares. This could include almost anything. Have you an enormous porcelain-enameled skillet? An antique brass mortar and pestle? Earthenware cooky jar? Old bottles? A set of stainless steel kitchen tools? French knives with wonderful wooden handles? A copper chafing dish? A teak tray? A marble cheese board? Ice bucket? Your mother's favorite rolling pin?

Don't forget to include pots of herbs or any other plants you like. Or candle holders. Or demitasse cups. Take inventory of all your stuff, whether of coarse pottery or fine bone china, whether of new teakwood or old pewter. Somehow, all kitchen things look well together. And everyone's collection is bound to be unique. It is unlikely that you will find anyone else will have the same assortment of kitchenwares that you accumulate over the years.

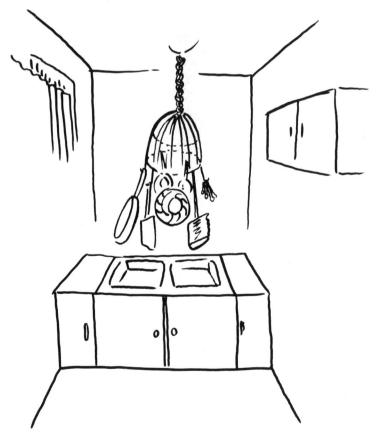

Stare a while at your collection; then return the least interesting, least lovable things to the cabinets and drawers from
which they came. Sort the remainder into things that can hang
from hooks (skillets, a clock, wire whisks); things that must
stand on shelves (salad bowl, cannisters, chafing dish); things
that could stand in a plate rack (plates, small bowls, ceramic
tiles); or things that could hang from a ceiling rack (paella
pan, ladle, colander).

Select the things to go in the space you've decided on. Things
you enjoy looking at and using. Here are some display ideas:

From a ceiling rack, hang one bright-colored item amid several metal ones. An orange skillet could mingle with stainless
steel saucepans, for example, or a brilliant blue colander could
accent a cluster of copper pots.

From a wrought-iron or chrome rack, hang utensils that are
all silvery, such as stainless, chrome, or aluminum. Mix utensils
and saucepans.

Arrange decorated plates symmetrically on both sides of a
bowl, tile or trivet on a plate rack. Make a plate rack easily by
nailing and gluing a strip of wood molding to a wooden shelf.
Mugs or espresso cups can stand in front of the shelf, with a
narrower molding attached to the front and side edges.

Make cookbooks part of your decorating scheme. Hang a

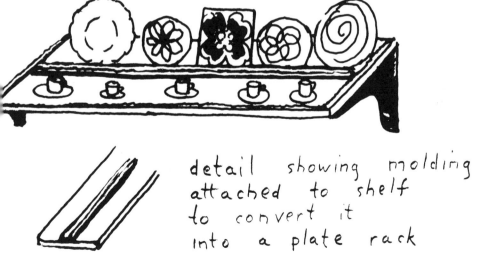

detail showing molding
attached to shelf
to convert it
into a plate rack

long floating shelf on the wall directly above the table, or behind a counter. Make suitable bookends by filling large decorative bottles (wine bottles, perhaps) with sand or pebbles, and use to support a small group of cookbooks on top of the refrigerator.

Build up a wall arrangement of assorted plates and tiles, interspersed with a clock, a planter, a hanging light fixture

and/or a shelf of cookbooks. Go right on up to the ceiling!

Run shelves or racks completely around the room just below the ceiling and create a continuous frieze of decorative plates, pots, plants or what-have-you; incorporate the tops of pantry cabinets and refrigerator into your frieze, too.

Attach shelf brackets on either side of a window and place shelves (of glass to let light through) across. Display plants, spices, a collection of old bottles, cannisters or cookbooks. Or an assortment of some or all of these.

Group ceramics of all kinds—mugs, vases, figurines, candle holders—or a bottle or old glass collection on a group of shelves.

Pegboard Can Be Beautiful

Does the efficiency with which a hook-filled pegboard holds a variety of objects appeal to you?

Does the appearance of pegboard, so familiar from countless store installations, turn you off?

If you answer both of these questions in the affirmative, read on.

Pegboard can be transformed into a decorative asset for kitchen, bathroom and closet storage. The simple solution is *color*!

Color—lots of bright color—can be painted on pegboard in a minute. Avocado, mustard, persimmon, flag blue, wine red, plum. Custom-color your own pegboard wall in one of these decorator shades. Or try sunflower yellow, ebony, mahogany, purple, salmon—any color on the paint store's color card. Just buy a can of enamel and brush on; two coats for complete coverage. Pick up an accent color from your favorite casserole to use in the kitchen; from towels or tiles to use in the bathroom; from a bedspread or comforter for boudoir or children's room.

Pegboard can be cut to any size. Cover an entire wall, a long narrow area, the inside or outside of a closet door. Turn a small patch of blank wall into a useful, interesting spot. The side of a cabinet that sticks out can also be converted in this way.

More than one color can be used effectively. Paint a large

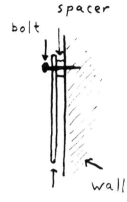

spacer

bolt

cross-section showing
how to install pegboard

wall

pegboard

pegboard checkerboard style—in black and red, or blue and green, or purple and white. Or have pegboard cut into several smaller panels, paint in different colors and hang as scattered rectangles on a wall.

In arranging objects on your decorator pegboard, try for a good balance of shapes and proportions. Rearrange until the objects themselves form part of the design. It is amazing how a good strong color on the pegboard background will call attention to itself and minimize the less interesting objects hanging from it.

Pattern and texture can be added to pegboard along with color, by covering it with an adhesive-backed material (burlap, vinyl or foil) or by pasting on fabric. Six easy steps do this striking job:

1. Cut desired covering material to exact size of pegboard area to be covered, and set aside.

2. Install pegboard on wall, using special spaces and screws (get this when you get pegboard), designed for this purpose, in each corner. Hang assorted hooks and suspend objects from them to form a pleasing arrangement.

3. *Important.* Make a chart showing where each hook and tool is to go. Draw dots for each hole in the pegboard and sketch the outline of each utensil in its proper place.

4. Remove all hooks and utensils and set aside.

5. Use white glue to attach fabric to pegboard; let dry. Or cover with adhesive-backed material.

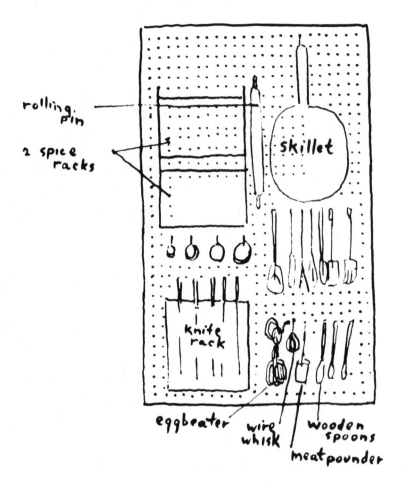

rolling pin

2 spice racks

skillet

knife rack

eggbeater   wire whisk   wooden spoons

meatpounder

6. Press covered pegboard with fingertips to locate holes. Install hooks and hang up tools, following the chart you made earlier.

That's all there is to it. I have used this trick in the kitchen, where a foot-square patch of shiny foil-covered pegboard over the sink keeps an assortment of scrubbing brushes handy—and somehow you don't really see the brushes, only the silvery foil. Also in my kitchen, on a dead-end wall above the side of the stove, is a large pegboard covered in a bright-patterned vinyl that matches the counter tops; it holds a knife rack, measuring cups, my favorite orange skillet, a rolling pin and other kitchen tools.

Closets and How to Stretch Them

Once upon a time, a friend of mine lived in a small apartment in an old building in New York. This friend is a super-meticulous housekeeper, and the thought of not having the ideal "place for everything and everything in its place" was driving her up her old cracked plaster walls. When she realized that the purchase of one more pair of shoes would totally upset the balance of her closet, she decided to take drastic action.

She took a day off from her job and spent the day moving furniture around in her bedroom until she found an arrangement that left an entire end wall free. Then she called in a carpenter and, with him, designed a built-in floor-to-ceiling closet that also contained bookshelves and a deeper shelf for a television set. The empty end wall became the rear of the closet, thus saving on construction costs. My friend determined exactly how much space she needed for handbags, how much for shoes, how much for hanging skirts, dresses, blouses, coats and gowns and how much for out-of-season storage; she designed her personal closet accordingly. And after the carpenter was finished, in came the painters, doing the whole thing up in the same shade of gold as the walls of the room.

My friend has since moved to a spacious apartment in a new building in the suburbs. In her bedroom there is a walk-in closet only a little larger than the room I am writing in right now. Still imaginative, she has lined its walls with felt and carpeted it—much easier to keep clean with a vacuum, she says, than the usual painted walls and linoleum floor are to scrub. She has used upholstery braid as a border around the felt, and attached everything with a staple gun.

I am properly jealous. The walk-in closet in my bedroom is only a little smaller than my friend's bathtub. And I have had to resort to lining its walls with hooks and towel bars, to hold tote bags and belts, scarves and stoles, robes and aprons, and even an occasional skirt or blouse whose hanger has temporarily disappeared.

The dramatic accessories needed for today's fashions create their own storage problems. Heavy metal belts, long scarves, pantyhose and other "undies" in varied colors—it seems every

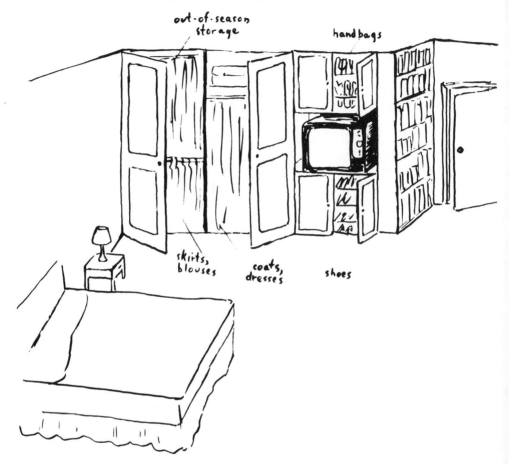

new season brings another "look" to strain the capacity of all but the most spacious of dressing rooms. Herewith some of my favorite solutions to accessory storage problems:

Pantyhose. Hang a large shoebag with twelve vinyl see-through pockets. Use adhesive-backed labels from the stationery store to organize your own "filing system." I have marked separate pockets for black, brown, navy, taupe. Hose with snags or minor runs below the calf are in pockets labeled "wear with boots," while those with more prominent damage but still wearable are filed under the label "wear with pants." It's easy to pull out the right pair of pantyhose when I'm in a rush, which is usually. Any pockets that are left over can hold matching sets of underwear, foot socks, gloves.

Metal belts. These were always slipping to the bottom of a drawer, snagging scarves and negligees and blouses as they went. If hung up, they'd bang against and scratch each other. Another vinyl shoebag files them, along with those thin leather shoestring belts that always fall off other belt hangers. Extra pockets can hold handkerchiefs or small chiffon scarves.

Long scarves, shawls, stoles. Attach a towel bar to the inside of the closet door and drape them over it. One bar can hold quite a few of these long, light accessories. If your silk shawls slide off the towel bar, cover it with adhesive-backed felt (sold for cushioning lamp bases).

Silk squares or kerchiefs. Hang these over a multiple-armed blouse hanger.

Tote bags, shoulder bags. These can hang from large hooks high on a closet wall.

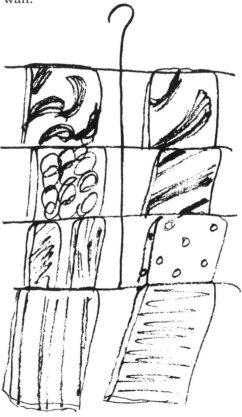

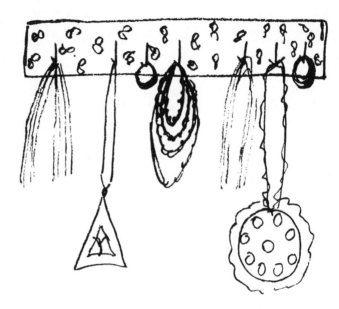

Hair ribbons, necklaces, bracelets. Cover a long, narrow pegboard rectangle with adhesive-backed vinyl or any decorative fabric you choose. Hang on a wall and plug in enough pegboard hooks to hold all your ribbons and love beads. If your jewelry is really interesting, set it up as a wall decoration near your dressing table.

Boots. I wish I knew! Too top-heavy to stand on my shoerack, they are cluttering my closet floor. I'd like to buy another pair, but I don't dare until I think of a better place to keep the several I already have.

"Dead" Storage

I don't know why things needed so seldom that they can be put away for long periods of time are referred to as being in "dead" storage. It has been my experience that, while you may go for months without needing things like extra pillows or suitcases or the electric meat grinder, when you do want them you want them in a hurry and don't want to unpack a crammed closet to get at them. In an ideal home, all storage areas would be accessible. Interior space, however, is at such a premium for most of us that I suppose anyone is ahead if he can store unused luggage or bedding or appliances anywhere at all. These are the things that (in a simpler age, when houses were much larger and possessions much fewer) used to be stored in the attic, there to be rummaged for when needed.

Someone once pointed out to me that, while we make efficient use of the floor areas of our homes, the overhead spaces are totally neglected. Could all that air up there under the ceiling really be superfluous?

When I first heard this, I walked around with my eyes turned upward for a week, trying to imagine how I could convert this vast reservoir of potential storage space to use. I dreamed of all the clutter I could get out from under foot and put up under the ceiling instead.

In the end, I had to get back down to eye level. Even though our ceiling is fairly high, I couldn't see lowering it and boxing our living space in with storage units. And I really didn't need any more out-of-reach storage than I already had. When I stopped to think of it, I was already making good and practical use of quite a bit of that under-the-ceiling storage. That's where the top shelves of all of my closets and pantry cabinets were, and they were barely within reach from the top of my stepladder.

However, my research into the problem turned up a good idea for an overhead storage unit that looks built-in, is simple to construct and provides large amounts of stow-away space without taking up any living space.

If you can read a ruler and hammer a nail, you can install an open shelf in almost no time. All you need is a narrow area, such as a hall, with two side walls to form the sides of your storage unit. Look for other good spots to use this idea in a powder room or kitchen. Here's how to do it:

1. Measure the distance between the side walls. Subtract 1 inch for ease in fitting, and you have the length of your shelf. The depth (front to back) is up to you.

2. Get a slab of clear pine (or any other even, unwarped wood —a good quality plywood would do), about an inch thick, and have it cut to your dimensions at your lumberyard. Get two pieces of wood shelf molding cut to the depth measurement.

3. Mark your walls where the top of the molding is to come; this is where the shelf will rest.

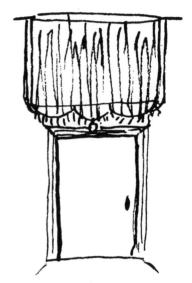

4. Hammer the molding into the wall; just hammer two nails halfway into each molding strip. (Make sure the edge of the molding that will support your shelf is facing *up.*) Place shelf in position and check to make sure that it is level.

5. Remove shelf, and hammer moldings securely to wall, placing nails about every 3 inches across molding. Put shelf in place.

6. Paint shelf the same color as hall; or paint moldings and cover shelf with wallpaper or self-adhesive vinyl.

7. To disguise an open shelf like this one, you can install a decorative window shade across it just below the ceiling, pulling it down to conceal the suitcases or linens or whatever you've heaped on the shelf. Or hang cafe curtains across. Or attach louvered shutters to act as a cabinet door.

A shelf like this will fit between any existing walls that are not too far apart; about 3 feet is a good maximum distance. Beyond that, the shelf is likely to warp or bend under the weight of its contents unless it gets additional support, such as angle irons attached beneath it and to the wall to absorb some of the weight.

A variation of this open shelf is a full-fledged cabinet built at over-the-head level in a larger area, perhaps 5 or 6 feet across. In this case the basic shelf will have to be supported by angle irons on all sides. This could be designed to fit into a

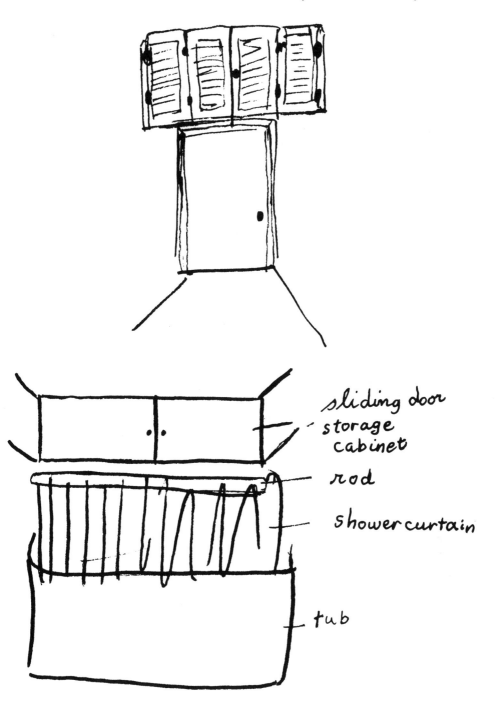

sliding door
storage
cabinet

rod

shower curtain

tub

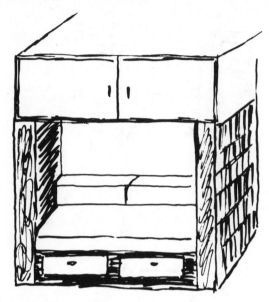

bathroom above the tub, or over a bed or at the end of a narrow bedroom. You might even build a bed into the support system. (This version requires a skilled handyman, who might add such refinements as sliding doors and bookshelves.)

❧ VIII ❧

Put-ons

To put on you, that is. How about a hostess skirt that doubles as a poncho, made from leftover scraps of yarn? Or a side-wrapped apron skirt that fastens easily over a jumpsuit or a dress and can be made in every length from mini to maxi? Or some aprons you wouldn't mind being caught in? Or a belt that turns into a headband? These are among my favorite quick-and-easy-to-make Put-ons.

Put-on Patchwork

Patchwork, long a popular way to use up leftovers, is becoming fashionable again. The hand-crafted look is chic. And crochet is popular. Put them all together and you get crocheted patchwork using leftover yarn. But, instead of making granny squares, which have become such a commonplace that even machines can turn them out, make afghan patches. Afghan patches are modules that can be used to make anything from a hat to a blanket.

The afghan stitch works up quickly into a warm solid fabric, without the lacy holes that make linings necessary for so many other crochet patterns. Afghan-stitched patches are ideal pick-up work, easy to do while traveling or watching television, or during odd moments. If you keep your work near the telephone and have mastered the knack of talking "no hands" (or if you have one of those useful phone shoulder rests), you should be able to finish at least one patch a day during phone calls.

You simply crochet patches until you have enough to make the article of your choice. Work up the patches in the sizes as listed with each diagram below. Then follow the diagram to join the patches. And that's all there is to achieving a very smart-looking combination of the patchwork and crocheted looks.

With afghan patches you can put an accumulation of odds and ends of yarn to good use. I like to coordinate my leftovers by buying enough yarn in a harmonizing or contrasting color and working a quarter or a half of the patches plus the border or trim in this color. Interesting effects can be achieved by working with two or more different textured and different colored yarns together—beige wool and orange mohair, for example, or brown tweed and yellow wool.

If your odds and ends are a mixed lot of baby- sports- and worsted-weight yarns, combine two or three strands of the lighter ones to equal one strand of the heavier ones. Work two-inch samples of each yarn or yarn combination to test how many stitches and rows you need. If, due to different yarns, you do wind up with patches of different sizes, don't fret about it. Simply work enough rows of single crochet around the smaller patches to bring them up to the same size as the larger patches.

If you have never held a crochet needle before, or if your skills are a bit rusty, see Chapter IX for diagrammed instructions for these basic crochet stitches: *chain, single crochet, slipstitch* and *afghan.*

Work with an afghan hook, the special long kind of crochet needle. Size 10 or J is about right for these patches, but if you can only get size 8 or size K, that's all right too. Simply work up a test patch about 2 inches square and then figure out how many stitches and rows it will take to make a patch the size you need. This is your gauge. For my sample gauge I used a number 10 needle and knitting worsted; I started with a 16-stitch chain and worked 15 afghan stitches to a row for 13 rows, and made a 3½-inch square. Make it a 4-inch square by working one row of single crochet all around; a 5-inch square with 3 rows of single crochet all around. (*Important:* Always finish off an afghan patch by working a row of single crochet across the top; see instructions in Chapter IX.)

If patches come out just slightly more or less than the required measurement, if they are not quite square or if they curl up at the edges, they must be *blocked*. Either (1) measure out squares of the required size and brown paper, pin paper to ironing-board cover and pin patches to paper; or (2) pin patches directly onto a cutting board marked off in 1-inch squares. Steam lightly with a warm iron, using a press cloth, if you don't have a steam iron. Leave patches pinned until they are completely dry.

There are two easy methods for joining crocheted patches:

1. Working on wrong side, *sew* together through loop in back of each stitch along matched edges.

2. Working on wrong side, *slipstitch* together through loop in back of each stitch along matched edges.

Always work in loose ends on wrong side of finished article.

Almost any combination of colors is effective in patchwork. Consider one of these.

A *checkerboard* pattern in either a striking contrast such as black-and-white, red-and-black or blue-and-yellow; or a subtle two-tone effect, such as pink-orange, purple-lavender, or red-wine.

Diagonal striping in three shades of the same color, such as bright, medium and baby pinks; olive, kelly and dark green; or yellow, gold and brown; or in sharply contrasting shades such as black, white and yellow or orange, green and brown.

A *random* arrangement of related colors such as blues and greens; or of several shades in the yellow-brown family, such as rust, gold, beige, orange and brown; or of black, white, and several shades of gray or black-white tweeds.

The first afghan patch design, a bolero, is a good project with which to explain the basic method. After that, follow the diagrams to make a jacket, beret, a variety of skirts, a skirt-poncho and even an afghan-patch afghan and matching throw pillow. Wear the bolero, made as you like it in bright or subtle

X	O	X	O	X	O
O	X	O	X	O	X
X	O	X	O	X	O
O	X	O	X	O	X
X	O	X	O	X	O
O	X	O	X	O	X

Checkerboard Pattern

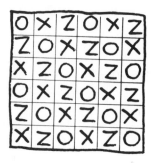

Diagonal Striping Pattern

colors, as a sophisticated accent for a favorite at-home costume. It will top a jumpsuit, a hostess gown, pants or a skirt-and-shirt with equally dashing results.

AFGHAN-PATCH BOLERO

Directions are for small, medium and large sizes.

MATERIALS:
 afghan hook, #10 or J
 knitting worsted, 2 4-ounce skeins or the equivalent, in varied colors
 frog closing (optional)

HOW-TO:
 1. Crochet 54 3-inch afghan patches, following directions in chapter 9.
 2. For large size only: Work edging around each patch. Attach contrasting yarn along any edge of patch and with right side of patch facing you work one single crochet (sc) in each stitch and three sc in each corner stitch. When you get back to where the yarn was attached, slipstitch (ss) in starting stitch, chain (ch) 1 and turn so that wrong side of patch is facing you. Row 2: sc in each sc of previous row, work 3 sc in each

Afghan- Patch Bolero

diagram

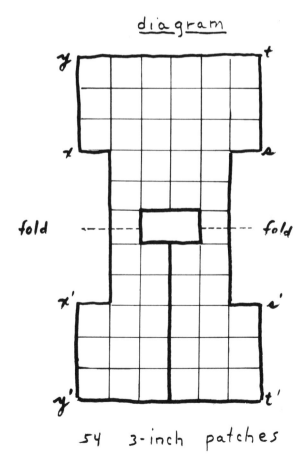

54 3-inch patches

corner stitch; ss in first stitch of row, ch 1 and turn. Repeat row 2 once more, working on right side; break off yarn.

3. For all sizes, join patches following diagram, leaving spaces as shown for armholes, neck and front openings.
4. Fold bolero at shoulders and join side seams x-y to x'-y' and s-t to s'-t'.
5. For medium and large sizes: Work 1-inch border all around. Attach yarn in border color along any edge with right side facing you and work 1 sc in each stitch and three sc in each corner stitch. When you get back to where the yarn was attached, ss in starting stitch, ch 1 and turn so that wrong side faces you. Row 2: sc in each

Afghan- Patch Jacket

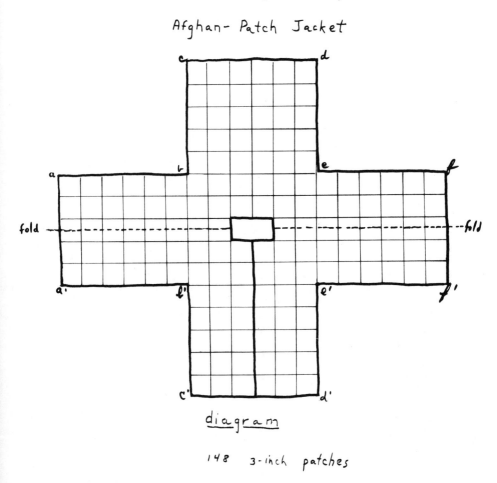

diagram

148   3-inch patches

sc of previous row, work 3 sc in each corner stitch, ss in first stitch of row, ch 1 and turn. Repeat twice more, until there are four rows of crochet for border. Break off yarn.

6. For small size only: Work one row of sc all around, attaching yarn and working 3 sc in each corner stitch as above.
7. Turn work to wrong side; weave all loose ends invisibly into back of work.
8. Sew frog to top front edges as shown (optional).

AFGHAN-PATCH JACKET

Now . . . turn the bolero into a jacket. Follow the diagram and the above directions. Join sleeve seams ab to a'b' and ef to e'f'; join side seams bc to b'c' and de to d'e'. Work border as for bolero. If you like, you can turn it into a coat. Simply add more afghan patches at the bottom.

AFGHAN-PATCH BERET

1. Make 16 3-inch patches. Join together as diagrammed, in two rows of 8 patches each, and join x-y to x'-y'.
2. Crochet crown: Work 99 sc around one edge of joined strip. Put a paper clip or tie a piece of thread into work to mark last stitch of each round. When you finish the following round, remove the marker and insert in the last stitch. Next round: sc in first stitch of preceding round, work next 2 sc together (a decrease) and continue around. There will be 66 stitches. Next round: work 2 sc together all around; there will be 33 stitches. Decrease 11 stitches on each of the next two rounds; there will be 11 stitches left. Break off yarn, leaving a long end. Draw it through remaining stitches, pull tightly and knot to fasten off, and weave yarn invisibly into wrong side. Cut off end.
3. Crochet lower edge: Work 99 sc around lower edge. Mark last stitch of round. Next round: sc in each of the first 7 stitches, work next 2 stitches together (decrease) and repeat all around; there will be 88 stitches left. Next round: sc in each of the first 6 stitches, work 2 stitches together (decrease) and contine around; 77 stitches. Continue to decrease 11

Afghan - Patch   Beret

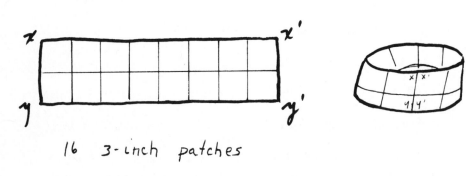

16 3-inch patches

diagram

stitches evenly spaced on each round until 44 stitches are left. Work 5 rows even and fasten off, weaving end invisibly into wrong side.

4. Top beret with a pompon if desired.

DIRNDL SKIRT

Who knows where skirts will end next? Make a Dirndl in the length of your choice. Follow the diagrams for any length from micro to maxi. Or hedge your bet and try one of the sketched hemline variations that combine the long-and-short of it. You'll never have to feel stuck when the fashion or your

Dirndl Skirt

mini ...

maxi ...

and other hemline variations ...

Dirndl Skirt

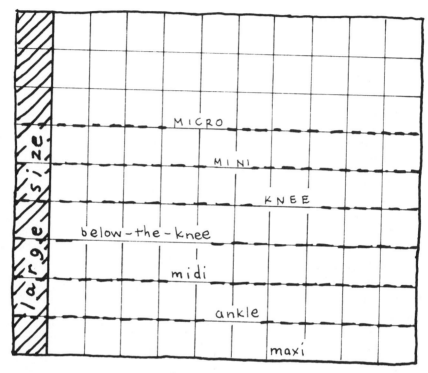

diagram

mood changes if you have a patchwork skirt. Whenever you get tired of the length you've got, simply add or subtract the afghan-patch modules until your skirt length is what you want.

Here's how to make the basic Afghan-Patch Dirndl:

1. Make the number of patches required for the size and length you want.

2. Join patches together, following diagram, and joining x-y to x'-y'.

3. Make waistband: With right side facing you, work 1 row of sc around waistline. Row 2: ch 3, skip 1 stitch, sc in second stitch of previous row, ch 2, skip 1 stitch, sc in next stitch; repeat around waist. Row 3: ch 1, work 1 sc in each ch-2 space and each sc of previous row; join last stitch of third row to first stitch of third row with a slipstitch. Fasten off.

diagram

number of 4-inch afghan patches required for:

	small size (8-12)	large size (14-16)
micro	30	33
mini	40	44
knee	50	55
below-the-knee	60	66
midi	70	77
ankle	80	88
maxi	90	99

4. Work 1 row sc around bottom edge or skirt (or more, for a deeper border). Add fringe if you like.

5. Make drawstring: Using a double strand of yarn, make a chain about 54″ long. Fasten off. Weave in and out through ch-2 spaces in waistband. Make two 3-inch tassels (see chapter 9) and attach one to each end of drawstring.

SKIRT-PONCHO

This double-duty pattern is a striking at-home skirt to wear over a body stocking during the cooler days; but then flip it over your head to ward off the outdoor chill of fall and spring. When you wear it as a skirt, let the points dip front and back, or side to side; either way, it's an effective split-level hemline.

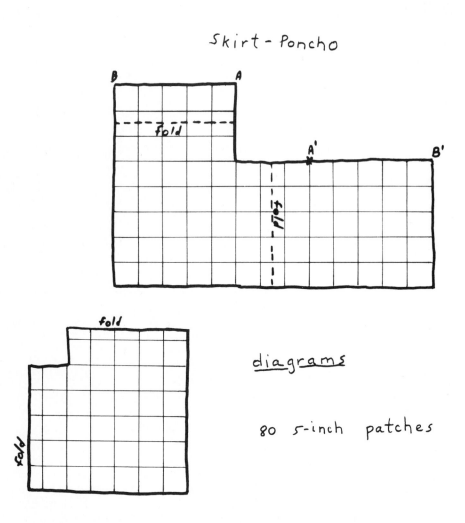

Skirt - Poncho

diagrams

80 5-inch patches

1. Make 80 5″ patches (or 80 3½″ patches with three rows sc worked all around each in a coordinating color).

2. Join patches together as diagrammed, joining AB to A′B′.

3. Work two or more rows sc around bottom edge. Attach knotted fringe if desired.

4. Make waistband and tasseled drawstring as in instructions 3 and 5 for Dirndl Skirt, above.

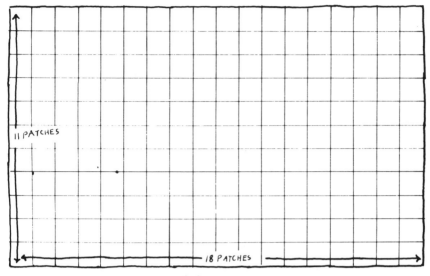

diagram

AFGHAN-PATCH AFGHAN OR THROW

And make an Afghan-Patch Afghan, or throw for a bed.

1. Make the number of patches in the size required for the size throw you want.

2. Join patches together as diagrammed.

3. Work 4 rows of sc around entire piece. Add fringe all around if desired. (Long fringe can turn a throw into a floor-length bedspread.) Or attach thick 4-inch tassels at the corners.

diagram

small afghan 41″ by 66″ 18 rows of 11 patches each=
197 3½-inch patches
single-bed throw 68″ by 99″ 19 rows of 13 patches each=
247 5-inch patches
double-bed throw 78″ by 99″ 19 rows of 15 patches each=
285 5-inch patches

Note: Only the small afghan is diagrammed. Dimensions of the larger throws are listed. A 5-inch patch is used for the larger throws.

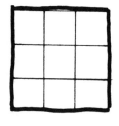 

<u>diagram</u> 18 3½- or 5- inch patches

Afghan - Patch Throw Pillow (make 2)

THROW PILLOW

And make a throw pillow, or several, to match.

1. Make 18 3½-inch patches.

2. Work 1 row sc around each.

3. Join together as diagrammed, making two squares of 9 patches each.

4. Work 2 rows sc around outside of each square.

5. Join squares on three sides, insert 12″ pillow form and sew up last side. Attach tassels at corners if desired.

Note: Or make a 15″ throw pillow using 9 5-inch patches to a side.

Put-on a Pillowcase

Today's colorful designer sheets and pillowcases are beautiful enough to wear—and that's just what I've been doing with two pillowcases that took my fancy. They proved to be the perfect solution to one of my perennial problems—finding aprons that cover up most of me and look good at the same time. The second Pillowcase Apron also doubles as a shift or

Pillowcase Pinafore-Apron

vertical fold in half

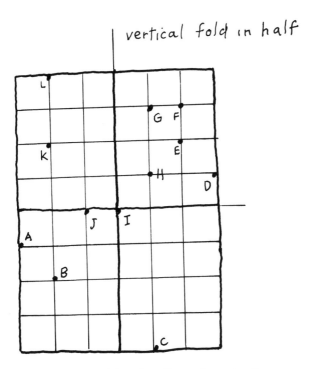

tunic; it was inspired by the charming pinafore worn by a doll that recently joined our household. Try these, if you have some extra pillowcases on hand. Or when your store has a white sale you can stock up on a year's supply of the basic material for these original, colorful aprons.

PILLOWCASE PINAFORE-APRON

MATERIALS:

1 pillowcase (or a piece of fabric 38″ by 42″)
bias binding or other trim
4 snaps

HOW-TO:

1. Open hem and all seams of pillowcase. Fold back to original shape.

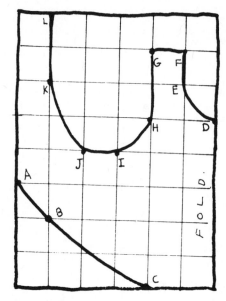

2. Make a pattern from a sheet of wrapping paper cut to
   38" by 21". (I opened up a large paper bag and cut it
   to this size.) Fold paper vertically in half and then in
   thirds, pressing creases sharply with fingers. Open
   paper and mark fold lines with crayon or marking pen
   (mark them quickly, not carefully; if the lines wiggle
   a bit it's all right). Follow the diagram to mark dots
   A through L on the pattern; note that all dots are
   located at crossings of the marked lines. Then connect
   the dots as shown, using a freehand curve. If the curve
   doesn't look right the first time, try it again; you'll cut
   away the "wrong" line, or you can cross it out.

3. Pin pattern to folded pillowcase, placing edge marked
   "fold" on the fold of the fabric. Cut out pinafore and
   unpin pattern.

4. Stitch bias binding all around.

5. Sew two snaps to each shoulder strap, matching them
   so that the short straps will go straight up over your
   shoulders, and the long straps will go under your arms
   to cross behind your back before snapping onto the
   opposite shoulders.

6. If you like, cut patch pockets from the extra fabric and
   sew to front of pinafore.

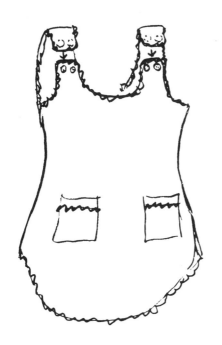

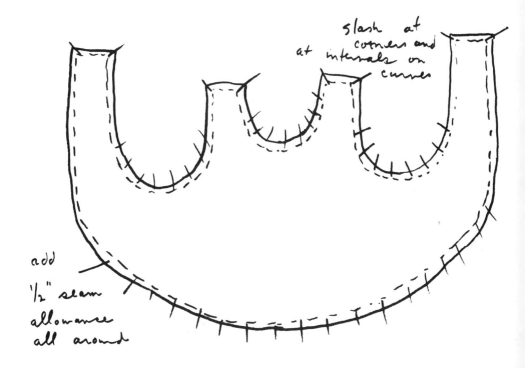

slash at
corners and
at intervals on
curves

add
½" seam
allowance
all around

7. To make this pinafore-apron lined or reversible: place two pillowcases together and cut out pattern as above, adding ½" seam allowance on all cut edges. Place both pieces of fabric with right sides together and stitch around ½" from all edges, leaving a 5" opening at the bottom. Slash at strap corners and at intervals on curves. Turn right sides out and sew up bottom opening. If desired, topstitch all around apron ¼" from edge. Sew on snaps at shoulder as above.

PILLOWCASE SHIFT-APRON

MATERIALS:

1 pillowcase
bias binding or other trim

HOW-TO:

1. Open seams (not hem) of pillowcase, and fold back to original shape.
2. Cut as in diagram.
3. Cut six 10" pieces of bias binding. Fold each strip in

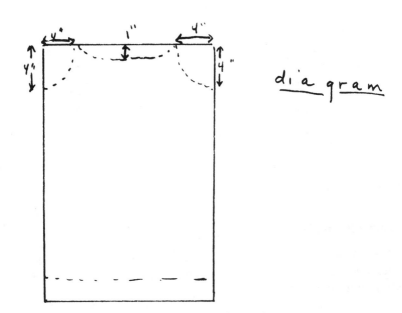

Pillowcase Shift-Apron

diagram

diagram

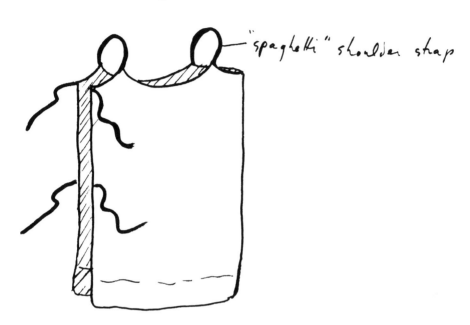

"spaghetti" shoulder strap

half lengthwise and stitch edges together to make narrow "spaghetti" straps.

4. Sew binding around all edges.
5. Sew one end of a spaghetti strap to each point of right shoulder; repeat for left shoulder. Sew other four to side opening as ties.

Note: The slim figure (size 10 or less) might want to wear this as an over-the-head shift. Do not open side seam; omit four side ties.

Another note: To make it longer, as apron or shift or both, open and let down the hem; trim with bias binding.

And Still More Put-ons

Try these, too—an apron that doubles as a hostess skirt, a bolero with bounce, and a silk belt (no one will ever guess what you made it from!).

Side - Wrap Apron Skirt

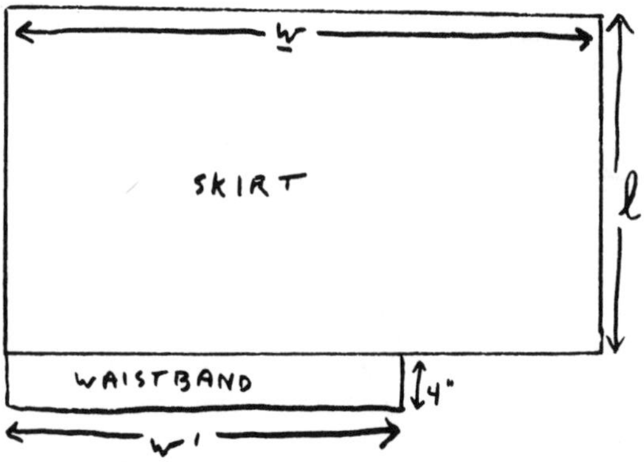

diagram

w = hip measurement + 10"

w' = waist measurement + 3"

l = for mini length: 16"

" knee " , 23"

" midi " : 30"

" maxi " : 37"

⎫ + 3"

SIDE-WRAP APRON SKIRT

MATERIALS:

1½ yds. fabric, approximately (for exact amount, figure out dimensions from diagram)

velcro or skirt hooks

iron-on seam binding (optional)

braid or other trim (optional)

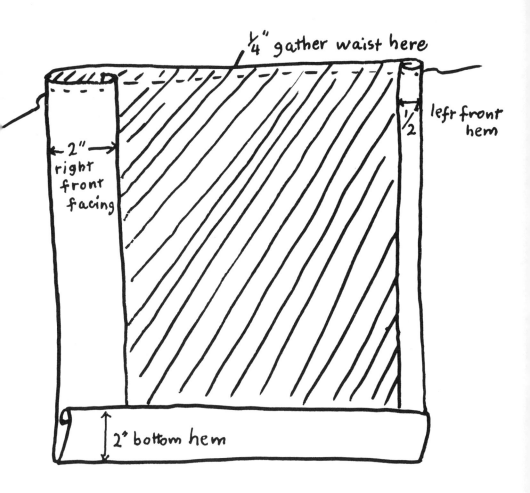

How-to:

1. Cut skirt of apron, and waistband, following diagram.
2. Fold under ¼″ at left front edge, then fold again for ½″ and stitch left front hem (or take a shortcut and use an iron-on seam binding).
3. Fold under ¼″ at right front edge, then fold again to make a 2″ facing, and stitch (or use iron-on binding).
4. Make bottom hem 2″ or 2½″ deep.
5. Gather waist ¼″ from top, pulling thread to make waist measurement plus 2″. Fasten off gathering securely.
6. Try on. Skirt opening should overlap at your left hip.

Move gathers around so fullness is at sides, or where you want it. Pin through gathers to hold fullness in place.

7. To sew waistband to skirt: place right side of one long edge of waistband against right side of skirt with ½″ of waistband extending beyond skirt on each side. Stitch together just below gather line of stitching. Fold waistband ends in ¼″, fold waistband up at stitch line, then fold unstitched long edge of waistband ¼″ to wrong side. Fold waistband over and stitch long edge to wrong side of skirt on previously stitched line.

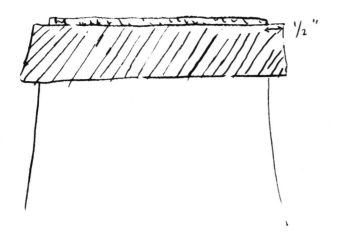

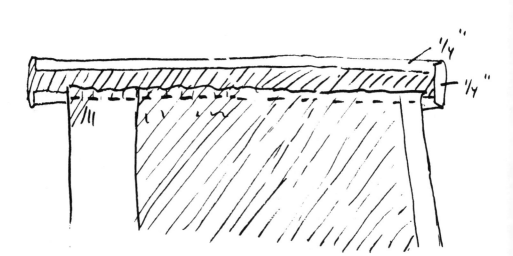

8. Sew velcro or hooks to waistband at opening.
9. If you like, sew a border of braid or other trim down the front edges and on hem.

BOUNCY BOLERO

A bolero like this one, trimmed with multicolored stripes of ball-fringe, was selling in a Fifth Avenue shop last Christmas for $37. Plus tax! I kid you not. You can make yours in a jiffy from a discarded man's shirt and a few dollars worth of ball-fringe, upholstery braid, ribbon or other trimmings.

MATERIALS:

1 man's shirt

several yards of ball-fringe or other trim (leftovers will do, but you'll probably have to add a few yards in your favorite colors)

HOW-TO:

1. Cut bolero background from shirt:
   a) Cut just inside of armhole stitching, all the way around each armhole.
   b) Fold shirt in half through center back and cut back of collar off, cutting just below collar to shoulders.
   c) Keep shirt folded and measure down 17″ from center of back of neck; mark with pin. Measure 8″

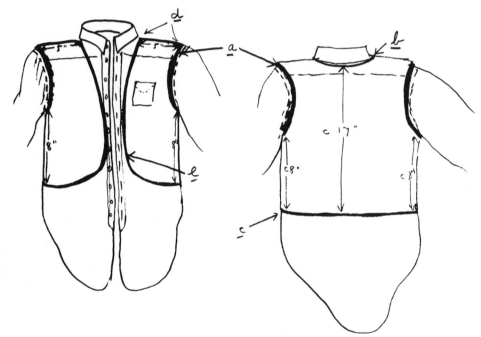

down from underarm at side seam and mark with pins. These three pins should form a straight line; adjust until they do and cut straight across.

d) Place fronts together, pinning at shoulder and wherever necessary to hold. Measure 5" across front shoulders from armhole to collar and mark with a pin.

e) Use pencil to draw the freehand curve of bolero front (shown from x to y on diagram). Or cut a paper pattern, try it against you and when it's right pin it to shirt front before cutting. You may want to use a large dinner plate to trace around to get the curve at bottom front just right. Note that both button and buttonhole front edges of shirt are cut away and discarded.

2. Fold all raw edges under ¼″ and stitch down.
3. Starting at center back of neck, pin and sew on ribbon or braid, going completely around outer edges of bolero. Starting at underarm, pin and sew on braid, going completely around armhole. Repeat for other armhole.
4. Starting at bottom of bolero directly below armhole, pin and sew braid on in a vertical strip up side seam to armhole. Continue to pin and sew braid in vertical stripes, placing each strip alongside the one before. Work on both sides of the underarm seam and cut off braid as it reaches the braid bordering the armhole. Then pin and sew stripes of braid up from front bottom over shoulder and down to back bottom. Repeat on other side. When both shoulders are covered with braid, fill in any unbraided portions of bolero by pinning and sewing vertical stripes to fit remaining space.

Note: If you are small, and your man's shirt is too big, use an old blouse or shirt of your own instead. Try the shirt on. If your shirt fits snugly, you may have to cut armholes a little deeper, and you may have to include part of the shirt front in your bolero front.

Idea! To make a lined bolero, cut the basic shape from two shirts. Sew trim to one, omitting both step 2 and the all-around trimming of step 3 above, and start with step 4, being sure to end all vertical stripes of braid about ¾″ from raw edge of bolero. When bolero is filled with vertical stripes, place it and other bolero cutout together with right sides facing and sew around armholes ⅜″ from raw edges. Sew around all other edges too, leaving an opening of about 4″ at bottom. Turn right sides out through bottom opening and sew it closed. Now go back to step 3 and pin and sew braid completely around each armhole and around all edges.

Another idea! Make this bolero for a little girl, using her big brother's shirt.

SILK BELT

If you're searching for *the* accent to wear with pants, skirts or a simple dress, try a colorful silk belt that gets together in a wink and goes on with style and dash. Make it from a lined necktie and curtain rings!

How-to:

1. Cut off the narrow end of the necktie, leaving a 46″ or 48″ piece. Remove labels but be careful to leave lining—probably a colorful silk—and interlining—the coarsely woven off-white or gray fabric that holds the necktie's shape—in place.
2. Fold cut edge ¼″ to wrong side and pin. Slip through 1½″ curtain rings, fold over ½″ and stitch down.
3. To wear, push loose end through both rings, then fold over and bring back through one ring and pull down.

Idea! Wear it as a headband, too!

⌇ IX ⌇

Getting It All Together

Acrylic Paints and Mediums

When you paint with acrylics, you are actually applying a film of plastic. Because these plastic paints are quick-drying, water-soluble, and adhere to virtually any surface, they are a basic addition to any list of crafts equipment.

Buy acrylic paints in starter sets or larger sets, or by the tube or jar. Use any brushes. Thin with water only. Wash brushes with soap and water after using; do not let paint dry on brushes. Paint on paper, cloth, canvas, wood, plaster, clay or plastics.

Before acrylic paint dries, smudges can be removed with water. After drying, acrylic-painted surfaces are waterproof; they can actually be cleaned with soap and water without being damaged.

Use a plate or a piece of foil as a palette. If you are working with several colors, a plastic ice-cube tray is a good palette.

Keep your paints soft from one session to another by covering tray or plate with foil or plastic wrap.

There are several polymer mediums—versatile accessories to use with acrylic paints—that have many independent uses as well. They come in the starter sets in small jars, but can also be bought in larger, more economical sizes in art supply stores.

Polymer medium or gloss medium. A thin, translucent fluid that brushes on to give a glossy surface and protective finish; can also be used as an adhesive for collage and other craft work.

Polymer gel medium. A thick, pasty substance that is excellent for gluing large objects such as shells, rocks, wood and so on; gives a glossy protective finish also, but takes longer to dry than the thinner polymer medium.

Polymer matte varnish. A transparent protective finish that brushes on, is not glossy or shiny; can be added to acrylic paints to reduce shine.

Adhesive-backed Materials

There's hardly anything, it seems, that doesn't come in an adhesive-backed version. And the convenience of getting everything from foil to wood on your walls or furniture without a gluey mess has spurred the adhesive-backed "revolution." Here's a brief rundown of some of the available materials.

Vinyl. Available in colorful patterns and solid colors, wood-grain and marble looks, velvet, flock, wet looks and felt, too. Also available in a heavy-duty vinyl. Buy it by the yard.

Aluminum foil. An extra-heavy-duty foil, which can be used for various projects and as a wall-covering. Buy it by the yard.

Foil tiles. 12" square tiles, in marbleized or solid-color designs; can be used anywhere you'd use adhesive-backed vinyl.

Burlap. Available in several decorator colors; use to cover almost anything. Buy it by the yard.

Wood tiles. 12" square tiles of a thin sliver of real wood bonded to an adhesive backing; several wood-grain finishes; can be cut with scissors.

Vinyl floor tiles. Square tiles in several sizes, usually 12", in a variety of patterns including marbles and wood grains.

Can be laid over wood, concrete or vinyl or linoleum floors. Can also be used on walls, table tops, window sills and other furniture. Cut with scissors.

Carpet tiles. Available in a variety of colors, textures and patterns. Some are adhesive-backed, and some adhere to floors by means of double-faced carpet tape.

Adhesive-backed Tapes, Decorative

Velvet ribbon. Available in several widths and cutout patterns, in many decorator colors. Use to trim almost anything, border a wall or a ceiling, a window shade or a wastebasket. (Also available in an iron-on version for adhering to fabrics, such as slipcovers or draperies.) Available at upholstery supply stores and in notions and trimmings departments.

Plastic. Available in two widths and several colors and patterns, some matching by-the-yard vinyl designs. For decorating and repairing.

Cloth. Available in two widths, several colors. A strong, waterproof tape that is as useful as it can be attractive.

Metallic. Available in two widths, several metal-look finishes.

Wood grain. Actual wood veneer with an adhesive backing, in several wood-grain finishes.

Adhesive-backed Tapes, Functional

Double-faced. So paper, fabric and other lightweight materials adhere invisibly to each other. Use to secure felt appliqués without gluing; to attach prints or photos to a felt, burlap or enamel surface; to hold foil to itself.

Double-faced, extra-strong. Designed for use with metal, concrete, fabric, glass, wood, paper, plastics, tile, leather. Will hold any of these to itself or to each other. Try it to stick down a patch of wallpaper that always comes loose; to secure scatter rugs; to fasten heavy braid or fringe to window shades or draperies.

Strapping tape. Will hold almost anything in place.

Striping tape. Masking tape with removable center strips of ⅛" and larger so you can paint on wide or narrow stripes without worry.

Foam rubber. Available in several widths. Intended for use as weather stripping, but useful for all sorts of projects and repair jobs too. Use a strip of it along the bottom of the back of a picture frame to prevent marking the wall and to help hold the frame in place. Or use it to cushion ashtrays or lamp bottoms, or inside a door frame to prevent door from slamming.

Appliqué

This used to be a tedious method of putting a design of one fabric on top of a background of another fabric. Now you have a choice of streamlined methods. Note that no turn-under allowance is required for any of these methods.

1. Cut your design from non-fraying felt or leather and
   a) glue (white glue or fabric glue) to background
   b) sew to background, using a
      zigzag or satin stitch on machine or
      tiny, close-together satin or blanket stitches by hand.

2. Cut your design from iron-on bonding tape or patches (available in various colors of closely-woven cotton, as well as corduroy and denim) and iron directly onto background.

3. Use any fabric at all. Before cutting out your appliqué designs, press the fabric to an iron-on interfacing or bonding material (such as Wonder Under). Do not remove the paper backing on the reverse side of the bonding material. Trace your appliqué designs onto the paper backing; cut out; remove paper backing and iron appliqué to background. If you want to add decorative stitching around appliqué, go right ahead.

4. To appliqué narrow bands of ribbon or braid without sewing, use an iron-on bonding ribbon (such as Stitch Witchery); simply sandwich bonding ribbon between decorative braid and background fabric, pin to hold, and iron to set the "sandwich" permanently.

Crewel

A kind of embroidery, using wool yarns and usually worked on a linen or homespun cloth background. The word "crewel" comes from *crule,* meaning wool, an English word in use some six hundred years ago. Simple embroidery stitches are used to create simple shapes, usually vines, flowers and animals. See *Embroidery*.

Crochet, four basic stitches

1. *Chain stitch (ch)*. This is the beginning of all crochet work.

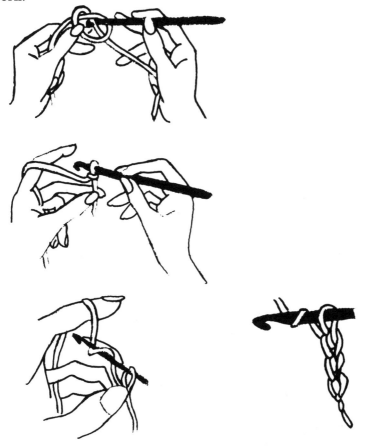

a) Make a slip knot at the end of yarn, and put hook through.

b) Wrap yarn over hook and pull it through the loop of the slip knot. Repeat for as many chain stitches or as long a chain as required.

2. *Single crochet (sc)*. Chain for desired length.

a) Insert hook into second chain from hook, under the top strand of stitch.

b) Wrap yarn over hook and pull it back through the chain stitch. There are two loops over the hook.

c) Now wrap yarn over hook again and pull it through both loops on hook. One single crochet made. Repeat to end of chain.

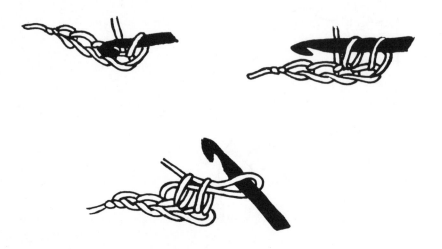

3. *Slip stitch (sl)*. Chain for desired length. Used for joining rows or ending off work.

a) Insert hook into second chain stitch from hook, under the top strand of stitch.

b) Wrap yarn over hook, pull it back through chain stitch *and* through loop on hook in one motion.

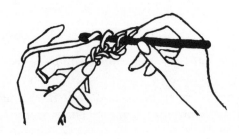

4. *Afghan stitch*. Chain for desired length. Always worked with a long afghan hook.

a) Start first afghan row. Insert hook in second chain stitch from hook, wrap yarn over hook and pull it back through chain stitch. There are now two loops on hook. Do not work off loops.

b) Insert hook in next chain stitch, wrap yarn over hook and pull it back through chain stitch; three loops on hook. Continue pulling up a loop in each stitch of chain, keeping all loops on hook. Do not turn work at end of row.

c) At end of row, wrap yarn over hook and draw it through last loop made. Wrap yarn over hook and draw it through last two loops on hook. Continue wrapping yarn over hook and drawing it through two loops at a time, until only one loop is left on hook. This will become the first loop of the next row.

d) Second and every succeeding afghan row: insert hook under first vertical bar of preceding row, wrap yarn over hook and pull it through bar, drawing up a loop on hook. Repeat in every vertical bar across row. To complete second afghan row, work off loops as before (see *c* above).

e) Final row: finish by working a row of single crochet across, inserting hook into vertical bars formed by last afghan row.

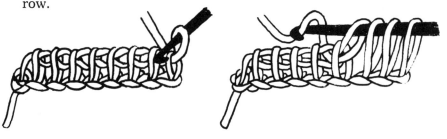

Embroidery, basic stitches

See following ten diagrams. Crewel work uses same stitches.

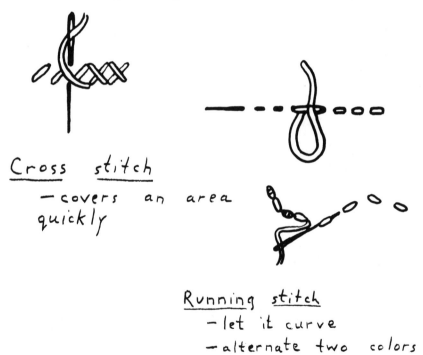

Cross stitch
— covers an area quickly

Running stitch
— let it curve
— alternate two colors

Satin stitch
— used to fill in
an area

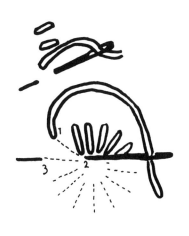

Back stitch

Stem stitch
or Outline stitch

Straight stitch
— it goes in any
direction

Chain stitch
—use it to outline,
or for a stem or a
vine
—or work concentric
rows close together to
fill in an area

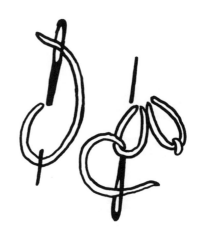

Lazy daisy stitch
—instead of joining
chain stitches, work
individual ones in
a circle

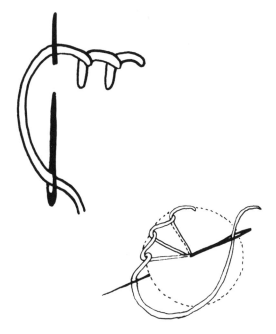

Blanket stitch
— work it in a single
row as a border, or
in neighboring rows to
fill in an area
— or work it in a
circle

French Knot

Embroidery, fabric for

Use unbleached muslin; burlap (don't use burlap for throw pillows unless you don't mind if they shed or feel rough!), or any loosely woven, nicely textured background fabric. Linen and linen-weave synthetics are just fine. Cloth napkins about 14″ square, in a wide range of colors, can be found for as little as fifty-nine cents, and a pair of them make a perfect pillow. Place mats can be used, too. Dish or glass towels of linen or linen-weave would be good for hangings, especially in kitchen or dining room; they can also be cut or folded in half to make throw pillows. Use your imagination when it comes to fabric; don't even discount the oxford shirt off your husband's (or your own) back.

Embroidery, finishing and mounting

Block embroidery if necessary by placing it face down over a terrycloth towel, covering with a damp press cloth and steaming lightly. Be careful not to put the full weight of the iron on the embroidery or it will be flattened. Leave embroidery on towel until thoroughly dry.

Mount embroidery on cardboard for framing. Trim background fabric to 1″ larger all around than size of mounting cardboard. Place fabric right side down over a terry towel on working surface. Position cardboard on top of fabric. Fold fabric margin up and over to back of cardboard and glue in place, mitering corners neatly. Use only enough white glue, being careful not to get any on the surface of the embroidery. Put glue on the back of the mounting cardboard only. (Or secure fabric to back of cardboard with masking or adhesive-backed cloth tape.) Frame work as desired. (Mount other fabric work, such as felt appliqué, in the same way.)

Felt-tipped Markers

Now available in truly marvelous colors, and with "points" or brushing ends that range from thick to thin. Some uses you may not have thought of are:

Tint foil to the metallic color of your choice: If you make a "mistake" you can wipe it off with a dab of turpentine.

Save old markers, even if they're frazzled at the ends but still have an ink supply left. Use them for special effects, such as fancy lettering or drawing softer-looking flowers.

"Paint" a border on a plain white window shade.

Instead of sticking shelf edging on the front of the pantry or closet shelves, "paint" a colorful design along the edge.

Fixatives

These are transparent sprays that will protect any surface. They are available in 16-ounce spray cans, in both matte and glossy finishes. Available in art supply and some hardware stores.

Fringe, how to make it yourself

If you can't find fringe in a special length or color, make it yourself from yarn, cord or silk-twist embroidery floss.

1. Cut a piece of heavy paper the desired width of the fringe plus ½", and about three inches longer than the desired length. (If you need a great deal of fringe, you may have to work several shorter lengths and then join them when you sew them to the article to be decorated.)

2. Wrap the yarn or cord over the cardboard, placing each strand next to but not overlapping the one before. End on the same side where you started.

3. Secure ends with Scotch tape. Stitch across that same end ½" from the edge, catching every strand in the stitching. Use a zigzag stitch if your machine can do it; if not, work

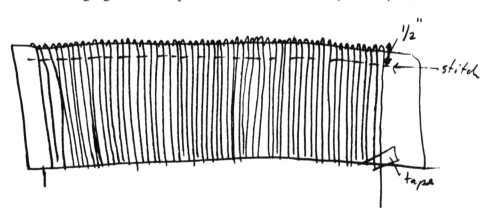

one row of stitches ½″ from the edge and two more rows between it and the edge.

4. Cut through the looped strands on the other edge, and tear away the bottom part of the paper.

5. Pin fringe in place on article to be decorated, remove top part of paper and sew in place.

Fringe, knotted

a) Attach fringe to fabric. Divide each section in half, and knot half of one fringe section to the half of the adjacent fringe section, spacing knots evenly below fabric.

b) Divide each new fringe section in half and make a second row of knots to alternate with the first. Trim off ends evenly.

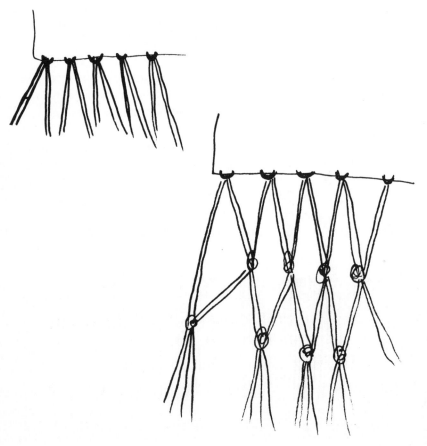

Glue, most useful varieties of

A basic glue "wardrobe" that will handle most projects and emergencies should start with at least white glue and contact cement. Then you can add epoxy and rubber cements.

Every substance listed under a particular glue can be attached to itself and to every other substance in the same listing.

1. *White glue*

wood	cloth
plastic	leather
paper	styrofoam
cardboard	pottery

Do not use for photographs, metals, or anything that will have to be in water. Dries transparent.

2. *Contact cement*

wood	foil
plastic	tile
metal	fabric
leather	glass
rubber	

Use contact cements sparingly on fabric; they come through yellowish. Clean up excess instantly, because contact cements set quickly and are almost impossible to remove when dry.

3. *Epoxy cement*

metal	china
wood	glass
rubber	

Mix epoxies carefully; use a piece of foil or a plastic container lid to mix in; lollipop or ice cream sticks, or toothpicks to mix with. Try epoxy in capsule form to eliminate variations in quantity that could interfere with the hardening capacity of the cement.

4. *Rubber cement*

paper	foil
sponges	foam rubber (polyurethane)
leather	

Let rubber cement dry and then use fingers to rub off any excess.

Glue, special-purpose

Plastic model cement. Use for all plastics.

Polymer mediums. See *Acrylic Paints*, above.

Liquid solder. For attaching most metals to each other.

Liquid thread. For mending and appliqué work on most natural (non-synthetic) fabrics; test synthetics before using.

Marine epoxy or epoxy cement and filler. For a putty-like filler that dries as hard as stone while permanently bonding two surfaces together. Use for leveling legs or base of furniture, vases, etc.; for attaching things like rocks and driftwood permanently to a base; for any out-of-doors project.

Linoleum paste. Attaches vinyl and linoleum sheet or tiles to floors, walls and other surfaces; also use for securing cork panels to walls or furniture.

Wheat paste. Standard wallpaper paste, for attaching ordinary wallpaper, brown wrapping paper to walls; can also be used for papier-mâché.

Heavy-duty wallpaper paste. For plasticized or vinyl wall-coverings, fabric, etc.

Spray adhesive. For covering large areas with fairly fragile materials; to put foil or fabric on a wall or on any wood surface; follow instructions on spray can.

Glue, tips and tricks

1. Always be sure that surfaces to be glued are clean (free from old dirt and grease) and dry. It may be necessary to roughen a wooden surface with sandpaper (or an emery board) or a metal surface with coarse steel wool to make the glue adhere better.

2. When gluing into a "tight spot," which happens especially when repairing furniture, be sure to push the glue in as deep as possible with a toothpick or other pointed instrument.

3. To hold two things together until glue sets, try wrapping a length of masking tape around them. For small pieces, try rubber bands.

4. Always follow directions on the container of glue that you are using.

Needlepoint, basic stitches

See following six diagrams.

Continental stitch
— work from right
to left.

Half-Cross stitch
— do not use on
single-mesh canvas
— work from left
to right

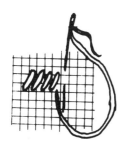

Slanted Gobelin stitch
— count 1 square over
and 2 squares up
— works up quickly for
large pattern areas

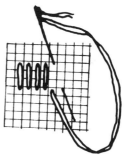

Straight Gobelin
stitch

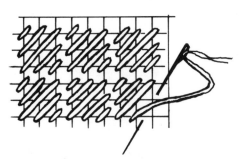

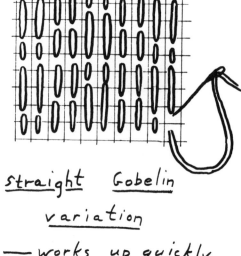

Mosaic stitch
— a slanted Gobelin variation worked in "boxes" of 9 meshes, 3 rows of 3 meshes each

Straight Gobelin variation

— works up quickly for backgrounds or geometric patterns

Needlepoint, canvas and yarn

Needlepoint canvases are woven either of single threads or two threads at right angles to each other, forming meshes of various sizes. For a starting project, use "mono" or single-thread mesh canvas, or a canvas with only a few meshes to the inch. If you use double-mesh canvas, work in the large meshes or squares only.

Work in knitting worsted or tapestry yarn on 9- or 10-mesh-to-the-inch canvas. Work with rug or thick acrylic yarn on 4- or 5-mesh-to-the-inch canvas.

Use a 20″ or 24″ length of yarn in needle (the thicker the yarn the longer it can be, up to a point); if yarn is too long, it will get frayed while working. To thread needle easily, fold end of yarn over eye end of needle; slip out needle so that you are left holding a firm loop. Push loop into eye of needle. Use a special blunt-pointed tapestry needle.

If you make a mistake, it's best to cut the bad stitches out. Trying to remove them by working backward will only result in weakening the canvas and fraying the yarn.

Needlepoint, finishing and mounting

To block needlepoint, mark desired shape and dimensions on a piece of wood or a cutting board. Dampen needlepoint, using a sponge and cold water. Stretch it to shape and pin, using rustproof pins, needlepoint to outline. Leave it pinned to board until thoroughly dry, about two days.

To mount needlepoint on cardboard for framing: cut cardboard to fit into frame exactly. Work needlepoint to exact size of cardboard. Trim canvas to about 1½" beyond stitching. Block needlepoint. Place it face down on a terry towel placed over working surface. Spread cardboard *lightly* all over with white glue. Press glued surface of cardboard into position over needlepoint. Be sure glue does not come through to right side of work. Cover with a sheet of waxed paper or foil, and weight with a telephone directory to keep the work flat while glue dries. When glue is completely dry (next day), fold canvas margin up and over to wrong side of cardboard and tape down neatly with masking or other adhesive-backed tape. Miter corners neatly. For a really complete finish, cut a piece of adhesive-backed vinyl, felt or burlap to the exact size of the cardboard and cover back of mounted work with it. Put cardboard-mounted work into frame.

To mount needlepoint on wood: work needlepoint to ½" bigger all around than dimensions of wood you want to mount it on. Trim canvas ½" from stitching. For a wall-hanging, use ¼" plywood. After needlepoint is blocked, position it on plywood, pulling stitched and canvas margin around to

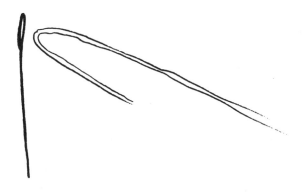

wrong side with small upholstery tacks spaced at even intervals. Fasten opposite straight sides first; then fold corners neatly and tack. For extra support, use adhesive-backed cloth tape to secure canvas edge to back of wood.

To mount needlepoint on box tops (wood or cardboard): work needlepoint to ½" *less* all around than dimensions of finished box top. Trim canvas ⅜" beyond stitching line. Position needlepoint on object and glue (white glue) in place; glue canvas border down, too, being careful not to get glue on stitching. Cover canvas margin by gluing suitable braid over it. Use upholstery braid; or make a matching braid by simply braiding together three groups of three or four strands each of tapestry yarn. End with a neat knot and cut threads evenly to make a tassel hanging from one corner of box top.

Tips: Protect finished work by spraying with a fabric-protective silicone spray. Before beginning work, bind raw edges of canvas with masking tape. When transferring a design to canvas, use only waterproof felt-tipped markers. If you draw your design on wrapping paper first, using a black marker—the outline will show through the mesh of the canvas and you can trace it on directly.

Painting, to make things easier during

1. Instead of removing things like picture hooks and curtain rod hardware, or getting globs of paint on them, as well as to prevent splatters on doorknobs and light switches, wrap all of these up with small pieces of masking tape. Also, tape windowpanes where they touch wood frame edges. Other places to mask include ceiling- or wall-hung light fixtures, wall-mounted shelves and shelf supports, and even the outer edges of wall-to-wall carpeting. Use the widest masking tape possible for efficient coverage.

2. Wipe up smudges as soon as possible, before they have a chance to dry out and set. Use a water-dampened rag for latex-based paint, and turpentine for other paints. It's a good idea to get a small can of turp and keep it around, because even weeks after a paint job you're likely to come across a previously unnoticed smudge.

3. To protect tables, chairs and other furniture at painting time, cover them with the largest plastic trash bags you can

buy. Simply slip the bags right over a chair or a table with a lamp on it (disconnect the lamp first, of course). To cover something too large for one bag, use two or three; slit the sides, slip the bags over the object and overlap edges, holding them in place with a strip of masking tape. Now you don't have to worry about paint-covered drop cloths ruining your furniture.

Polyurethane (foam rubber)

Available already cut to standard cushion sizes or by the yard in various thicknesses; also by the pound-bag of scraps. Mark with ball-point pen. Cut with scissors, electric knife, razor or saw. Use rubber cement to join two pieces together. You may notice that polyurethane changes to a yellowish color after a while, but this does not change any of its properties. Save trimmings from major projects and use to stuff toys, pin cushions or throw pillows.

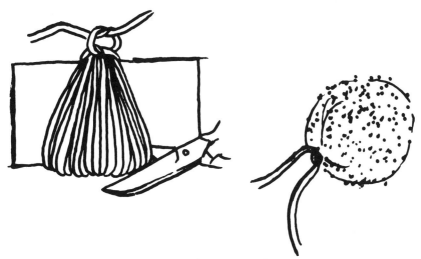

Pompons, how to make

1. Cut cardboard about 6" wide and as long as size of pompon desired.

2. Wind yarn around cardboard 40 or more times, depending on thickness of yarn. Cut off.

3. Place a 12" length of matching yarn between the wrapped yarn and the cardboard and pull it to the top; tie tightly. Cut through bottom loops and remove yarn from cardboard.

4. Holding ends of tying piece, roll and fluff cut yarn into a ball-like shape. Trim ends with sharp shears to complete shaping of pompon.

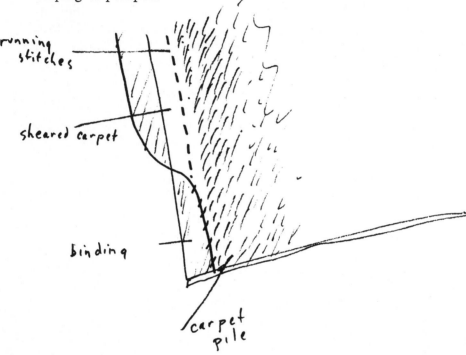

Rugs, trimming or binding of

Always vacuum carpeting first, on bottom as well as on top, to remove loose dust, lint and "fluff" that might otherwise get in the way of a neat job.

Use blackboard or tailor's chalk to mark cutting lines on underside of carpet or rug.

Cut with sharp shears or a linoleum knife. Put heavy cardboard or board underneath carpet when cutting to protect the floor.

Apply rubber cement over cut edges to prevent fraying.

Before adding binding or fringe, shave off carpet pile where the edge of the trim will cover it. Shear pile off with a sharp scissors held horizontally. If you put newspaper underneath, you can scoop up all the trimmings neatly.

Use spring-type clothespins to hold ends of trimming in place at side of carpet.

Sew on trim, using a heavy carpet needle with a 3-sided point. Use carpet or button thread, and pull it over a piece of beeswax for extra strength. Use a heavy-duty thimble. Work with single thread and make small stitches, if possible concealing them in the fringe edging or on the edge of the binding next to the carpet pile.

When sewing on binding, put about one-third of the width of the binding under the carpet and sew in place with running stitches or back stitches. Fold binding up and over the edge of carpet to cover the stitches. Then fasten it with neat, small overcasting stitches along the edge, hiding stitches close to the pile.

Fringe for carpet may be cotton or wool, 2″ to 4″ wide, and may match or contrast in color.

Shelves, instant

Support lengths of stock shelving on large clay flower pots. Whether you use glass or wood shelves, the effect is original, the job is quickly and inexpensively put together and you can add a lot of display and open storage space in a short time. It all comes apart quickly when you move. For more space between shelves, stack two flower pots, gluing their rims together. To prevent slipping of shelves, cover bases of flower pots with adhesive-backed foam or felt.

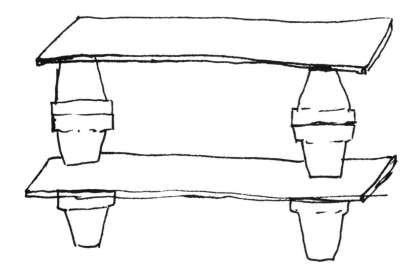

Tassels, how to make

1. Cut cardboard about 6″ wide and as long as length of tassel desired. Wind yarn around cardboard twenty times or as many times as needed for thickness of yarn used and tassel desired. Cut off end of yarn.

2. Slip a 12″ length of yarn between the wrapped yarn and the cardboard and pull it to the top. Tie tightly.

3. Cut through bottom loops and remove from cardboard.

4. Wrap another length of yarn ½″ or 1″ below top of tassel and knot tightly; clip ends off close to knot.

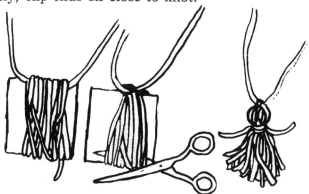

Tie-Dyeing, basic equipment

pots and saucepans, 2-quart to 5-quart sizes and/or glass
   measuring cups, 8-ounce and 1-quart sizes
rubber gloves
rubber bands or string
long stirring sticks (wooden spoons will do nicely)
plastic wrap or plastic sandwich bags (optional)
hot water and cold water

Tie-Dyeing, basic dye "recipes"

1. 1 bottle liquid dye or 2 packages powdered dye to 1 gallon hot water (use 5-quart pot).

2. ½ bottle liquid dye or 1 package powdered dye to 2 quarts hot water.

3. ¼ bottle (¼ cup) liquid dye or ½ package powdered dye to 1 quart hot water (use 2-quart pot).

4. ½ ounce liquid dye to about ¾ cup hot water (use measuring cup).

Rosette

Donut

Gathering a stripe...

or stripes

Note: for a stronger color, use a little more dye or a little less water. Double the quantity of dye for true black and navy; add about half again as much dye for dark greens and browns. Remember that the strength of the dye bath becomes diluted after use; so unless you want a paler version of the color, add more dye or start again for a second or third project. Follow label directions for amount of time to leave in dye bath, or see below, Basic Procedure, step 3.

Tie-Dyeing, basic knots

1. *Rosette.* This is the basic tie-dye knot. Pinch up a clump of fabric and fasten with string or rubber band.

2. *Donut.* This is a rosette knot with an extra twist. Pinch up a long rosette knot. Then push the top down through the center of the rosette and fasten with string or rubber band.

Sunburst

3. *Stripe.* Fold fabric into accordion pleats and fasten across folds at intervals.

4. *Sunburst.* Make a long rosette knot, and twist the end. Fasten at intervals with rubber bands or string.

Tie-Dyeing, basic procedure

1. Wet fabric in clear water; wring out excess.

2. Tie fabric in the knots of your choice, using string or rubber bands.

3. Place knotted and tied fabric in prepared dye bath, stirring to cover fabric evenly. Leave until the color has developed to a shade darker than desired, which can be anywhere from 5 to 40 minutes, depending on the type of fabric, the quantity of dye, and the size of the object being dyed.

4. Remove fabric from dye bath and rinse in cold running water until only a faint tint of the color comes off. Remove rubber bands or string and rinse again until water runs clear.

5. Set dye by ironing fabric while it is still damp.

6. To dye fabric in more than one color, or to keep portions of fabric background undyed, use plastic wrap or bags fastened with rubber bands to cover any portions of the fabric that are not to be dyed in the first dye bath. Rinse thoroughly before removing plastic wrap. If a second color is to be used, you can either a) wrap all portions of fabric not to be dyed in second color, or b) let second color show through clearly on previously undyed fabric while blending with first color on previously dyed fabric.

7. Experiment, experiment. There's no limit to the effects you can achieve. Try new knots, combinations of knots, combinations of colors. Use an eye dropper to put small quantities of strong dye solution right into the folds of a knot. Dyes "take" differently on different fabrics; blend differently with the original fabric colors. There's almost no predicting in advance exactly what a tie-dyed project will look like when it's finished. But all tie-dyed fabrics will have a soft, handcrafted, original look, and that is what you're after.

8. Although you can't tie them, you can dye such things as unfinished wicker and wood. Use 1 part liquid dye to four parts hot water. Wear rubber gloves. Place object to be dyed on a thick wad of newspaper. Rub wood with liquid sandpaper to smooth it, if necessary. Apply dye with a sponge and let soak into wicker or wood. Let dry overnight. Spray with protective vinyl finish, or brush with shellac or varnish (the wood will probably need it).

Wood, antiquing

Paint or stain wood in the color of your choice. Let dry thoroughly. Brush over the surface a contrasting color (gold, white, gray, green, silver, black or whatever). Use oil paint or enamels. While still wet, wipe with a clean dry cloth (cheese-cloth or any lintfree fabric), removing most of the color but leaving only streaks or a film to provide the antique effect. If piece is very large, work on a foot-square area at a time. If it doesn't come right the first time you wipe it, wipe it all off and try again. Let antique coat dry. Brush or spray with clear varnish or vinyl for a protective finish.

Wood, stain

Use commercial wood stains, of course, but for special color effects, paint or rub wood with oil paint or acrylic thinned to the consistency of thick cream. The wood grain will show through the color of the paint. Acrylics dry quickly, in a matter of minutes, so you can use the item almost immediately. Oils take several days to dry, giving you time to lighten or darken the surface if you think a change is necessary.

Wood, unfinished

Raw wood and most of the unfinished furniture that is sold as stock pieces must be properly prepared before it can be given its final surface treatment, whether that is to be paint or anything else. Two simple steps will prepare any wood surface for painting, staining or being covered with fabric, wallpaper or adhesive-backed material.

1. Rub wood all over with sandpaper, and wipe with a rag to remove all dust.

2. Brush with shellac or a primer coat of paint, letting it sink into the wood and dry thoroughly before starting to apply the final finish.

✤ X ✤

Design Portfolio

The designs in this chapter are those I have used for various projects, or special ones from my files, chosen because they are adaptable to appliqué, embroidery, needlepoint or painting. Many of them start out as simple shapes which can be given tremendous variety by means of adding a few lines or curves.

Designs 1 through 6 were suggested by some Mexican and other Latin American pieces in my collection of folk art. I used them, in felt and yarn appliqué, for the felt banner described in chapter 6.

Design 7, taken from two drawings by my daughter, was worked in needlepoint for a throw pillow (I used half-cross stitch for design, mosaic stitch for background).

Design 8 shows some ways in which decorative lettering can be used attractively; any word will do.

Designs 9 through 14 are simple shapes, elaborated into different designs. The final design can be as starkly modern or as fanciful as you wish to make it.

Designs 15 through 19 are especially prepared for needlework; you can do them free-hand with needle and floss or yarn, without having to draw them on canvas or fabric first. And 20 consists of designs particularly suited to use in kitchen or dining room wall hangings.

To use these sketches, slip a sheet of carbon paper under the page, place a sheet of plain paper under that and trace with a dull point (a used-up ball-point pen is excellent). Go over your tracing with felt-tipped marker to make the lines sharper.

To enlarge design, fold your tracing in eighths. Take a larger piece of paper, cut it to the size desired and fold it in eighths. Now copy the lines in each box. *Note:* this method will work only if paper lengths and widths are in the same proportion to each other. For instance, if your traced design is 3″ by 6″, you can enlarge it by this method to 6″ by 12″ or 12″ by 24″. Or try to sketch it freehand.

Use these designs to get started; then begin searching out and filing designs that you discover. Here are some ideas for other designs and places to find them:

Copy the signs of the zodiac from a book or chart; use your sign, or "his and hers."

Trace around your shoes, or the shoes of other family members; trace around gloves; trace around new socks or stockings.

Trace around your eyeglass frames.

Trace around jars, glasses, cups, mugs and plates to make circles of every size.

Copy a child's drawing, or trace around a favorite rag doll, a toy truck or other plaything.

Find an idea in a coloring book or a favorite story book.

Find an idea in a fashion advertisement.

Copy or trace drawings or flowers or leaves from a field guide or identification chart.

Find designs in your home right now, on dinnerware, casseroles, tea towels, ceramic or vinyl tiles, wallpaper, a scarf and, of course, in magazine articles and advertisements.

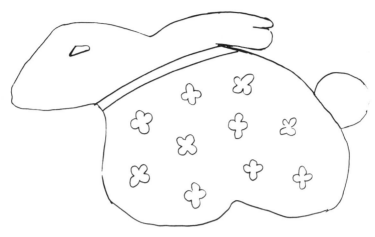

#1: MEXICAN RABBIT

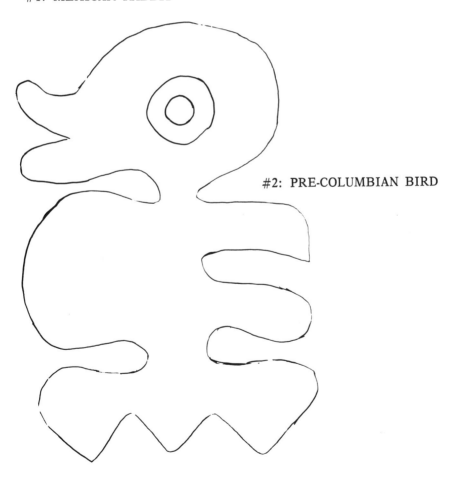

#2: PRE-COLUMBIAN BIRD

#3: MEXICAN OWL

#4: MEXICAN BIRD

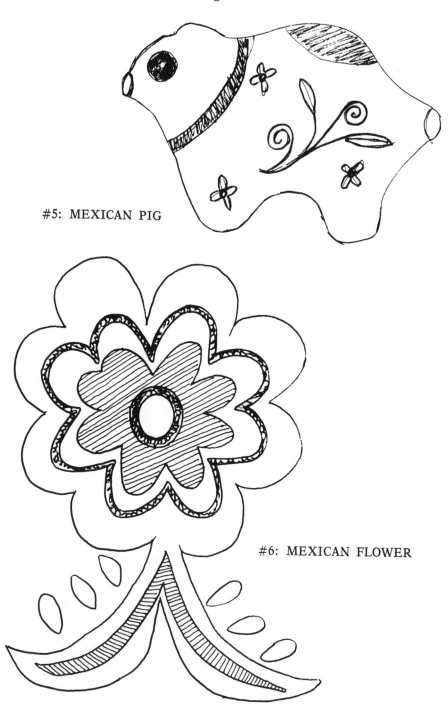

#5: MEXICAN PIG

#6: MEXICAN FLOWER

#7: "LOLLIPOP TREE AND FLOWERS"
a needlepoint design by Nina Katz, age 5

#8: ANY WORD WILL DO . . .

LOVE, PEACE or your name...

— copy other lettering styles from newspaper headlines and advertisements; cut them out and play with different arrangements.

#9: SEVERAL FLOWER SHAPES

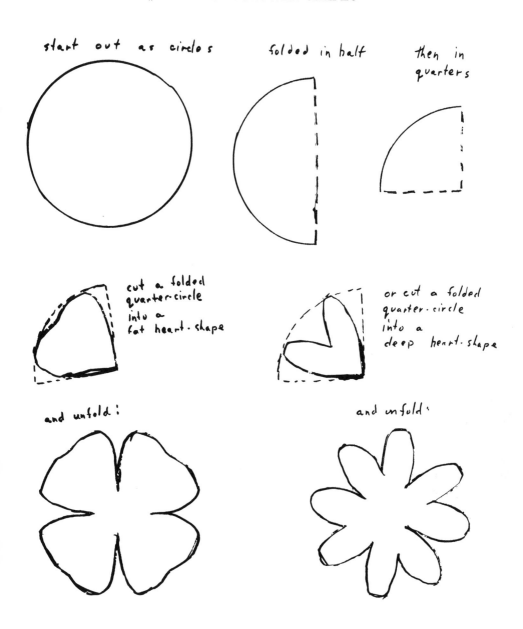

start out as circles

folded in half

then in quarters

cut a folded quarter-circle into a fat heart-shape

or cut a folded quarter-circle into a deep heart-shape

and unfold:

and unfold:

add contrasting circles
for centers ...

... or make the same flower shape out
of two or three circles of different sizes
and arrange them in layers so the larger
petals show behind the smaller ones.

... a very different
effect is the result
of repeating the basic
flower shape with
uneven concentric curves.
Work these in different
shades of The same
color, with an occasional
contrasting band

#10: MORE FLOWER SHAPES

add a stem —
just a simple curved
line. Leaves are ovals
attached on alternate
sides of the stem; or a
spiral that starts from
the stem.

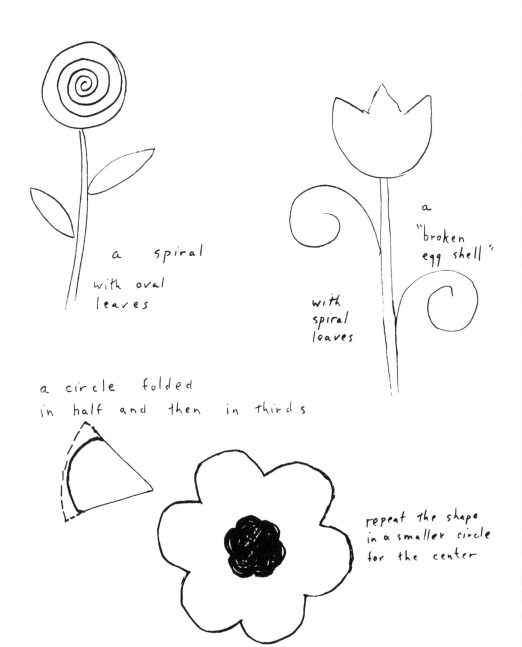

a   spiral

with oval
leaves

a
"broken
egg shell"

with
spiral
leaves

a circle folded
in half and then in thirds

repeat the shape
in a smaller circle
for the center

#11: SIMPLE ANIMAL SHAPES

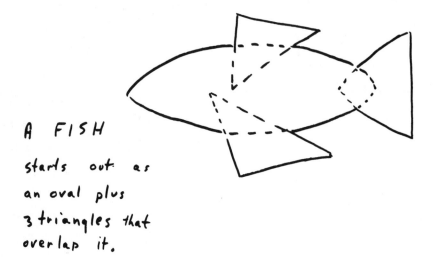

A FISH

starts out as
an oval plus
3 triangles that
overlap it.

make the
triangle sides
wavy.

... a butterfly is two hearts...

... add a center oval that extends for feelers, and repeat the basic shape

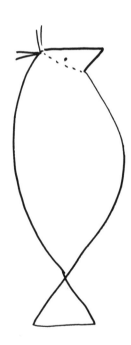

a bird is an oval with two triangles...

... change the shape slightly and add "L's" for legs. A "U" indicates a wing.

A WHALE

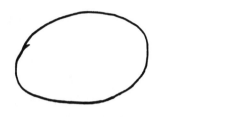

... start with a fat oval   ... add a half-moon

... a U and a shallow S

Flatten one end of the oval, put all the shapes
and send some water spouting up

Flatten one end of the oval, put all the shapes together
and send some water spouting up

#12: PAPER DOLLS

To make PAPER DOLLS:

begin with
accordion-folded paper
and draw half-doll as shown;
then cut through all layers,
and unfold.

#13: START WITH A COMMA

The basic Paisley shape is a fat comma, something like a crook-necked squash.

Enlarge it, repeat it, and tuck them in next to each other to create your own variation of a classic Paisley. Work it in concentric rows. Fill in the center or any row, with a contrasting pattern.

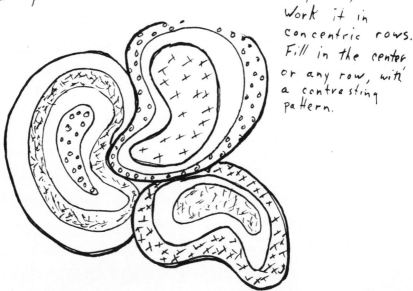

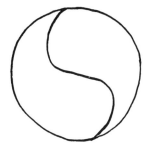

Make the Yin-Yang symbol with a shallow S-curve across the center of a circle, forming 2 Paisley units.

overlap two Paisley units and extend the center oval to form a flower shape

repeat the outer curves, add a few small ovals, a stem, and a heart-shaped leaf

#14: BUILD A SKYLINE OR A CITYSCAPE

make paper cut out "blocks" and put them next to and on top of each other. Fill in windows and doors if you like

start with

shapes like these:

#15: BULL'S-EYE

For embroidered throw pillow or wall hanging, work in two or more colors, using worsted or mohair yarn on homespun or burlap.

Start with a French knot for center of bull's eye. Change colors, work a circle of chain stitches around French knot. Change colors, work a second chain stitch circle around and close to the first. Continue changing colors and working concentric circles until your bull's-eye is as big you want it to be. It doesn't have to be in the center of your pillow or hanging.

Then start a second bull's-eye nearby, with a French knot in the center as before and concentric circles of chain stitch in alternating colors around it.

Add a third bull's-eye, or as many as needed to fill your fabric area. Vary the size of the bull's-eyes as desired. Work chain stitches loosely so as not to pull the fabric out of shape. If a bull's-eye is going to collide with one already worked, pretend it is partially hidden behind the first one and work only ⅞ of the circle, or however much you can work without overlapping.

#16: LAZY DAISY

For an embroidered throw pillow or wall hanging, work in embroidery floss or crewel (or sport) yarn on linen or homespun.

For a throw pillow, you can use a linen table napkin as the background. Limit yourself to two or three shades of each of two or three colors. (I used shades of pink and orange on a yellow napkin.)

Work lazy daisy stitch flowers at random all over the fabric. Make French knot centers. Vary sizes of flowers. Change colors. For variety, scatter some straight-stitch flowers between. Trim pillow or hanging with drapery rope or braid in one of the colors you've used.

#17: STARFLOWERS

For embroidered wall hanging or throw pillow, use embroidery floss or crewel (or sport) yarn on linen, or worsted on heavier weight fabric such as homespun.

This design is most effectively done in two shades of one color on a contrasting background. (I used two blues on a tawny gold homespun.)

Make starflowers on fabric by working double cross stitches of various sizes at random.

Vary it for a hanging by attaching each flower to a long straight backstitch or outline stitch stem. Have all stems absolutely straight and parallel to each other, all ending on a cross-stitched bar or ground. But make flowers of different sizes and at varying heights.

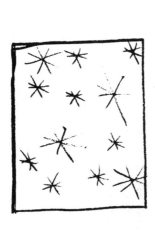
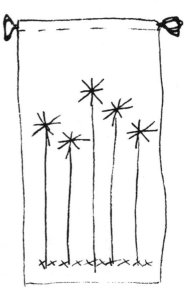

#18: PANES

For embroidery or needlepoint throw pillow or wall hanging, work in embroidery floss or crewel-weight yarn on linen or homespun; needlepoint or worsted yarn on burlap or 8 to 10-mesh canvas; or rug yarn on 4 to 5-mesh canvas. (This basic geometric, and the several sketches in #19, can also, of course, be adapted to paint and canvas or plywood, too.) Use at least two colors, as many as five.

1. Start at center of fabric by working a square with three vertical stitches each covering three squares of canvas or six threads of fabric.

2. Change colors and work a concentric square around center, keeping stitches same size and going in the same direction (you are actually working in 3-stitch blocks). Make two more concentric squares of vertical stitches, changing colors for each.

3. When the fourth square is completed, do not change colors; continue working with same color to make the fourth concentric square of the adjoining pane, which will share one side of its outermost square with its neighbor. Then work two concentric squares inside, and last the 3-stitch center.

4. Count threads or meshes to figure where to start the next pane. Continue to work this way, in concentric squares, until you cover your fabric or canvas.

diagram of "Panes"
designed for 4 colors

D	D	D	D	D	D	D	D	D	D	D	D	D
D	C	C	C	C	C	D	C	C	C	C	C	D
D	C	B	B	B	C	D	C	B	B	B	C	D
D	C	B	A	B	C	D	C	B	A	B	C	D
D	C	B	B	B	C	D	C	B	B	B	C	D
D	C	C	C	C	C	D	C	C	C	C	C	D
D	D	D	D	D	D	D	D	D	D	D	D	D
D	C	C	C	C	C	D	C	C	C	C	C	D
D	C	B	B	B	C	D	C	B	B	B	C	D
D	C	B	A	B	C	D	C	B	A	B	C	D
D	C	B	B	B	C	D	C	B	B	B	C	D

#19: DIAGRAMS OF OTHER GEOMETRICS
FOR EMBROIDERY AND NEEDLEPOINT

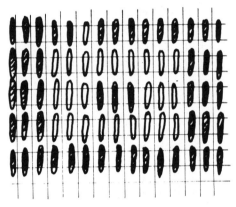

needle point design
using Gobelin stitch
and two colors

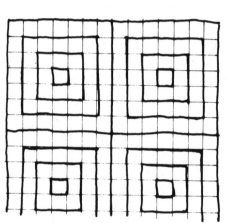

make your own diagram
on graph paper and
use crayon to test
color schemes

C	C	C	C	C	C	C	C	C
C	C	C	C	C	C	C	C	C
C	C	B	B	B	B	B	C	C
C	C	B	B	B	B	B	C	C
C	C	B	B	A	B	B	C	C
C	C	B	B	B	B	B	C	C
C	C	B	B	B	B	B	C	C
C	C	C	C	C	C	C	C	C
C	C	C	C	C	C	C	C	C

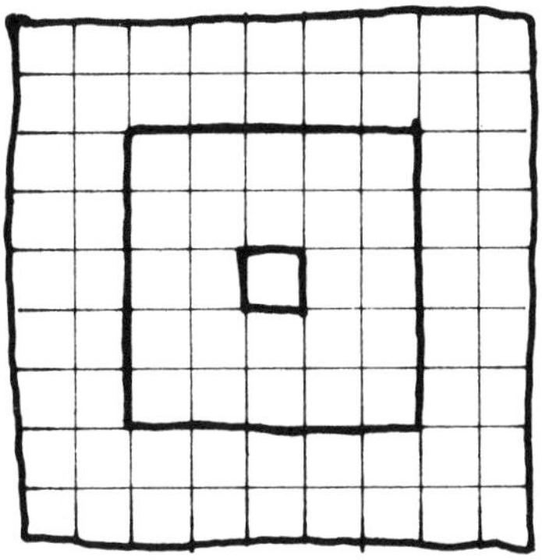

D	D	D	D	D	D	D	D	D
D	D	C	C	C	C	C	C	C
D	D	C	C	B	B	B	B	C
D	D	C	C	B	B	A	B	C
D	D	C	C	B	B	B	B	C
D	D	C	C	B	B	B	B	C
D	D	C	C	C	C	C	C	C
D	D	C	C	C	C	C	C	C
D	D	D	D	D	D	D	D	D
D	D	D	D	D	D	D	D	D

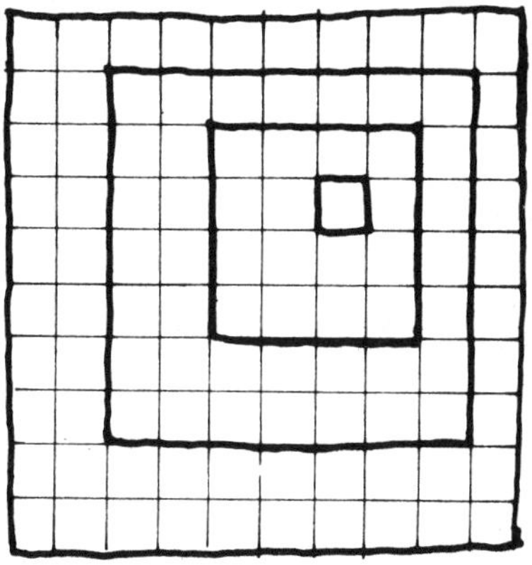

—keep repeating
them to fill your
cloth or canvas

This one has an
"op art" quality —
if the colors gradually
darken toward the
center, it will seem
as though the center
is getting further away
from you as you look
at it. But if the
colors gradually get
lighter or brighter
toward the center,
it will seem as
though the center is
coming toward you.

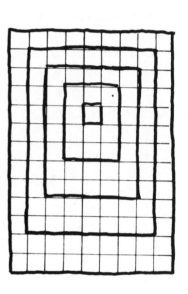

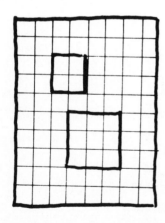

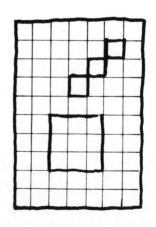

#20: DESIGNED FOR DINING

Work a bright hanging for a dark kitchen corner on a linen dishtowel, on a place mat, or a table napkin. Or on anything else that you have around the house.

For your design, draw whatever is typical of *your* kitchen.

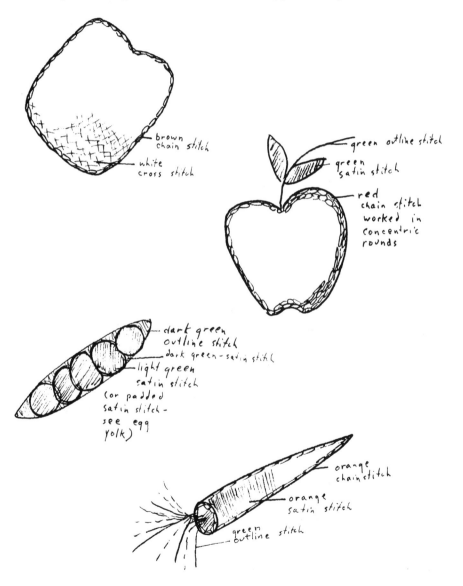

brown
chain stitch

white
cross stitch

green outline stitch

green
satin stitch

red
chain stitch
worked in
concentric
rounds

dark green
outline stitch
dark green - satin stitch
light green
satin stitch
(or padded
satin stitch -
see egg
yolk)

orange
chain stitch

orange
satin stitch

green
outline stitch

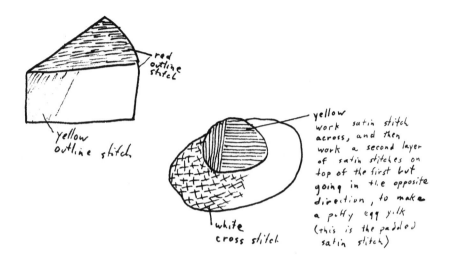

Copy the pattern of your dinnerware (put a piece of wax paper over a dinner plate, and trace with felt-tipped marker; transfer your design to fabric with carbon paper). Or sketch a favorite casserole or salad bowl; create a "still life" by arranging the fruits and vegetables in your refrigerator crisper on the table; or trace around your eggbeater, meat pounder and rolling pin. You can also copy some of your favorite kitchen wares from magazine and department store advertisements. Or copy my designs.

Use a variety of stitches—whatever you feel like. Your stitches can create such varied textures as a waxy cheese covering (closely worked rows of outline stitch), a spongy slice of bread (rows of cross stitches), a shiny apple, a puffy-yolked sunny-side-up. Do your embroidery free-hand, placing stitches next to each other by using your eye. You do not have to draw each cross stitch first!

Trace or draw designs on paper first. Then cut them out and place them on your fabric in an arrangement that seems right. Pin paper patterns in place on fabric, trace around them, remove and embroider.

❧ XI ❧

Something Else

Or, What Something You Would Otherwise Throw Away Can Be Turned Into

Or *recycling*. These days, finding new uses for old things instead of throwing them out is fashionable. Everybody's talking about recycling; what are you doing about it?

One girl collects empty whiskey and wine bottles from restaurants, cuts off the tops and sands the rough edges smooth, producing beautiful tumblers and vases with a hand-crafted look. Her minimal investment in special glass-cutting and polishing equipment was recouped when her output was accepted for sale at a New York department store.

Turning orange crates into bookshelves is an old story. But how would you feel about a coffee table whose top is a black steel subway grating or manhole cover that rests on a cinder-block base? What can you say about a sofa found in an auto junkyard (that's right—it was the rear seat!)? Or a lamp table that's really a black-enameled stack of car wheels?

Time magazine recently coined the word REJASE—recycling junk as something else—to describe what is happening as people try to find new uses for old stuff that would otherwise be thrown away. And their researchers uncovered some pretty far-out ideas. Would you believe place mats made from old X-rays? Or an old-woman-in-the-shoe table centerpiece featuring real, used Army boots? Or a sofa that was once a bathtub (the old-fashioned kind with legs) with one side cut away?

Among the weird recycling projects I've heard about are sculptures made from discarded throat swabs (by a doctor who removes the cotton tips and sterilizes the swabs before gluing them together), and ponchos knitted from yarn spun from dogs' hair combings!

A few of the projects uncovered by *Time* sounded better.

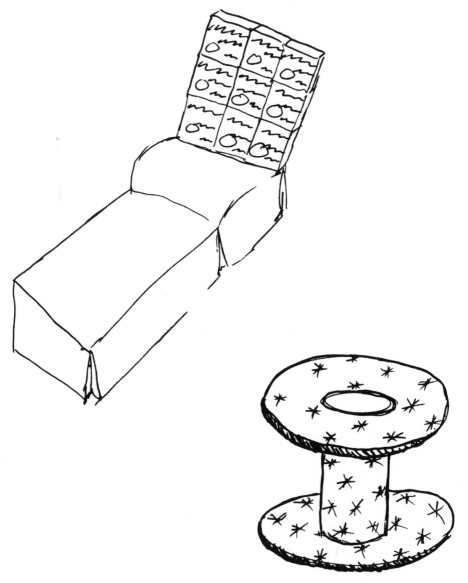

I like the pop art headboard made for a child's room from discarded cereal or snack boxes glued directly to the wall (I'd use wallpaper paste and spray with clear vinyl afterward). As soon as I find a spare wall I'm going to try gluing styrofoam packing materials onto it for a fascinating sculptural effect. And someday I'll make a patio or cocktail table from one of those enormous spools that hold industrial cable.

But you don't have to be ecology-minded to like the idea of creating something new and useful out of something old and useless. You could be the kind of pack-rat who can't discard a bleach bottle or coffee can without thinking, "Shouldn't I save it . . . perhaps some day I'll think of something to do with it." This, of course, is exactly my problem.

My first recycling project dates me: as a little girl, I used the gauze strips that protected Band-Aids as curtains for doll house windows. Nowadays, I find myself accumulating too much junk because it might someday be useful. Periodically, I donate my collection to a children's arts and crafts class, and see the mturn wire hangers into bird-like sculptures, coffee cans into drums and all sorts of odds and ends into imaginative collages. Since I couldn't possibly find time to use all the waste our family produces, this is an ideal solution.

Even if, like us, you are sorting your trash and separating reusable paper, cans and bottles for recycling, you undoubtedly accumulate pounds of other possibly useful junk every week. So here are some of my favorite ideas for recycling otherwise useless materials.

#1: A SECOND USE FOR NEWSPAPER

When old newspaper, tissue paper and paper toweling are used to make papier-mâché, they can be turned into bud vases, trays, pad-and-pencil caddies, and all manner of useful things. Don't buy the commercially prepared papier-mâché mixtures; what is the point? You can make up a batch yourself with very little fuss and put waste products to good use at the same time. And you can score a double for ecology by using supermarket packaging leftovers, such as meat and vegetable trays and plastic berry baskets, as the bases for several papier-mâché projects.

There are countless ways to produce papier-mâché. My favorite recipe starts with about 48 pages of the *New York Times* (double the number of pages if your raw material comes in tabloid form!), torn up into small pieces and heaped in a large pot or bowl. (Let the children help; this can be a tedious, as well as dirty, part of the job. Tearing up all that paper is a great hostility-releaser for children.) Cover the torn paper with warm water, stir around well with your hands, and let stand at least an hour or even overnight. Paper should be good and mushy. Pour off any excess water, and set pulp aside.

Into another bowl measure approximately two cups of pulp (three or four handfuls). Add the contents of an 8-ounce container of white glue and knead together well. *Or* blend together 1 cup flour, 1 cup water and 1 tablespoon salt, and knead into pulp; add ½ cup white glue and knead again. This is my *Gluey Pulp* method.

An alternate recipe also starts with torn newspaper (or tissue paper) heaped in a bowl. Tear strips about 1" by 2". In a small cup or bowl, mix 1 part white glue and 1 part water. To cover something with papier-mâché: dip a paper strip into glue mixture until it is saturated and place it on object to be covered. Dip a second paper strip and place it overlapping the first. Continue dipping and overlapping the glue-saturated paper strips until object is covered with five or six layers; or more if greater thickness and strength are desired. I call this the *Strip* method.

Make a bud vase. Take a large handful of Gluey Pulp, bunch or roll it into a cylinder about the length of your hand, and squeeze gently to form a narrow neck section. Holding this section firmly in one hand, use the other to poke a pencil or other long object down into the center of the cylinder. With fingers pack pulp firmly about pencil. Twist pencil and pull gently to remove. Tap closed bottom of cylinder gently on table a few times to make the base level. Use fingers to pinch out top of cylinder into a decorative top for vase. Add more Gluey Pulp if needed to extend or smooth edges. Use fingers to smooth vase all over as much as possible. Let dry (stand it on a plate or pie tin, or on waxed paper or foil). When dry, you can rub with sandpaper to smooth a bit more. Despite your

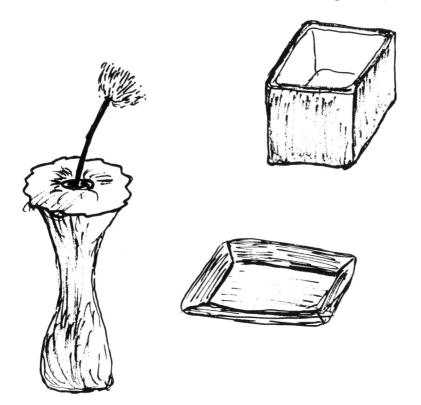

best efforts, however, it will retain a certain bumpy texture that is its greatest charm. Then decorate. It will hold one perfect rose, or dandelion.

Make a planter. Start with one of the plastic or cardboard containers that berries are sold in. Take a clump of Gluey Pulp and press it onto the outside and inside of the berry basket. Keep taking clumps of pulp and pressing them onto basket, being sure to cover it all around and on both sides of the bottom. Press pulp to thin it out as much as possible; it will still have a chunky, solid look, however. Let dry with basket inside. *Or,* cover berry basket with the Strip method, inside and out. This will result in a much thinner-walled container. When dry, decorate. Insert a flower-holder, arrange flowers and greenery and use as a centerpiece. Or place a plant in a clay pot inside. Make a row of planters for a shelf or window sill.

Make a serving tray. Start with one of the plastic, styrofoam or cardboard trays that meats or fruits are sold in. Cover by Strip method. You can build up the sides to make them higher by simply extending the strips of glued paper. Trim and level the sides while still damp, using a sharp scissors. Let dry, and decorate.

Make a pad-and-pencil caddy. Start with a large flat container such as a 12-inch round cake pan, skillet, plate or tray. (I used the lid of a covered mixing bowl.) Rub this mold with oil or vaseline. Either press Gluey Pulp into it, or use six or more layers of Strips to cover it completely. It should be about ½″ thick. This is the caddy back. Take a cardboard meat or fruit tray and cut it in half. One half will form the pocket for a notepad. Cut the other half in half again. One of these small sections will form the pencil holder. Use Strips to attach the two pockets to the caddy back and cover pockets with Strips, too. With fingers or a knife, cut a small semi-circle out of the top of the caddy back and insert a screw eye, slanted slightly toward the back, for hanging. Secure screw eye by pressing papier-mâché about it firmly and then add several narrow Strips of glue newspaper. Let caddy dry. Remove from mold and decorate.

Papier-mâché can be decorated by painting with acylics or enamels. If you use poster or tempera paint, a coating of shellac is needed. Or you can tear colored tissue or crepe paper into strips and glue them on over newspaper, as in the Strip method. Spray with clear vinyl for a hard, protective finish.

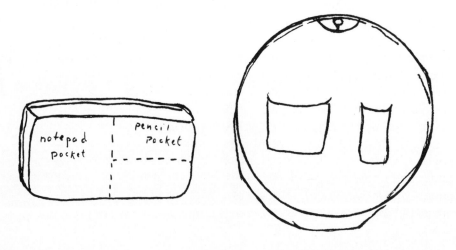

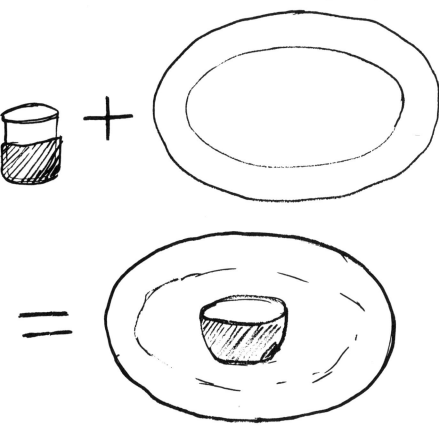

The tissue- or crepe-paper colors will show up more clearly if strips of white tissue paper are used for a layer or two directly underneath.

You can mold papier-mâché in or around almost anything, provided that the object is first coated with vaseline or oil, or wrapped with waxed paper. Try making a chip-and-dip server by molding a large platter or tray and a bowl or cup, and then attaching the cup shape in the center with glued strips of newspaper. When dry, decorate as desired, and spray with two coats of clear vinyl for an easy-to-clean surface. If you use paper plates or paper cups as molds, they can be left in place under the papier-mâché covering. (And if you reserve once-used paper plates and cups to use as the base of papier-mâché projects, you get a gold star for Recycling Junk As Something Else!)

#2: USE BROKEN CRAYONS AND CANDLE STUBS

My daughter brought home from school this easy way to make use of waxy odds and ends, and taught me how to make chunky, colorful candles.

Make new candles. Save candle stubs and broken candles. Every bit of wax counts—the leftover skinny birthday candles as well as the too-short leftover tapers. And save broken crayons (or ask a friend with young children to give theirs to you; since children break crayons at a prodigious rate, you'll receive an ample supply). Use plastic sandwich bags to sort both candle stubs and crayons by colors. You'll also need other leftovers: thick cotton string, once-used paper hot-drink cups, and some ice-cream or lollipop sticks. (You get two gold stars for this project!) You can label a shopping bag "candle-making materials" and accumulate your leftovers in it. When the shopping bag is loaded, you're ready to get to work.

You'll need a double boiler, a small bowl or pan, a scissors and wooden spoon or ruler for stirring. If you don't want to risk a good double boiler, you can improvise by setting a soda or coffee can in a saucepan. If you do, pinch the rim of the can first to make a pouring lip. Always melt wax over hot water; never heat wax directly over the flame or it may splatter.

Bring some water to a boil in the bottom of the double boiler. Cut candle stubs to remove old wicks. If you don't have enough wax from old candle stubs, you can always buy a package of paraffin. Place wax pieces in top of double boiler and let stand over simmering water until melted.

Meanwhile, cut crayon into teeny pieces by twisting through a pencil sharpener and collecting the shavings, by grating on a wire grater held over the pot of wax, or simply by scraping with a knife. Stir crayon pieces into the hot wax until they melt and the wax is either marbled or evenly tinted throughout, as you prefer.

Cut cotton cord an inch or two longer than the heights of the paper cups you are using to mold the candles. This will be the wicking. Tie one end of wicking around an ice cream stick or anything else—a butter knife, perhaps—that is long enough to fit across the top of the paper cup but not so heavy that it would tip the cup over. Hold on to the stick and dip the wick-

ing in melted wax, and place on a plate or on waxed paper to set. Dip end of wick in melted wax again, and drop into cup, placing stick across top of cup. Slowly pour in melted wax, filling the paper cup as high as you like, or up to about ½" from the top.

Meanwhile, fill a small bowl or pan with cold water. Carefully, so as not to disturb the wicking, lift a wax-filled paper cup and place in cold water. This will set the candle quickly. Add ice cubes to the cold water for faster action. Or simply set filled cup aside until candle hardens.

When candle is set, tear off paper cup, cut off wick holder, and enjoy your candle.

Wick note: Candle will harden from the outside in. When the outside is hard but the inside, although somewhat cooled, is still soft, the wick can be inserted with the fingers.

More notes: 1) Use the bottom three or four inches of a milk container instead of a paper cup.

2) It's a good idea to wear a smock or an apron when making candles.

3) If wax gets on clothing, remember that hot water or a hot iron will melt wax out of cloth.

Idea! Make striped Christmas candles. Save green and red crayons all year, and make up two pots of melted wax, one in each color. Pour an inch of red into your candle mold first, dip in ice water until partly set; then pour in about an inch of green wax. Dip again to set, and continue until your mold

is filled. Or pour in red wax and set the mold on its side in ice water; when partly hardened, pour in green wax and turn to set another side. Continue pouring and turning mold until it is filled with alternate uneven vertical stripings of holiday colors.

#3: TURN A WOODEN TRIMMING RACK INTO...

A Mug Rack

MATERIALS:
>   wooden trimming rack (your local notions or trimming shop will probably be glad to save its discards for you)
>   4 cup hooks
>   4 rectangular lead weights
>   a small piece of felt (adhesive-backed if possible)
>   sandpaper and enamel or acrylic paint

HOW-TO:
1. Remove paper from trimming rack by pulling it off and, if necessary, soaking in water to remove the rest.
2. Sand rack if necessary.
3. Paint as desired. Leave bottom of broader end (base) unpainted.
4. Turn rack upside down. Mark underside of *top* of rack at equal intervals—you should have four marks about 2 inches apart. Insert cup hooks at marks.
5. Glue weights to bottom of base to make it sturdy.
6. To cover bottom of base with adhesive-backed felt (or glue on plain felt): trace around base on paper backing of felt. Cut just *outside* of traced outline. Felt

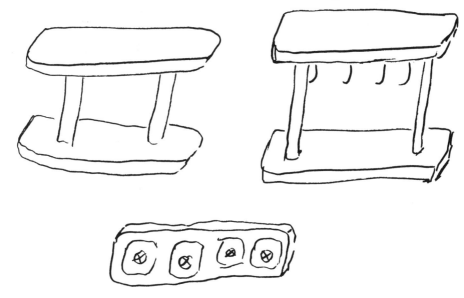

is somewhat stretchy and you can easily work it with your fingers to fit around weights.

Idea! Place cup hooks a bit closer together and hang six after-dinner coffee cups. Tack narrow moldings to top of rack to form a snug place for the saucers.

Another idea! Loop necklaces, bracelets or hair ribbons over cup hooks, and place rack on dressing table instead of kitchen counter.

Or a Pipe Stand

Do it the same way, but omit cup hooks. Instead, you'll need white glue, and about 2 yards of sisal twine or a thick rope like clothesline.

1. Follow directions above (except for 4).
2. Measure length of rack; cut piece of twine twice as long as this measurement. This will form the support for the pipe stems. Double-knot twine around each post of rack, about halfway between top and bottom. Pull ends to knot tightly, and cut off ends close to rack. Turn rack upside down and squeeze white glue on underside of knot and into crevice between twine and post. Let dry.
3. Meanwhile, make the supports for the pipe bowls. Cut three or four 8-inch lengths of twine. Take one between

fingers and loop into a double ring with ends together. Squeeze white glue on ends and between two strands, gluing completely around ring. Hold for a few minutes until glue begins to set and ring holds its shape, or use a spring-type clothespin to clamp. Set aside to dry, and make rings of the other short pieces of twine.

4. When all glue is dry, or almost dry, glue rings into place at intervals across upper side of rack bottom.
5. Brush all rope with 1 part white glue diluted with 1 part water. Let glue solution sink into rope. Let dry.

#4: NEW USES FOR OLD BOXES

There's more than one way to cover a box, and the easiest (and sometimes the sloppiest) is with paint. Simply brush or spray, inside and/or outside of box, with the paint of your choice. Enamel is best—it won't rub off on fingers after it dries, as tempera will; and it will thoroughtly cover up the original box.

To cover a box with paper, foil, fabric or adhesive-backed vinyl, you can try

1. *The One-Side-at-a-Time Method.* Measure each side or face of box. Cut a separate piece of covering material to fit each side and glue in place (white glue will do for most materials that are not adhesive-backed, and for most boxes). When all sides are covered, cover up the edges—and any "mistakes" such as gaps or lumpy spots—with narrow adhesive-backed cloth or vinyl tape, or by gluing narrow ribbon, lace or braid along edges. You can line a box by this method, too, one inside panel at a time.

2. *The Bottoms-First Method.* Cut covering material ½" larger all around than bottom of box. Glue to bottom. Slash margin diagonally at corners and turn up, folding neatly around bottom edges. Cut a rectangle of covering material long enough to go around all four sides of box plus 1", and the height of the box plus 1". Glue around box, creasing sharply at corners and overlapping the extra inch at one side. The excess 1" in height should be sticking up at the top. Slash

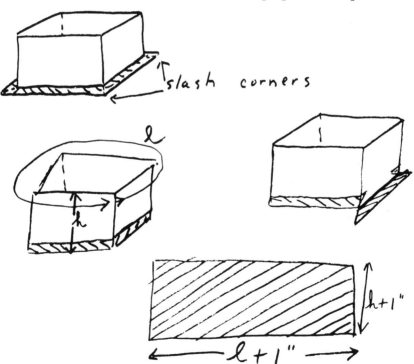

slash corners

ℓ

h

$h+1$"

$\ell+1$"

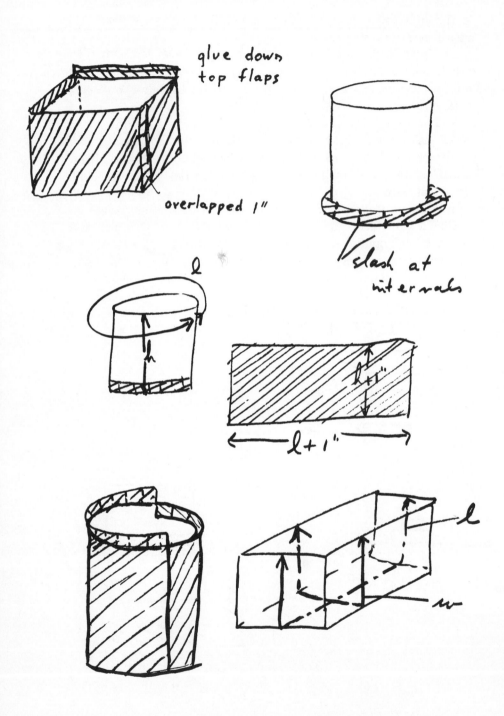

glue down
top flaps

overlapped 1"

slash at
intervals

ℓ

$\ell + 1"$

$\ell + 1"$

ℓ

w

it through the corners, fold each of the four flaps neatly to inside and glue in place.

Bottoms-first is the best way to cover a round container, like a coffee can, an oatmeal box or an ice cream carton. Slash top and bottom margins at intervals of about ¾" all around and fold down or up neatly; glue in place.

3. *The All-Together-Now Method* works best for smaller boxes. Cut covering material into a rectangle whose length is the total of two opposite sides plus the bottom and whose width is the total of the two *other* opposite sides plus the *other* measurement of the bottom (follow diagram). Glue bottom. Cut out corners. Glue sides up. Glue trim over edges.

Get double recycling points by covering boxes with wall-paper leftovers or samples; newspaper (try color comics or the financial pages, sprayed with clear vinyl); a montage of greeting-card cutouts; or fabric remnants.

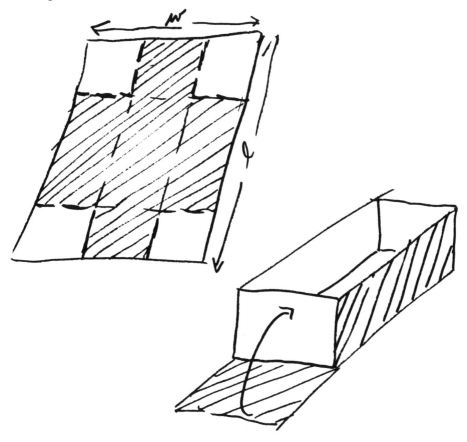

Trim a box with:

a) Adhesive-backed cloth or plastic tape, foil or wood-grain tape;

b) Glued-on grosgrain ribbon, rickrack, soutache or other braid, bright acrylic yarn, twine, whatyouwill;

c) Glued-on frogs to close as well as trim; use matching ribbon for added decoration.

Make a recipe file. Cover a shoebox and its lid with magazine pages of recipes and pictures of foods or utensils, using the One-Side-at-a-Time method. Spray with clear vinyl for a wipe-clean surface. Line with adhesive-backed vinyl to match your kitchen shelves. Glue the bottom of an egg slicer (get a plastic one in a coordinating color) to the lid; its slots will hold your recipes so you can read them while you cook.

Make a toy or storage chest. Take two heavy corrugated cardboard cartons, or 1 carton and a large sheet of corrugated cardboard. Cut top off one box, using a craft knife or razor blade. Cut off labels and any tape on the box that is not needed to hold the box together. Spray-paint the outside of the box. If necessary, to make the box stronger cut a section of cardboard (either from the second box or from the sheet of cardboard) to fit exactly inside the bottom of the box, and glue it in place.

Make a lid for the chest by cutting a piece of cardboard (from the second carton or the sheet cardboard) the length plus 6″ and the width plus 3″ of the box (see diagram). Use

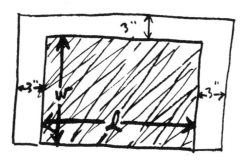

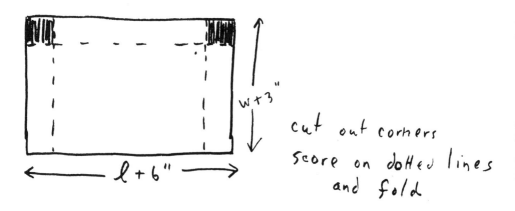

cut out corners
score on dotted lines
and fold

a razor blade and straight edge of ruler to score or cut partly through cardboard. Cut out corner square and fold on scored lines. Spray paint outside of lid.

Spray paint inside of box and lid, or line with felt or with adhesive-backed vinyl.

Trim box with contrasting adhesive-backed cloth tape. Use

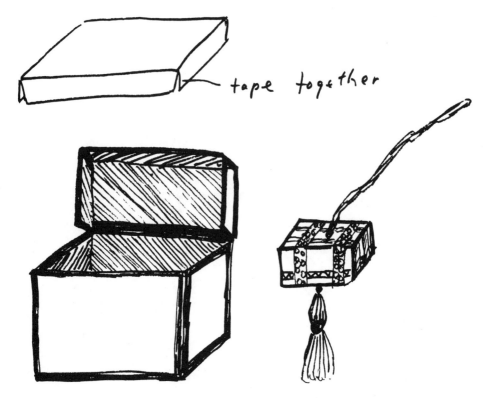

tape 1½ inches wide and center it on edges; fold tape to make a ¾″ border around each side of box. Use tape to attach front edges of lid to each other, taping inside and out. Place lid in position on box and tape across back at both outside and inside to form a hinged attachment. Add any other desired designs—shapes cut from felt and glued in place, or cut from adhesive-backed vinyl. Or add more cloth tape trim.

Make a light pull. Cover a small (3″ to 6″ long) box with colored paper or adhesive-backed vinyl. Cover bottom as in the Bottoms-First method; then cover the rest of the box, top and all, as in the All-Together-Now method. Trim by gluing narrow braid, lace, sequins or what you will on covered box. Thead a yarn needle with a yard of brightly colored acrylic rug yarn and push needle completely through box. Make a tassel out of more yarn and knot it onto yarn just below box. Or string a bead or button on the bottom and knot yarn securely. Fasten long end of yarn to the chain of the light fixture.

Make a twine caddy. Cover a 1-pound coffee can as desired, using the Bottoms-First method. Cut two holes in the plastic lid—a round hole in the center, and a rectangular one at one side. Put a ball of twine in can, pushing end of twine through hole in center of lid. Replace lid on can and insert point of scissors in rectangular slot.

Make a sewing box. Cover a cigar box as desired, using adhesive-backed cloth tape to reinforce hinge of lid both inside and out. Glue pin cushion to lid. Hammer 1½" nails up through bottom at intervals for spool holders. Make a needle box by trimming a cylindrical plastic pill container to match box; poke a hole in its plastic lid with a large needle. You can quickly slip a needle into this container through the hole in the lid, but the hole is too small for the needles to fall out.

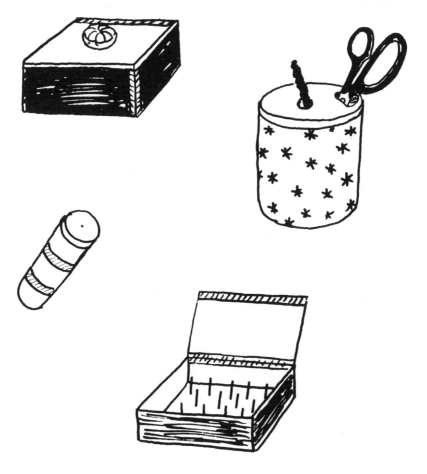

#5: WHAT YOU CAN DO WITH PILL CONTAINERS

You can turn them into a *makeup caddy* that becomes the striking focal point of a dressing-table set.

1. Attach four or more small cylindrical plastic pill containers to each other and be sure to keep their bottoms even. Use white glue, polymer medium or plastic model cement used for painting model airplanes. Glue to inside of the plastic lid from a coffee can. Let dry. Paint to suit your bedroom or dressing-room decor, using acrylic paints or the small jars of enamel for painting model airplanes. Caddy holds several lipsticks, mascara tubes and makeup brushes.

2. Make a *dressing-table tray* to match, from an inexpensive picture frame. Remove glass, mat and backing. Discard mat, and cover the frame and backing as desired (see directions in chapter 4). Leftover wallpaper or fabric from bedspread or other bedroom furnishings can be used to cover backing; use a coordinating solid-color adhesive-backed vinyl for the frame. Replace glass and backing in frame. Attach adhesive-backed rubber bumpers (from hardware store) to wrong side of frame, one in each corner, or cover wrong side of frame with felt.

3. Then make a *comb-and-brush caddy* by covering a juice or coffee can to match (use Bottoms-First method described for previous project). Line with contrasting color.

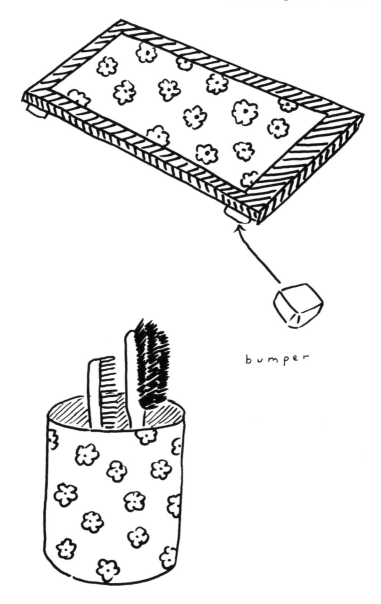

bumper

4. Other accessories you might want to cover to match: a table-top scrap paper basket from a 2-pound size coffee can or a cardboard ice cream container; a curler tote from a coffee can; a picture frame; an address book. See project 3 in this chapter for a jewelry rack you can also design to match.

#6: USE EMPTY EGG CARTONS

As a Wall-Covering. Even your best friend won't be able to tell how you achieved that marvelously sculptured, colorful effect. But you'll know you did it this way:

Save empty egg cartons; and ask everybody you know (except the friend you might want to fool) to save them for you, too. Cut off the lids (recycle them as serving trays by covering with papier-mâché; see project 1) and nest the compartmented sections for neat storage. When you've got several dozen, you're ready to get started.

Spread wallpaper paste (the kind used for vinyls and other heavier wall-coverings) over a section of your wall, and press an egg-carton bottom into it. Then press another and another, adding more paste when necessary, until your wall, or a large section of it, is covered. Arrange the cartons horizontally, vertically, or in a zigzag combination—whatever you like. (Spread them out on the floor to get the effect. You can use string to mark off an area on the floor that is the size of the wall area to be covered, and test your arrangement in it, while at the same time you check to see whether you have enough egg cartons.)

Let dry thoroughly—at least three days. Then spray-paint with two coats of a bright gloss enamel—red, yellow, electric blue. Cover adjoining wall and floor areas with newspaper and masking tape to avoid paint fallout. Simply stunning.

As a ring and earring box. Keep lids on egg cartons for this one. Brush or spray-paint with enamel, inside and out. Glue a 5″ circle of velvet into each egg cup, spreading glue completely around the upper edge of the "cup" and letting the center of the velvet circle fall in a soft crush into the bottom. Glue a narrow strip of lace or ribbon to cover the raw edges of velvet around the top of each "cup." Place a set of earrings, a ring, a pin or any small single piece of jewelry into each compartment.

As a mold for permanent Easter eggs. Rub vaseline over the inside of each eggcup. Press papier-mâché (see project 1 above for recipe) into each cup, bringing it up to the top of each cup and making a half eggshell ¼″ to ½″ thick. Let dry. Remove half eggshells from egg cups; trim rims and fasten two

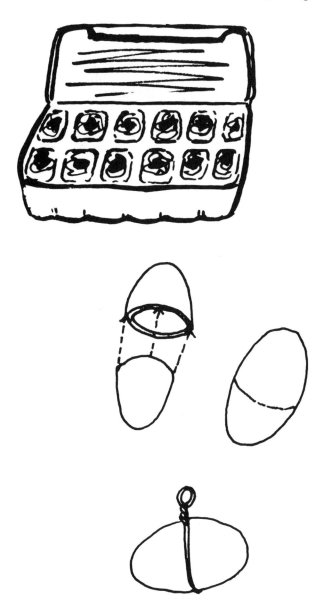

half shells together with glue-saturated strips of tissue paper, making one egg. Let dry, and paint or decorate as desired. (To use these as Christmas decorations instead, twist a 3″ piece of picture wire into a loop and insert between egg shell halves and secure with glued paper strips. Decorate appropriately.)

#7: USE OLD WRAPPING PAPER

And cover a wall. Save the wrapping paper from packages, bundles of laundry and so on. Save brown paper grocery bags, cut open on the side and bottom seams and flatten them. Fold all the brown paper neatly and store it away until you accumulate enough for your wall-covering project. Then buy wallpaper paste and 1 can of brown paste-wax shoe and boot polish.

Crinkle up a sheet of brown paper, smooth it out and paste it to your wall, starting in any corner. Crinkle up another paper and paste it to the wall, slightly overlapping the first. Continue crinkling and pasting until your wall is covered. Cut paper to fit around doors, moldings and other built-in features. Don't worry if you find that you've used up all your paper and covered only half of your wall. Just live with half a wall until you accumulate enough paper to complete the job. Half a wall done is better than none!

When paste is thoroughly dry—allow three nights at least— take a sponge or a soft cloth and rub shoe polish, a little bit at a time, onto the papered wall. Rub it on smoothly, just as you would if you were polishing a shoe. It will build up in the folds and cracks and produce an interesting leathery texture. Just keep rubbing until the paper, a large section at a time, is covered. Then buff wall lightly with a clean soft cloth. Spread polish on another section and buff until entire wall is covered.

Try this to perk up a dull, end-of-a-room wall or to add interest to a hall.

Idea! Make a jewelry box for a man by using old wrapping paper, crinkled, pasted and polished as above, to cover a cigar box. Edge with narrow gold braid, and line with green or brown felt.

#8: AND USE FROZEN-JUICE CANS

To cover a ceiling. A ceiling? Yes, of course. To create a fascinating, mysterious textured surface from which light bounces and flickers, reflected in dozens of miniature shades, to cast an exotic dappled glow over a room.

First, accumulate the small cans that frozen juices come in. The lightweight aluminum ones are best. Clean cans thoroughly. Leave as is, if you like. Or spray-paint with gloss

enamel in the color of your choice, inside and out. Test your ceiling to determine the proper adhesive to use. Try either linoleum adhesive or wall paneling adhesive for starters, getting a small can if possible. If you know what the finish on your ceiling is, you can ask your paint, lumber or hardware

dealer for suggestions. Following the directions on the can of
adhesive, spread it on a section of your ceiling and place a
juice-can bottom side up, in position, twisting it into the adhesive. Hold it in place for a minute or two, until adhesive begins to set. While holding the first can, you can add two or
three others next to it, supporting them all at the same time.
If your ceiling is cooperative, you should have the beginnings
of a smashing effect. If not, it may all come smashing down.
In that case, try try again with a different adhesive.

You can place cans in neat rows, side by side, or you can alternate them. Either way, the effect is fascinating. Try bright
yellow or green cans for a kitchen ceiling, gloss black for a
den. If there is a ceiling fixture, arrange cans in a neat square
or circle around it. And start your ceiling here, working outward to the walls. Otherwise, start in the most prominent
corner.

Index

Acrylic paints and mediums, 233–34. *See also* specific uses
Adhesive-backed materials, 234–36. *See also* specific types, uses
Adhesives. *See* Glues
Afghan patchwork, 207–20; pillow of, 71–72
Afghan stitch, 239
Afghans, afghan-patch, 219
Aluminum foil, adhesive-backed, 234. *See also* specific items
Aluminum frames, 111
Animal design, 266
Antiques, 13–14; restoring frame, 111–12
Antiquing furniture, 259
Apple embroidery design, 287
Appliqué, 236. *See also* specific items, *e.g.*, Pillows, Window shades
Aprons: pillowcase pinafore-, 220–24; pillowcase shift-, 224–25; side-wrap skirt-, 226–29
Area rugs 57–58
Art, 95–150 (*See also* specific kinds); do-it-yourself, 125–50; galleries, 99–101 (*See also* Galleries, art)
Assemblage, 138–42; kitchen, 191–95
Austrian curtains, for canopies, 48
Auto collages, 137

Backstitch, 241
Baking center, 182
Ball fringe, uses for, 61, 91–93
Banners, wall-hanging, 154–58
Bars, rolling, 184, 185
Bathrooms: galleries in, 101; storage in, 188–90
Beams, painting, 54–55
Beds, 206; cereal-box headboards, 290, 291; cover-ups for, 43–48; in Environments, 23ff.; pictures over headboards, 102
Bedsheets for spreads, 43–44; tie-dyed, for wall hangings, 166
Belts: silk, 232; storage of, 201
Berets, afghan-patch, 213–14
Bird designs, 263–65, 274
Blanket stitch, 243

Boleros: afghan-patch, 210–13; bouncy, 229–31
Bonding tape, for appliqué, 236
Bookcases, rolling, 185-86
Books (*See also* Bookcases; Bookshelves): cookbooks in decorating, 193–94
Bookshelves, 180ff.; in Environments, 24ff.
Boots, storage for, 202
Boxes: decorating, uses for, 300–9; for headboard, cereal or snack, 290, 291; lucite (*See* Lucite)
Bracelets, storage ideas for, 202, 299
Braid (*See also* specific items to be decorated): appliquéing, 236
Branches mounted, 173–75
Bread embroidery design, 287
Bud vases, papier-mâché, 292–93
Building fragments, as sculpture, 142–43
Bulletin boards, 25, 181
Bull's-eye embroidery design, 281
Burlap: adhesive-backed, 234; for embroidery, 244; for picture backings, 114; for picture galleries, 169
Butcher blocks, as sculpture bases, 118–20
Butterfly design, 274
Buttons, as pillow decoration, 93

Cabinets: bathroom, 190; "dead" storage, 204–6; doors for galleries, 101; in Environments, 27; filing, 24, 180, 181; rehabilitating, 20, 22
Caddies. *See* specific uses
Café curtains, 37, 38
Candles, making. 296–98
Canopies, bed, 46–48
Canopy valances, 31–37; for beds, 47
Cans, uses for, 308, 309; for ceiling cover-ups, 312–14
CanTop assemblage, 139–40
Canvas. *See* specific uses
Cardboard. *See* Boxes; specific uses
Carpet tiles, 235

Carpeting, 13, 16; area rugs from, 57–58; in Environments, 27; remnants for patch-work rugs, 56; trimming and binding, 253–54; walls, 52–53
Carrot embroidery design, 287
Casters, 181–88
Ceiling cover, from juice cans, 312–14
Cellulose fiber wood filler, use of, 21
Chain stitches: crochet, 237; embroidery, 242
Chairs: in Environments, 24ff.; seat cover-ups, 58–60
Checkerboard afghan patchwork, 209, 210
Checkerboard floor cover-ups, 57
Cheese embroidery design, 287
Chests, 183; in Environments, 24ff.; rehabilitating, 20, 21–22; toy or storage, from boxes, 304–6
Chip-and-dip servers, papier-mâché, 295
Christmas candles, striped, 297–98
Chrome, in Environments, 27
Cityscape design, 280
Closets, 199–202; in Environments, 23ff.; rolling, 184
Cloth tape, adhesive-backed, 235. *See also* specific items to be decorated
Clothes: making, 207–32 (*See also* specific items); storage of, 199–202
Coffee tables, 183, 186
Coin collector's collage, 137
Collages, 136–38; wall cover-ups, 51
Color (*See also* specific items): collage, 138; for Environments, 27; scheme, 12, 14–17
Comb-and-brush caddies, 308, 309
Constructions, 145–50; cardboard tube, 146–47; hardware, 148–50; lucite, 145–46; scrap wood, 147–48
Contact cement, 247
Continental stitch, 249
Cookbooks, in decorating, 193–94
Cork panels, 181; in Environments, 25, 30
Cork wastebaskets, as sculpture bases, 120
Cotton batting, as pillow stuffing, 69–70
Cotton napkins, for pillows, 70
Cover-ups, 31–64

Crayons, candles made of, 296–98
Crepe paper, to decorate papier-mâché, 294–95
Crewel work, 236–37; pillows, 71, 74–75
Crocheting, 237–39. *See also* Afghan patchwork
Cross stitch, 240
Cross-stitched open seam, 164
Cup racks, from trimming racks, 299
Curler totes, from coffee cans, 309
Curtain rods. *See* specific uses
Curtains, 37, 38–40; Austrian, for canopies, 48
Cushions, seat cover-ups for, 58–60

"Dead" storage, 202–6
Designs: as art hang-ups, 125–36; portfolio of, 261–88
Desks, in Environments, 24ff.
Diamonds and boxes design, 284–86
Dirndl skirts, afghan-patch, 214–17
Dolls (*see also* Paper dolls): pillow, 76, 77
Donut tie-dye knot, 256, 257
Doors: as part of galleries, 101; paintings on, 54
Double-faced tape, 235. *See also* Mounting tape
Draperies, striped, 38–40
Drawer-pulls, removing and cleaning, 20
Drawers: as chairside tables, 17–18; in Environments, 23, 25; in rehabilitating furniture, 20, 21–22
Drawings, 123. *See also* Designs
Dressers (*See also* chests): pictures over, 102
Driftwood art, 171–72
Dry cleaning, for delicate fabrics, 151
Duck design, 263
Dyeing (*See also* Tie-dyeing): wicker and wood, 259; window-shade decoration, 41–42

Earring boxes, egg-carton, 310
Easter eggs, permanent, 310–11
Egg cartons, uses for, 310–11
Egg embroidery design, 287
Embroidery, 240–44 (*See also* Crewel work); design portfolio, 281–88; on pillows, 71, 74ff.; on wall hanging, 160–62
Environments, 22–30
Epoxy cement, 122, 247; Marine Compound, 122, 248

Fabrics, 16. *See also* specific kinds, uses
Feather pillows, for throw pillows, 67
Felt: appliqué, 236 (*See also* specific items to be decorated); banners, 154–58; "headboards," 44–45; pillows and covers, 70–71, 77–79, 82, 86–87, 88; -tipped markers, 244–45; wall covering, 51–52
Files, recipe, 304
Filing cabinets, 180, 181; for desks in Environments, 24
First-apartment collage, 137
Fish design, 275
Fixatives, 245
Floor pillows, from feather pillows, 67
Floor plans, 16; for Environments, 24–27
Floors (*See also* Carpeting): cover-ups, 56–58
Flower designs, 266–67, 269–73, 279, 281–82
Flower pots, for instant shelves, 254–55
Flowers, mounted, 173–74
Foam rubber, 252; pillow forms and stuffing, 58–60, 67–68, 69–70, 77; tape, 236
Foil (including adhesive-backed foil), 234; for box trim, 304; for picture-frame covering, 116; for plywood-slab frame covering, 113–14; tinting with markers, 244; for wall covering, 54
Formica supersculpture, 143–44
Frames, picture, 9, 111–17. *See also* specific uses
Free Association collage, 141–42
French knot, 243
Fringe, 245–46 (*See also* Tassels; specific items to be decorated); ball, uses for, 61, 91–93; wall hanging of knotted, 159, 160
Frogs, as box trim, 304
Furnishings, 12–13. *See also* Environments; specific items
Furniture (*See also* Floor plans; Wood; specific items): Environments made of unfinished, 22–30; Found, 17–22; Instant Upholstery, 58–60; protecting from paint, 252; refinishing (*See* Wood)
Furniture tips, collage of, 141

Galleries, art, 99–101; burlap 169; in Environments, 29
Gardening supplies, storage of, 183
Gift-wrap wall hang-ups, 98
Gimp, for lampshade decoration, 61
Glues, 145–46, 247–48 (See also specific uses); special-purpose, 248; tips and tricks, 248
Gobelin stitches, 249–50
Goodwill Industries, 11
Graphics, 123

Half-cross stitch, 249
Hallways, for galleries, 99–101, 102
Hangings, 151–66, 173; embroidery designs for, 281–88
Hardware, 188; construction, 148–50; removing, cleaning, replacing, 20
Headbands, from silk neckties, 232
Headboards. *See* Beds
Hobby collage, 137

Ice Cap collage, 141
Iron, removing rust from, 20

Jackets, afghan-patch, 212, 213
Jewelry, storage of, 202, 299; egg-carton box for, 310; wrapping paper for box covering, 312, 313
Junk, "recycling," 289–314

Kapok, for pillow stuffing, 69–70
Kerchiefs, storage of, 201
Kindergarten blocks, as sculpture bases, 118, 119
Kitchens: collages for, 137; embroidery designs for, 287–88; as galleries, 101; storage ideas for, 181–82, 184, 190–95, 198
Knots (*See also* Macramé; Tie-dyeing): French, 243
Knotted fringe, 246; wall hanging, 159, 160

Lace, as pillow decoration, 93–94
Lamps, 9, 13–14
Lampshades, cover-ups for, 60–64
Lazy daisy embroidery design, 281–82
Lazy daisy stitch, 242
Leather: appliqué, 236; square pillow, 79–82
Leaves, mounted, 173–75
Legs, in rehabilitating furniture, 20
Lemon oil, 21

Lettering designs, 268
Light pulls, 306
Linen: for embroidery, 244; pillows, 70, 71
Linoleum, for checkerboard floor covering, 57
Linoleum paste, 248
Liquid solder, 248
Liquid thread, 248
"Love" design, 268
Lucite: bases, 120, 121, 171, 172; construction, 145–46

Macramé, 173; wall hanging, 151
Magic Mounts, 110–11, 122
Mahogany, enamel for, 20
Makeup caddies, pill-container, 308
Maps, as wall hang-ups, 97
Marine epoxy, 122, 248
Markers, felt-tipped, 244–45
Mats, for pictures, 111ff.
Memory collage, 137
Metal (*See also* specific kinds): belts, storage of, 201
Metallic tape, adhesive-backed, 235
Mirrors: as hallway decoration, 99–101; as wall coverings, 53–54
Moldings: to decorate plywood frames, 112; wall, with fabrics, 52; as window cover-ups, 37
Montage, tissue-paper, 135–36
Mosaic, shell or pebble, 176–78
Mounting tape, 110–11, 122
Mug racks, from trimming racks, 298–99
Muslin, for embroidery, 244
Napkins: embroidering, for pillows, 244; for throw pillows, 70, 244; tie-dyed, 165
Nature, the art of, 170–78
Naval jelly, 20
Necklaces, storage of, 202, 299
Neckties: belts of, 232; for pillows, 85
Needlepoint, 249–52; design portfolio, 283–86; pillow, "presto-point" square, 87–89; sampler, mounted on plywood, 113
Newspaper: to cover picture mats, 117; for papier-mâché, 291–95
Night tables, 183; in Environments, 24ff.
Nylon stockings, as pillow stuffing, 67

Oak: refinishing, 20; waxing, 21
Open-weave hanging, 158–60

Opwork, 130–32
Outline stitch, 241
Owl design, 264

Pad-and-pencil caddies, papier-mâché, 294
Paint, 16 (*See also* specific items to be decorated); acrylic, 233–34; protecting furniture when painting, 252
Paintings. *See* Art; Pictures
Paintsplotches, 126–27
Paintstrings, 128–29
Paisley design, 278
Panes, embroidery design of, 283–84
Pantyhose: pillow stuffing, 67; storage of, 200
Paper (*See also* Tissue paper; specific uses): gift-wrap wall hang-ups, 98; papier-mâché, 291–95; wrapping, uses for, 312, 313
Paper dolls, 277; lamp-shade decoration, 62; window-frame decoration, 38
Papier-mâché, 291–95
Pastes, 248
Patchwork: afghan, 71–72, 207–20; circle pillow, 82–85; rugs, 56
Peas, as embroidery design, 287
Pebble mosaic, 176–78
Pedestal, for sculpture, 117–18
Pegboard, 196–98, 202
Photographs, hanging, 96–97
Picture frames, 9, 111–17. *See also* specific uses
Picture galleries. *See* Galleries, art
Picture hooks, 109–10
Pictures. *See* Art; Designs; specific items to be decorated
Pill containers, uses for, 308–9
Pillowcases: for "headboards," 46; for pinafore-aprons, 219–24; for shift-aprons, 224–25
Pillows. *See* Throw pillows
Pinafore-aprons, pillowcase, 220–24
Pipe stands, from trimming racks, 299–300
Pipes, painting, 54–55
Placemats: embroidered, for pillows, 244; tie-dyed, 165
Planters and plant stands, 190; hanging, 170; made from table, 18–19; papier-mâché, 293
Plants (*See also* Planters and plant stands): mounted, 173–74